HOLD THE
MARIANAS

The Japanese Defense

of the Mariana Islands

D. Colt Denfeld

White Mane Publishing Company, Inc.

This White Mane Publishing Company, Inc. publication
was printed by
Beidel Printing House, Inc.
63 West Burd Street
Shippensburg, PA 17257-0152 USA

In respect for the scholarship contained herein, the acid-free paper used in this book meets the guidelines for permanence and durability of the Committee on Production Guidelines for Book Longevity of the Council on Library Resources.

For a complete list of available publications
please write
White Mane Publishing Company, Inc.
P.O. Box 152
Shippensburg, PA 17257-0152 USA

Library of Congress Cataloging-in-Publication Data

Denfeld, D. Colt.
    Hold the Marianas : the Japanese defense of the Islands / D. Colt
Denfeld.
        p.   cm.
    Includes bibliographical references and indexes.
    ISBN 1-57249-014-4 (alk. paper)
    1. World War, 1939–1945--Campaigns--Mariana Islands. 2. Mariana
Islands--History.   I. Title.
D767.99.M27D46   1997
940.54'26'09967--dc21   97-8219
                                                             CIP

PRINTED IN THE UNITED STATES OF AMERICA

TABLE OF CONTENTS

Saipan Photographs

iv

Tinian Photographs

Rota Photographs

Guam Photographs

After the Battle Photographs

Saipan

ACKNOWLEDGMENTS

We have the opportunity to visit many relics of the Marianas campaign. The two responsible historic preservation offices and the U.S. National Park Service have done an outstanding job of preserving battlefield features. In the Commonwealth of the Northern Marianas the Historic Preservation Office has protected valuable sites on Saipan, Tinian, Rota and Pagan. While Guam's Historic Preservation Office has actively guarded the islands' World War II legacy.

During 14 years of field investigations in the Marianas many individuals have been generous in their assistance. No one has been more helpful than Scott Russell, the Deputy Historic Preservation Officer, Commonwealth of the Northern Mariana Islands. He knows every inch of Saipan and is eager to share his knowledge. Additionally Michael Fleming, the Historic Preservation Officer, and Jesus Pangelinan, Director of Cultural and Community Affairs, deserve thanks for their assistance.

Stell Newman created a powerful War in the Pacific National Historic Park (NHP), Guam, and encouraged researchers to pay attention to the Japanese side of the war. The National Park Service has honored Stell's memory by naming their Guam museum and archives, the Stell Newman Visitors Center. Superintendent Ralph Reyes, of the War in the Pacific NHP, has provided assistance. He has experienced the horror of the war. In 1944 he was a 17 year old who with his older brother worked on the Orote Airfield as forced laborers. Ralph was sent from Orote to a concentration camp at Manenggon, while his brother was taken to the north to build fortifications. The Japanese executed the older Reyes son and other Guamanian workers.

Staff at the Newman Center and also the Micronesian Area Research Center (MARC) both have gone the extra distance to locate materials. Richard Davis, the Guam Historic Preservation Officer, has made available documents dealing with Guam wartime features.

Stanley Hocoq of Tinian identified the locations of significant relics hidden in the jungle of that island. This included directions to the 6-inch gun battery, the battery responsible for the hits on the U.S. battleship *Colorado*. Thanks are due to Darlene Moore, Micronesian Archaeological Research Services, for sharing her survey documentation of the cliff defenses of Rota Island, and buried tanks in Guam.

The International Archaeological Research Institute of Honolulu has provided the opportunity to accomplish archival investigations of poorly documented issues such as mass burial of Japanese dead in the Pacific. Mikk Kaschko, a Pacific archaeologist, has pushed for the inclusion of historians in survey work at battlefields.

Mark Peattie, author of the comprehensive history of the Japanese in Micronesia, was a source of ideas. Another person always available to answer questions is a fellow member of the Coast Defense Study Group, Al Grobmeier.

The Memorial Service Association for Deceased Compatriots Overseas, Seoul, Korea, provided data on forced Korean laborers. Thanks are due to Min Ja Chong who translated these Korean laborers' documents.

Finally, I would like to thank my editors at White Mane, Martin K. Gordon and Barry W. Fowle, for their work in bringing this book to completion.

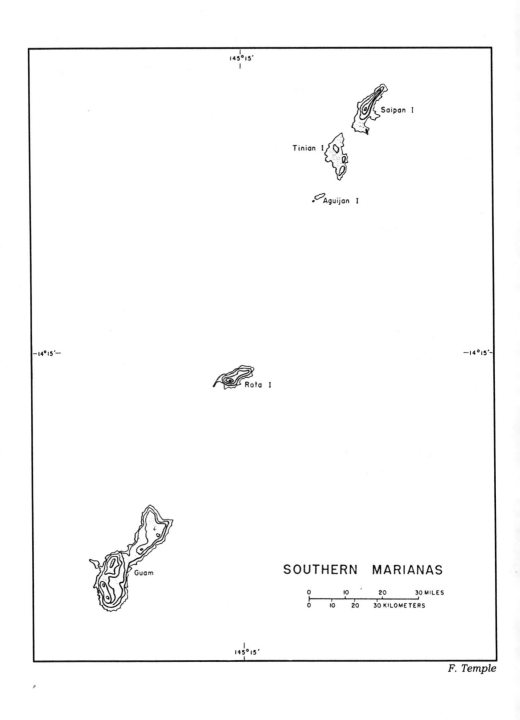

145°15'

14°15'—   —14°15'

Saipan I

Tinian I

Aguijan I

Rota I

Guam

SOUTHERN   MARIANAS

0		10		20		30 MILES
0	10		20		30 KILOMETERS	

145°15'

F. Temple

INTRODUCTION

This is the story of the Japanese in the Marianas, who conducted a heroic, but futile World War II defense of these islands. The book follows the Japanese presence in the Marianas from their 1914 acquisition from Germany to the fall of the Japanese defenses in 1944. Included is a brief review of their economic development and militarization. Military base construction in the Marianas started in the mid-1930s, well before the attack on Pearl Harbor. These were designed to be offensive bases in support of the Pacific strategy, in which aircraft and submarines operating from Mariana bases would chip away at the American fleet in preparation for the decisive sea battle. The anticipated Japanese victory would demoralize the American Navy, and America would relinquish the Pacific and Asia to Japan. By September 1943, with the American advance in the Pacific, the Marianas changed from an offensive station to a central point of an absolute final line of national defense. The islands were fortified and readied to halt the American drive.

Tokyo and the home islands depended upon the Marianas for their protection. Japan's military leadership feared the very heavy, long-range B-29 bomber. They knew it could reach the home islands from the Marianas. Despite recognizing the Marianas as of great importance, poor defensive planning occurred. Instead of effective defenses in depth, and taking advantage of the terrain, the various island commanders prepared thin linear beachline defenses. This method failed in the Marshall Islands. And, even after it failed again at Saipan, the Guam command stayed with this flawed doctrine.

To understand the poor planning requires a review of the defense plans to include the placement of coastal guns, troop tactics, and airpower. Generally the island military commanders and staff wore blinders and avoided honest appraisals of the battle conditions. This inability to confront reality and to change doomed the Marianas, and in the long run doomed Japan. Clearly the commanders contributed to their own undoing. They aided the landing forces by many poor defensive decisions, errors largely traceable to the Japanese military value system, a system out of touch with the warfare of 1944.

The Japanese military value system included: an emphasis on spirit, a rigid adherence to tradition, complete acceptance of authority, a bureaucratic military experience discouraging innovation, and a rigid belief in doctrine unshaken by failures. As a result of these values, the Japanese took actions that hindered a refined response to the American threat in the Marianas. For example, there was the belief that spirit was more powerful than steel. Armed with spirit the aggressive soldiers could overcome more powerful enemies. But what good was spirit when the soldier was under intense bombardment and could not even see his enemy? This spirit was no match for American firepower. The individual soldier was expected to make a greater sacrifice when the situation deteriorated, and this led to desperate acts, with the ultimate effect of weakening the defense.[1]

The Marianas are important as a crucial battleground determining the fate of Japan, and as the locale of unique events. On Guam the Japanese conducted the largest and best organized counterattack in the Central Pacific. At Saipan the largest final, all-out counterattack of the War in the Pacific occurred, when over 2,500 Japanese struck the American lines to die an honorable death. The Marianas were the first Pacific islands with the potential for urban warfare, each of the three assaulted islands had modern cities. These islands were also the site of rare large-scale Japanese armor attacks. Finally, the fall of Saipan forced the resignation of Prime Minister Hideki Tojo and his cabinet. Leaders more inclined to surrender replaced Tojo and his cabinet who were willing to lead Japan to total destruction.

Most of the Japanese records disappeared in the war and the island commanders did not survive to present their recollections. Among the limited existing documents are captured records, intercepted messages, and diaries. These materials offer on-the-spot views not colored by recollection or distance from the event. There are few oral histories, the few survivors have been hesitant to relate details of the island battles. One exception is the outstanding collection of personal accounts in Cook and Cook, *Japan at War: An Oral History*, 1992. A number of Guamanians have recorded their recollections and these records are available at the Micronesian Area Research Center (MARC) in Guam. In Korea, forced laborers and victims of the Japanese are now talking about their experiences.

Still photographs serve as an adjunct to battle histories, offering a visual accompaniment. Marine, Navy, and Army battle and after the battle photographs, located in the National Archives and Records Center, College Park, Maryland, are research tools. These photographs clarify and add data regarding the defenses. For example, there are five widely divergent inventories of Japanese weapons in Guam. Four were contemporary, compiled during or directly after the battle. The fifth was based upon the memory of Lieutenant Colonel Hideyuki Takeda, 29th Division, chief of staff, and compiled in October 1946.

Of the inventories, we would expect the III Amphibious Corps list, one of the four prepared soon after the battle, and based upon a field inspection, to be most accurate. However, it has glaring errors, listing no 120mm guns. The National Archives photographs show 120mm guns. Additionally, there are about six surviving 120mm dual-purpose guns, indicating their wartime presence. A careful comparison of photographs, field research, and the five lists indicate that the Takeda record, based upon memory, is the most valid.[2]

National Archives photographs are instructive in other ways. They show the degree of completeness of fortifications, camouflage techniques, and provide details regarding trenchworks and infantry positions. They also provide new details. For example, a set of photographs record the participation of a Japanese civilian woman in the Saipan mass counterattack. Another interesting group of photographs record the burial of General Saito, the Saipan commander, who the U.S. Marines laid to rest with full military honors. This was an unusual event, rarely were Japanese commanders buried in marked graves or with military honors.[3]

Another approach used to understand the Japanese defense was field surveys. The author has inspected the extant fortifications, gun positions, and weapons in the Marianas. Standing in these positions enables one to obtain a feeling for the Japanese defense and the situation confronting the American invasion forces.

ONE

Saipan: A Spanish, German and Japanese Colony

For three centuries Saipan was an unimportant Spanish and then German Pacific outpost. Then the Japanese turned the island into a colonial state, integrated into its empire, and made it a contributing economic partner.

The Mariana Islands stretch for some 425 miles in a north-south arc, located 1,600 miles east of the Philippine Islands. At the north end of the Marianas is Farallon de Pajaros, 335 miles southeast of Iwo Jima. On the southern end is Guam, 250 miles north of the Caroline Islands. Guam, Saipan, Rota and Tinian, the largest islands in the chain, are in the south. Guam is the largest, followed by Saipan, at 14 miles long and at its widest point 6.5 miles.

Archaeological research suggests that the Chamorro people lived in the Marianas 1,500 years before the birth of Christ. They were a self-sufficient race, believed to have migrated from Southeast Asia to this chain of islands. When Ferdinand Magellan landed in the islands, probably at Guahan (the Chamorro name for Guam), on March 6, 1521, there were about 25,000 Chamorros on Guam. Another 20,000 occupied the remaining islands of the chain.[1]

Chamorros welcomed the Magellan expedition as it anchored in Umatac Bay. Natives in canoes pulled aside, bringing baskets of fruits and foods for the half-starved ships' crews. Once aboard the ships the Guahan natives traded fruit for small items. Also, socialized in communal property, they helped themselves to loose pieces of iron. This Chamorro behavior angered Magellan, and he responded with a raiding party to attack an island village. The raiders burned down 40 huts and killed seven villagers. Still angry, Magellan, named

1

the islands Isles de Los Ladrones, or Islands of Thieves. The islands were renamed Las Marianas in 1568, in honor of Queen Mariana of Austria, who had provided support for Catholic missionary work in the islands. As late as World War II mariners referred to the islands as the Ladrones.

The Spanish had little interest in the Ladrones following their discovery. Spanish galleons on their westward passage stopped for food and water as they sailed from Acapulco to the Philippines. There was limited trading with the islanders on these remote outposts. This changed with the arrival of missionaries, in June 1668, who brought a permanent Spanish presence. Missionaries worked in the southern islands of Guahan, Saipan, Luta (Rota) and Tinian. At first the natives accepted the missionaries, but, religious conversion required rejection of traditional values. The Chamorros started to resist. On July 23, 1670 open rebellion broke out on Guahan. The Spanish Army fought back. Rebels escaping to Saipan and Tinian were hunted down and punished. Finally in 1693, the Spanish overcame the rebellion. Warfare and disease had decimated the native population, reducing it from 45,000 to 5,000.[2]

With the end of warfare a slow and gradual population increase occurred. Adding to the natural growth was migration to the Marianas. In about 1815, Caroline Islanders left their typhoon-stripped islands to resettle in the Marianas. Carolinians arriving at Saipan settled the village of Arabwal, naming it for the leafy green vine growing on its sandy beaches. Later this west coast village was renamed Garapan. Some Carolinians went to Tinian to work on the cattle ranch there. When the ranch failed in 1889 they moved to Saipan and established Talabogh village, later renamed Tanapag.

The Spaniards offered free land to encourage migration to Saipan. Chamorros in Guahan could obtain this free land by making the short voyage north to Saipan. Few accepted the offer and Saipan never became a significant colony of the Spanish Marianas.

During the Spanish-American War the United States captured Guam on June 21, 1898. The United States retained this island as a coaling station, allowing Spain to sell the remainder of the Marianas to Germany on July 1, 1899. On November 17, 1899, the German governor of the Marianas, Captain Georg Fritz, took control of the islands with his headquarters at Garapan, Saipan. Captain Fritz was more aggressive in the development of Saipan. He expanded the free land offer for Chamorros to relocate from Guam to Saipan, and welcomed more Carolinians in 1901. By the end of 1902 the population of Saipan had increased by over 30 percent.

Germany also made efforts to foster economic growth by establishing coconut plantations and exporting copra. Unfortunately a series of typhoons prevented the development of a successful copra export business. The German effort at economic improvement also included allowing Japanese trading companies to operate in the Marianas. In a few years these companies dominated the commerce in the Marianas, accounting for more than 80 percent of the German Marianas trade. Two Japanese firms, the Hiki Trading Company and Murayama Trading Company, virtually controlled the Micronesian trade. Their greatest enemies were each other, so to reduce competition they merged in 1908 as the Nanyo Boecki Kabushikigaisha (South Seas Trading Company, NBK) or better known as "Nambo".[3] Nambo became the leading economic entity in the Marianas, dominating fishing, copra, transportation, and passenger service. By World War I this firm had a monopoly of trade in Micronesia.[4]

The German era was short-lived. On August 23, 1914 Japan declared war on Germany and formed a naval task force to pursue the German East Asiatic Squadron in Micronesian waters. While Japanese ships challenged the German Navy in Micronesia, the top echelons of the foreign ministry and Navy debated the capture of German possessions in Micronesia. Some called for immediate territorial expansion, acquiring the German territories. Others urged a go slow policy so as not to upset Great Britain, a nation expressing concern regarding Japanese goals in the Pacific.

In the debate over territory, the territorial expansionists won. A naval task force set out to capture the German possessions. First, was Jaluit, in the Marshall Islands, occupied on October 3, 1914. By October 9, Pohnpei (Ponape), Kusaie, Belau (Palau), and Angaur with its phosphate mines, were under Japanese control. On October 14 the battleship *Katori* dropped anchor off Garapan, Saipan to complete the bloodless occupation of the former German colonies. Germany was too busy in Europe to contest the loss of its far distant Pacific islands. For the native peoples of these islands, never consulted regarding their desires, this latest occupation would have a profound impact.[5]

For the Spanish it was a religious mission. The Germans administered the islands as minor trading posts, even allowing the Japanese to dominate shipping and trade. It was much different for the Japanese, who made the Micronesian islands an integral and contributing entity of the empire.

The Japanese Navy administered these new territories from 1914 to 1922. Naval officers made laws, enforced rules and regulations, and supervised public works. They formed a bureaucratic colonial administration with total control, in strong contrast to the limited and aloof character of the German administration. In March

1922 a civilian government replaced the naval administration. Civilian rule was more acceptable to the League of Nations and its Mandate Charter of 1920. This mandate had conferred trusteeship to Japan to administer the islands for the benefit of its people. An advanced nation providing for the well-being and improvement of people not yet able to stand by themselves under the strenuous conditions of the modern world. It was a mandate imposing responsibilities on Japan for the social progress of the indigenous peoples.

Garapan became an impressive district administrative center, the headquarters for the Marianas. Even more impressive facilities were built at Koror, Belau (Palau), the headquarters for the mandates. The civilian government, the Nan'yo-cho, comprising home island officials, administered these islands. In turn the Nan'yo-cho picked local men to serve as district chiefs (Kutyo) and deputy district chiefs (Zyoyaku). These Saipanese leaders explained the laws to the residents and assisted in the collection of taxes. They also had some influence with the Japanese authorities.[6]

The Japanese made substantial progress in advancing health care, education, and the standard of living, as stipulated in the mandate. However, they failed to comply with nonfortification stipulations. Three agreements applied: the December 1920 Mandate Charter; Article 19 of the nonfortification pledge of the 1922 Washington Naval Limitations Treaty, and the February 11, 1922 United States-Japan Convention confirming the mandate not to fortify the islands. These three agreements prohibited the construction of fortifications and military or naval bases. A brief review of the pre-World War II Japanese administration, especially in Saipan, shows that military construction begun in the mid-1930s.

During the naval administration, 1914–1922, there was limited military activity. The Navy conducted ocean and harbor surveys, but did not construct any bases or facilities. Economic development was the primary focus of the Navy and early Nan'yo government. This included development of trade, integration of the islands into the Japanese economy, and using migration to bring laborers to the Pacific islands, and by doing so reducing overpopulation in Okinawa. Sugar was the key to realizing these economic and social goals. This was a potential profitable export, and one whose production required a large labor pool. Okinawan farmers, acclimated to the hot temperature and hard work in the sugarcane fields, were prime candidates for migration. In 1916 the Navy started sugarcane production in Saipan. It was a failure leaving hundreds of unemployed Okinawans stranded on Saipan.

The Japanese did not give up. In 1920, Haruji Matsue, a sugar expert, came to Saipan to evaluate the island's sugarcane potential. Matsue, a 1905 graduate of the sugar chemistry program at Louisiana State University, the world's leading sugar cultivation university, had already created a profitable sugar industry in Taiwan. He believed he could do the same at Saipan, an island he determined well-suited for large-scale sugarcane production.[7]

The Nanyo Kohatsu Kaisha or NKK was formed to develop the sugar industry. Laborers of the failed naval sugar effort and several thousand new workers started land clearing in 1921. Sugar was produced the next year confirming Matsue's assertion. Despite setbacks, sugar production reached 1,200 tons a day in 1928. In 1929–1930 sugarcane growing expanded to Tinian and Rota. By 1938 there were over 19,000 hectares of sugarcane and 3,200 tons of sugar processed per day in the Marianas.

Sugar became the largest income producer in the Japanese South Seas colonies. It was 60 percent of the export market, followed by fish processing, phosphate, coconut cultivation, and alcohol by-products of sugar processing. Matsue became famous, remembered as the "Sugar King". A larger-than-life statue of him was erected in Garapan's Central Park, where it still stands. A bullet in its left temple recalls the 1944 battle for Flametree Hill, as the Marines named the park with its colorful trees, still displaying their reddish-orange blossoms, and shading this pleasant park.

The profitable sugar industry changed the face of the Marianas. Saipan became a bustling Japanese colony. Garapan took on the appearance of a coastal Japanese town with neat streets lined with modern buildings. Missing was the South Seas village scene of thatched roof huts. Also, the foreign population rapidly overtook the native population. In the late 1930s there were over 42,000 foreigners and only 4,000 Chamorros and Carolinians.

Economic development in the 1920s brought construction, not war preparations. A narrow gauge railroad was built to connect the canefields to the sugar processing plant in Chalan Kanoa. In the private sector, businesses opened in Garapan, offering a full range of goods and services, including ice cream shops, tofu factories, sake breweries, and an umbrella store. There was a cultural conversion along with the economic development. The four thousand native residents had to adopt the Japanese language, values and life styles. A significant exception was religious freedom, with Catholicism surviving as the main Saipanese religion. Japanese medical care, provided at the modern hospital in Garapan, across the street from Central Park, improved native health.

Elderly Saipanese, interviewed in the late 1970s, remember the period before the war as a time of hard work but with close family life. Thomas P. Sablan recalls that "life was simple and strict. People had to work very hard. Every family had a garden or farm. This was necessary to supplement the very low income from jobs at the factories".[8] Of course all this changed during the war, which brought privations, death and destruction.

While the emphasis was on economic development there were civilian projects with military value. The major project of 1927 in this category was the dredging of Tanapag Lagoon to improve the harbor. It was similar to the 1930s American harbor improvements at Guam, Midway, and Wake, supporting the Pan American Airways Clipper Service. Both the Japanese and American harbor improvements had immediate civilian applications and potential military value.

The first Saipan military project was the airfield at Aslito on the southern end of Saipan. Surveyors arrived in 1930 to lay out this airfield and a second field on Pagan Island, 180 miles to the north. After the war Japanese officials claimed that Aslito was a civilian field. However, the building and facilities constructed were those of a Navy depot, far exceeding the needs of an airport on the Great Japan Airways' route.[9] Also in the early 1930s there were airfield surveys at Chuuk (Truk) and Belau, and harbor studies to identify potential anchorages. More harbor and sea data was collected in the 1933 Combined Fleet exercises held near the Marianas.

While the Aslito Airfield was under construction in 1933, Japan gave the required two-year notice for withdrawal from the League of Nations. This withdrawal did not include giving up the mandates. However, Japan did not go so far as to declare them sovereign territories. The Japanese continued to make annual reports to the League, while denying inspection or verification. Despite unilateral claims, the mandate requirements were probably still binding, but the League of Nations had no power to intercede.

A number of military projects were accomplished between 1934 and 1940. During this time period the Japanese government appropriated at least 14,456,800 yen ($3,939,478) for construction in the Mariana Islands. For the year beginning November 15, 1940, a minimum of 121,189,666 yen ($28,406,858) was spent in the Marianas, Carolines, and Marshalls, of which 15,605,885 yen ($3,658,019) went to the Marianas. Nearly one-half of the Saipan money was for airfield construction. The remainder was used to build fortifications, barracks, storage buildings, offices, water supply facilities, ammunition storage facilities and communications stations. Practically all the money allocated to Tinian and Pagan was earmarked for airfield construction.[10]

In 1934 a seaplane and naval base was built at Flores Point, on Tanapag Harbor. This base included two seaplane ramps, steel hangars, shops, and warehouses. However the limited ship anchorage prevented building Flores Point into a major base. Flores Point Base and Tanapag Harbor served as a fleet refueling and resupply facility.

As the Pacific situation worsened in the late 1930s, military construction was expanded. Naval construction battalions, each consisting of 800 Koreans supervised by 100 Japanese engineers, arrived to build bases. It was labor intensive work, since the battalions had no heavy equipment. Japan, at this time, was backward in the area of civil engineering. Never during the war could the Japanese match the remarkable construction achievements of the U.S. Navy Seabees and the Army Corps of Engineers. Large numbers of laborers were needed to make up for equipment shortages. These workers came from many sources, including prisons. In October 1939 over two thousand convicts, the majority from the Yokohama Central Prison, became laborers. They were organized into labor battalions with names such as the Sekiseitai or "Sincerity Battalion", giving them some espirit de corps.[11]

In early 1940 the prisoner battalions arrived at Tinian and Chuuk (Truk) to build airstrips. By the end of 1940 the prisoners had cleared the forests and accomplished the hardest work. With this done, the convicts were returned to prison and the naval construction battalions completed the airfield projects. Also, this year the military program included construction of "lighthouses" on various Micronesian islands. These "lighthouses" were heavily reinforced structures to serve as lookouts and fire control stations for gun batteries. Nearby were the guns, ammunition magazines, command posts, and barracks. Twelve "lighthouses", some of them actual navigational aids, were built on Saipan at a cost of 1,333,333 yen or $312,533.[12]

Two

From Outpost to Absolute Defense Line

Saipan was a backwater during the first years of the war. The only major military events were support of the Guam landings and staging duties during the Midway operations. Life on Saipan had a largely civilian character until the major military build-up in 1944.

There was little defensive construction in the Marianas. Japanese military plans for the Marianas had these islands backing the central war goal, a decisive sea battle. The role of the Pacific outposts was to strike at the American Pacific Fleet as it steamed west and toward the waiting Japanese fleet for a final confrontation. Aircraft and submarines stationed at Pacific bases, were to knock out American ships and through attrition reduce the Pacific Fleet to parity with the Combined Fleet. Once at parity, the assumption was that the advantage would go to the Japanese with their high quality ships and fighting spirit. With the destruction of the U.S. fleet a demoralized United States would sue for peace, leaving Japan in control of Asia and the Pacific. It was a war plan emphasizing the offensive. The only islands requiring defenses were those on the outer ring, such as Kiribati (Gilberts) and Marshalls. There was some worry on Saipan that American raiding parties from Guam might conduct landings. In February 1941, $23,440 built four reinforced-concrete blockhouses to defend landing beaches. Each of the semi-circular blockhouses held four 20mm guns spaced around the unit so that the gunners could fire seaward and enfilade fire up and down the beach. They were integrated into strong beach defenses of machine guns and infantry positions. American 1944 intelligence reports referred to them as "German type", since they resembled fortifications on the Atlantic Wall.

8

Important 1941 military construction projects at Saipan were: the inter-island radio station, a radio direction finder and a naval depot for the 4th Fleet Naval Stores Department. The total program allocated on September 1, 1941 was 1,500,000 yen ($351,600) for base construction including: barracks, baths and latrines, kitchens, infirmaries, shops, warehouses, torpedo storage sheds, garages and air raid shelters.[1]

Saipan received troop reinforcements in December 1940. The first unit was the 5th Defense Force, for defense of the Saipan sector of the 4th Fleet. The 4th Fleet, with headquarters in Chuuk (Truk), was divided into four sectors: Chuuk, Belau, Kwajalein and Saipan with each sector having a base defense force. Next, in January 1941 came the 4th Fleet Naval Stores Department and the 4th Naval Air Depot.

Troops of 500-man strong 5th Defense Force built defenses. They dug trenchworks at landing beaches and established a defense at the Flores Point Base. On June 1, they received orders to prepare for an offensive mission, the capture of Guam. Mission planning and training were immediately initiated, with a schedule requiring that they be ready for the assault by the end of November. Preparations included practice landings and assaults on fortified positions.

Aslito Airfield was also to play an important role in the capture of Guam. By October 1941 the Aslito Airfield had a coral-concrete runway, and depot facilities for maintenance and repair. There were steel hangars, shops, torpedo fueling and assembly plants, fuel and ammunition storage bunkers, a garrison, and a hospital. The main tenants were the 4th Naval Air Depot and an operational unit to bomb Guam, the 18th Naval Air Group.

The seaplane and naval base at Flores Point contained two seaplane ramps, semi-underground ammunition magazines, barracks, shops, warehouses, and nine air raid shelters. Three steel hangars stood on the edge of the aircraft parking apron. When completed the base had a total of 65 buildings. During October and November 1941, seaplanes stationed at this base made intelligence flights over Guam.

Life in Saipan in 1941 still had a civilian character. Sugar production was the main event. The military population was small and dispersed over the island, at Aslito Airfield, Flores Point Base, an inter-island radio station at Susupe, the radio direction finder, and a wireless station. The wireless, located on Mount Hanachiru in the northeast corner of the island, remained operational to the very end of the defense of Saipan.

1. Aslito Field in early 1944, before the preinvasion aerial and naval bombardment

National Archives

Just before 0600 on December 8 (East Longitude date) crews at Aslito Airfield started loading bombs on the planes of the 18th Naval Air Group. One hour later these aircraft lifted off the runway for a flight to the west of the direct southwest route to Guam. This flight pattern would avoid detection by the U.S. observation post at Ritidian Point. Opposite Apra Harbor, the 18th Naval Air Group turned left to come in over the harbor and Orote Peninsula to hit the Apra Harbor facilities.[2]

A second raid against Guam was carried out that afternoon by float planes from the Flores Point Base. Meanwhile, the 5th Defense Force transferred to Rota Island to await the South Seas Detachment, the main force for the capture of Guam. The 5th Defense Force, was now designated a Special Naval Landing Force (SNLF). It would join the Army 5,000-man South Seas Detachment in the landings at Guam. The Guam invasion convoy sailed into Rota Harbor on December 8 to load the SNLF. Early on December 9, the convoy steamed to Guam to land troops during darkness of December 9–10.

The third raid, carried out by the 18th Naval Air Group, struck Guam on December 9. During this and previous raids there was only ineffective U.S. antiaircraft fire and no planes had been lost. Returning aircrews brought back photographs of Guam documenting the destruction of the Guam naval force, and the absence of coastal defenses. Therefore, the South Seas naval task force had no need to conduct naval bombardment.

The Special Naval Landing Force got ashore quickly and in a short battle captured the island. Meanwhile the much larger Army force was delayed by landing at the wrong beach and then a long march to their targets. After the battle, the SNLF remained in Guam, redesignated the 54th (Keibitai) Naval Guard Force. With Guam a Japanese possession, duties at Saipan returned to resupply, maintenance, and fleet support. Activity picked up in May 1942 when Saipan and Guam were staging areas for the invasion of Midway. Twelve transports with two battalions of Special Naval Landing Forces left Saipan on May 28. Escorting this Midway invasion force was the light cruiser *Jintsu* and eleven destroyers. Two more destroyers and four cruisers departed Guam for Midway.

With the departure of the Midway forces, Saipan returned to a remote outpost. The military presence was small and life went on much the same as before the war. By 1943, Japan, drained by military losses, and threatened by American advances in the Central Pacific had to rethink the Marianas. Strategic reviews in the spring of 1943 considered the establishment of a defensive line of land-based naval air power. The Marianas could be turned into unsinkable carriers for naval air power. It was an unpleasant thought, a move from the offensive to a more defensive posture.

At an Imperial General Headquarters conference in September 1943, the war situation was reviewed. Coming out of the conference was an order to establish an absolute national defense sphere, a perimeter from Burma across Malaya, East Indies, New Guinea, Carolines, Marianas to the Kurile Islands. This perimeter was essential to Japan and had to be held. Bases forward of this line were to be held for six months and then abandoned if necessary. On the perimeter land-based naval air power was a central element. Aircraft were to hold back and reduce the American fleet prior to the decisive sea battle. Orders were issued to realize this defense, but reinforcement was slow.

Captain Mitsuo Fuchida, senior staff officer, 1st Air Fleet, and Vice Admiral Chuichi Nagumo inspected the Marianas in October 1943 to develop an air defense plan. Admiral Nagumo was at this time 1st Fleet commander in Japan, and scheduled to assume command of the Marianas naval area on March 4, 1944. Nagumo and Fuchida shared the opinion that air strength had to be greatly expanded. To accommodate a greater numbers of planes, Fuchida asked Nagumo to build a total of ten new air bases on the islands of Saipan, Tinian, Guam and Rota.[3]

The Marianas were critical in the defense of the home islands. Loss of this chain would open Japan to attack by long-range U.S. bombers. Saipan was only 1,272 miles from Tokyo, within range of the B-29 Superfortress. Holding it was imperative for home island security. The defenders had on their side, had they not been so blinded by tradition, the very defensible terrain of Saipan. Its natural features, properly used, would give the defenders an awesome capability. On the island sea approach was limited access, there are fringing reefs with few openings. Many of the beaches have mountains at their edges, denying maneuver space for landings. There is rough terrain, and cave-lined cliffs to provide cover and concealment for guns. The east shore is largely free of a fringing reef but the beaches are narrow and the sea pounds against steep cliffs. Off Laulau Bay (Magicienne) is a fringing reef; however, this wide bay was a potential landing beach. Historically, this bay was used as an anchorage with ships lightering their cargo ashore. Militarily, it could be denied to an enemy landing force. The mountains reach down almost to the shore, leaving very little maneuvering space. Defenses could be concealed in the heavy forest of these mountains.

The west shore has only a few potential landing beaches. And, fewer yet with coastal plains for maneuver room. Even when the landing beach had maneuver room there was another problem for the enemy and that was the fringing and barrier reefs along the entire west coast. There were only two gaps in the reef, one off Chalan Kanoa and the dredged entrance to Tanapag Harbor. The western beaches were under the observation and control of the central mountain spine with its commanding field of fire. The key terrain feature of the central region was Mount Tapotchau, the 1,554-foot-high mountain. Observers on this mountain could see most of the island to relay target information to guns sited on the hills below this high mountain.

In the south there were few landing areas, mostly narrow beaches in front of steep cliffs. All could be defended by dual purpose guns emplaced at Aslito Airfield. Together, coastal defenses and dual purpose guns at Aslito could lay a deadly barrage on the southern beaches.

Sheer cliffs at the sea, rough seas, and only a few small landing sites characterize the north. There was no maneuvering room at these landing areas, instead mountainous terrain. Defense of the north was largely accomplished by its rugged terrain.

Where Saipan realized exceptional defensibility was with its mountainous central region spine, including the dominant Mount Tapotchau. This central spine ran from above the southern Aslito plateau to the north end of the island. Its layout was ideal for development into a redoubt, as virtually all approaches to the spine channelized the invaders into long, narrow corridors, which could be raked by gunfire. On the outside of the spine were small knolls and hills for strongpoints. Many of these hills were pockmarked with caves, ideal for shelter and gun emplacements. On their reverse slopes were ideal locales for artillery and mortars. Additionally, these hills and mountains were covered with thick vegetation giving concealment. Properly developed, the central spine had great defensive potential.

The Saipan garrison also had two cities, Garapan and Chalan Kanoa, where urban fighting could inflict heavy casualties on the Americans. Both of these cities were near the western landing beaches, so they could serve as choke points, blocking road travel. Their modern concrete buildings were well-suited for urban defense.

Another factor favoring the defender was the weather. During the dry season, November through March, the roads are dry and passable, but water is scarce. In a prolonged defense, invasion troops would have a hard time finding water, while the defenders had stored water. The rainy season, April through October, brings plenty of water but turns the roads and trails into muddy morasses impeding the movement of any invasion force. Also this season has storms and typhoons which could put an invasion fleet in danger.

Despite its importance the reinforcement of Saipan was slow. In May 1943 the Navy's 5th Special Base Force was comprised of

919 troops and 220 civilians. One year later, the 5th had only grown to 1,437. The 1st Yokosuka Special Naval Landing Force, 1,500 strong, was sent to Saipan in late 1943, but 500 men were transferred to Rabaul in early 1944. Also, in early 1944 the 1st Air Fleet began its aerial reinforcement of the Marianas. Headquarters of this naval air unit was located at the Ushi Airfield on the north end of Tinian. Despite inadequate training and the fact that a number of the Marianas airfields were not ready, the 1st Air Fleet was on its way. To make matters worse, the flights to the Marianas ran into a typhoon, delaying fighter arrival to the last day of February.

A flight of bombers was able to get through the typhoon and landed at Ushi Airfield on February 21. At almost the same time Vice Admiral Marc Mitscher's carrier planes visited the Marianas. On February 22 a patrol plane from Tinian sighted Task Group 58.2 of Mitscher's force, as it steamed towards Tinian and Saipan (a second task group blasted Guam). The patrol plane made a contact report. Reading the report, Vice Admiral Kakuji Kakuta, commander of the 1st Air Fleet, that night dispatched 27 bombers and nine reconnaissance planes to an intercept location. They found the American task group, and in four attacks failed to hit one ship. None of the bombers returned to Tinian, and only a few reconnaissance aircraft made it back.

The next day Mitscher's planes struck the Marianas, hitting Saipan, Guam, Tinian and Rota. Kakuta got 47 bombers and 27 fighters into the air to challenge the Americans. Sixty-seven of his 74 planes did not return, and another 100 planes were destroyed on the ground. It had been a disaster for the 1st Air Fleet. And there was more bad news, Mitscher's raiders sank two freighters, and obtained needed photographs of the island military installations. Meanwhile, American submarines positioned to the west of the islands intercepted fleeing ships. On February 22 a five ship convoy was detected by the American submarine *Tang* which sent to the bottom the *Fukuyama Maru* and *Yamashimo Maru*. Lieutenant Commander Richard O'Kane commanding the *Tang* sank three more ships during the next three days. The *Sunfish* in the same patrol sank two freighters on February 23.[4]

Admiral Kakuta, wanted more planes from Iwo Jima and the home islands, but his request was refused. Higher headquarters feared the loss of replacements sent to Kakuta. He appeared willing to rush headlong into total destruction of his air force.

The fleet reorganization was realized in March. The new Central Pacific Area Fleet, commanded by Vice Admiral Chuichi Nagumo, established its headquarters at Saipan. Placed under the Central Pacific Area Fleet was the 4th Fleet, which had been mauled in the

Marshalls and in the February 1944 carrier raids against Chuuk. The 4th Fleet was left with the somewhat meaningless command of Chuuk, a bypassed island left to wither on the vine. Command responsibilities of the Central Pacific Area Fleet included the Japanese forces in the Central Pacific and Ogasawara Jima (Bonin Islands) to the north. While the Central Pacific Fleet commanded Navy and Army garrisons, it was an illusionary unified command. The 31st Army, which commanded all Army forces in the Marianas from its Saipan headquarters, refused to surrender its authority. A compromise was reached, that during combat the 31st Army would assume control of plans and operations. Friction between the Army and Navy was too ingrained to overcome and the Central Pacific Area Fleet came too late with too little. Resolving this debate between the Army and Navy wasted valuable time and energy, when they should have been working together to create a better defense.

A combat hardened division, the 13th, was selected to reinforce the Marianas. The 13th Division had been fighting in China since 1937, a proven unit. In October a 300-man detachment of the division left Central China bound for Guam. However, the division was held in China to serve in the South China campaign of late 1944.

A substitute division was not found until early 1944, it was the 29th Division of the Kwantung Army. In mid-February 1944, the 29th Division left Manchuria headed for the Marianas, to be followed by other units. Already considerable time had been lost in the defensive build-up of the Marianas. Additionally, the delays meant death for many of the troops on convoys. Increased U.S. submarine patrols and greater torpedo effectiveness had made the sea lanes much more hazardous for Japanese convoys.[5]

The 29th Division convoy to the Marianas was one of the unlucky sailings. As the convoy of four large transports and three new destroyers, the *Kishinami*, *Okinami* and *Asashimo*, neared the Marianas on February 29 it was intercepted by the submarine *Rock*. However, one of the convoy's escort ships spotted the submarine and fired on it with a 127mm gun. The *Rock* was damaged and forced to retreat, but not until the sub had sent a contact report. Later that day the convoy was discovered by the *Trout*, which made torpedo attacks, sending the *Sakito Maru* to the bottom and damaging the *Aki Maru*. Going down with the *Sakito Maru* was most of the equipment of the 18th Regiment, and 2,420 soldiers and ship's crew. The three destroyer escorts counterattacked and probably destroyed the *Trout*. It was never heard from again.

The next day, the *Nautilus* intercepted the convoy, and launched torpedoes which damaged two ships. This left the convoy badly hurt

2. Flores Point Naval Base leveled by the American preinvasion bombardment.
National Archives

and the 18th Regiment short of weapons and equipment. Saipan warehouses did not contain the equipment to refit the regiment. It was so bad that soldiers had to throw away oil–soaked uniforms and the only replacements were uniforms of the detested Navy.[6] With its arrival the regiment was sent to Guam, except for the 1st Battalion which stayed on Saipan.

Another March convoy carrying reinforcements, the 1st, 5th and 6th Expeditionary Force and Navy reinforcements, could not escape the American submarines. The *Kokuyo Maru*, a Navy transport with 1,029 reinforcements for Guam's 54th Naval Guard Force, was hit by a *Sandlance* launched torpedo and sank on March 13. An escort, the light cruiser *Tatsuta,* was also sunk and a third ship damaged in this attack.

The transports on their return trips to Japan evacuated civilians. These voyages were also dangerous, but the U.S. submarine focus was on inbound not outbound convoys. On March 6 the *Nautilus* attacked an outbound convoy as it sailed along the very northern Mariana Islands. Sent to the bottom was the *America Maru* loaded with 1,700 civilians; how many perished is not known.

In April 1944, the Marianas were assigned a special and high priority for the delivery of war materials. A regular convoy service, the Matsui Transport, was formed to deliver crucial items such as cement, reinforcing steel and weapons. The Matsui operation faced aggressive and now more effective American submarine patrols. Every ship sunk by torpedoes carried with it to the bottom pieces of the Marianas defense. There was neither time, material nor shipping to replace lost items.

The frustration resulting from lost ships of the Matsui transport was expressed by Major General Keiji Ikeda, the 31st Army chief of staff, in a message to the Central Pacific Area Fleet:

> We cannot strengthen the fortifications appreciable now unless we can get materials suitable for permanent construction. Specifically, unless the units are supplied with cement, steel reinforcements for cement, barbed wire, lumber, etc., which cannot be obtained in these islands, no matter how many soldiers there are they can do nothing in regard to fortifications but sit around their arms folded, and the situation is unbearable.[7]

This message, laying blame on the Navy, was only partially true. There was a large quantity of material sitting in warehouses. Unquestionably, valuable weapons and materials had not arrived. Convoys in April, May, and June suffered major losses. Lost to the submarine *Seahorse* on April 8 were the transports *Aratama Maru* (which made it to Talofofo Bay, Guam, where it sank) and the *Kizugawa*. The next day a convoy of twenty ships came under attack, with the *Bisaku Maru* hit and sunk. A submarine, the *RO-45*, fell victim on April 20 to the *Seahorse*. One week later the *Akigawa Maru* was destroyed and the submarine, *I-183*, with aviation fuel for the Marianas was lost on April 28, more American submarine victims.

Heavy losses were experienced, on May 10, when the *Silversides* sank the *Okinawa Maru*, *Mikage Maru*, *No 18*, and the converted gunboat *Choan Maru II*. A few days later the *Silversides* destroyed the *Shosei Maru* near Guam. More valuable aviation fuel was lost when on May 29 two fuel tankers, the *Shoken Maru* and *Horaizan Maru*, were sunk as they neared Saipan. A May 31 convoy bringing building materials was intercepted by the *Pintado* which sank the *Toho Maru*.

The 29th Division originally sent to Saipan was moved to Guam. This required another division, the 43d Division, for duty at Saipan. Formed in Japan in 1943, the division boarded ships in May 1944, bound for the Marianas. The convoy carrying one-half of the 43d Division was detected on June 1, but escaped undamaged. Units in this convoy reached Saipan organized and ready for battle. Luck was not with the second echelon of the 43d Division which left Tateyama Harbor, Tokyo Bay, on May 30. On June 4 as this convoy neared Saipan the submarine *Shark* fired torpedoes at it, but all missed their targets. The next day, the *Shark* attacked, this time sinking the *Tamahime Maru* and *Takaika Maru*. Later that evening torpedoes slammed into the gasoline-loaded *Kashimasan Maru* which exploded and sank. Next, the *Harve Maru* was sunk. The second 43d Division convoy had suffered dearly, large quantities of equipment were lost, 20 percent of the troops died, 5,000 of the 20,000 had lost their weapons, and the units were left disorganized. Five of seven transports were sunk. Troop losses were heaviest in the 118th Regiment, which lost 850 men.

Convoy losses caused unit reassignments. When the shot-up, Yap-bound 9th Expeditionary Force disembarked at Saipan, few of its 1,500 soldiers had weapons. The unit was ordered to remain here and reformed into a 600-man battalion of the 47th Independent Mixed Brigade, leaving another 900 as stragglers. Ill-equipped survivors of the 15th Regiment from a sunk transport were left at Saipan instead of their original destination of Koror.

Takeo Yamauchi has vivid memories of his voyage to Saipan and the subsequent battle. His trip was safe, but uncomfortable:

On May 14, 1944, the freighters carrying the Forty-Third Division left the Tateyama Harbor in Tokyo Bay, escorted by five warships. We were told for the first time that we were going to Saipan. We were laid out on shelves like broiler chickens. You had your pack, rifle, all your equipment with you. You crouched there, your body bent. You kept your rubber-soled work shoes on continually, so your feet got damp and sweaty. Water dripped down on you, condensation caused by human breathing. The hold stank with humanity.[8]

Once on Saipan, Yamauchi's unit, the 136th Infantry Regiment, headed for their assigned defense at Oleai. Yamauchi manned a position in the second line to the rear of the beach line trenches.

The administrative command for all Army troops in the Marianas-Ogasawara Jima-Marshalls-Carolines was vested in the 31st Army, commanded by Lieutenant General Hideyoshi Obata. General Obata had just come from the Army general staff and before that air command positions. He established his headquarters at Saipan, where he had little time to prepare defenses, before the anticipated invasion in November 1944. Optimism prevailed, the Army welcoming an American landing as an opportunity to crush the enemy, proclaiming, "now they come where we have been waiting."[9]

On June 5 General Obata and two senior staff personnel flew to Koror to conduct an inspection of the Belau (Palau) defenses, where he expected the next invasion. While at Koror the American assault struck Saipan. The surprised 31st Army commander boarded his plane to hurry back, but he could not make it, the air approaches to Saipan were blocked by American air cover. General Obata was forced to land at Guam, where he remained stranded, with only a minor role in the Marianas defense.

The central defense unit for Saipan was the 43d Division. In command of the division was Lieutenant General Yoshitsugu Saito, who was also the commander of the Northern Marianas Army Group, which included Saipan, Tinian and Pagan. Three regimental combat-type regiments, the 118th (commanded by Colonel Takeshi Ito), 135th (Colonel Eisuke Suzuki) and 136th (Colonel Yukimatsu Ogawa), made up the division. Supporting units included signal, transport, and ordnance companies, a field hospital, and quartermaster unit. The total division strength was 12,939 officers and men.

The 43d Division did not have the time for training in island defense. Even if they had the time, such training might not have been accomplished. Static defense was not in the manual, the best defense was seen as an aggressive offense. The defenders were completely new to island defense, while the invasion forces were well experienced in island warfare. These invasion troops had learned from each previous operation, fine-tuning their tactics. The American marines and soldiers had learned how to neutralize caves, expected night counterattacks, and knew the Japanese tactics. On the Japanese side there was little combat experience among the ground forces. Also many of the naval commanders had yet to engage in naval warfare. They had spent their time waiting for the big battle, the decisive sea confrontation, missing the most valuable training, combat.

Additional units at Saipan included an independent brigade, armor units, antiaircraft units, and straggler forces. Colonel Yoshiro Oka commanded the 47th Independent Mixed Brigade comprised of 2,600 officers and men. This was the former 1st Expeditionary Force redesignated in May as the 47th with four renumbered battalions: the 315th, 316th, 317th, and 318th. The 315th was sent to Pagan, while the remaining three numbered battalions remained at Saipan. Attached to the brigade were independent artillery and engineer units. Independent artillery at Saipan included the 3d Independent Mountain Artillery Regiment with two battalions, each organized into three batteries of four 75mm guns each. Another artillery unit was the 3d Battalion, 10th Field Artillery Regiment, with one battery of eight 75mm guns and two batteries of seven howitzers each. Antiaircraft defenses, the 1st, 2d, and 6th Batteries of the 25th Antiaircraft Regiment, guarded the important Aslito Airfield.

There were 13 straggler units, including the 9th Expeditionary Force, which was on its way to Yap, but stuck on Saipan. Other straggler units were the 150th Infantry Regiment, the 15th Infantry Regiment, the 1st Battalion of the 18th Infantry Regiment, and the 4th Independent Tank Company, minus its tanks lost in a convoy sinking.

Armor had reached Saipan in April 1944 with the unloading of the 9th Tank Regiment, commanded by Colonel Takashi Goto. The 9th Tank Regiment was divided among the Marianas with three and one-half companies to Saipan, with 36 Type 97 medium and 12 Type 95 light tanks. The 1st Yokosuka Special Naval Landing Force had three Type 2 (1942) Ka-Mi amphibious tanks, a model using the Type 95 chassis with two detachable pontoons added. Propulsion was by two screws and steering by two rudders.

The total Saipan Army strength was about 25,450.

On the Navy side to call the Central Pacific Fleet a fleet was a tremendous misstatement. It was not a fleet, but a collection of a few patrol boats. Sailors of the CPAF had infantry duties, to join the Army in the defense of Saipan. Commanding the Central Pacific Fleet was Vice Admiral Chuichi Nagumo, who had disappointing results at Pearl Harbor and Midway. He was now paying for his conservative approach, with this demotion in responsibility. He found himself in a command which existed largely on paper. A specialist in torpedo warfare he was again in a position where his expertise was not relevant.

The 5th Base Force which had been the island defender since before the invasion of Guam, was reduced in status. Rear Admiral Takahisa Tsujimura, the 5th Base Force commander, stepped aside, when the 5th was merged into the Central Pacific Area Fleet.

Manning the coastal defense guns was the 55th Naval Guard Force. In numerous positions at the Flores Point Base was the well-trained 800-man 1st Yokosuka Special Naval Landing Force. A straggler unit, the 41st Naval Guard Force of 400 men, headed for Chuuk, stayed on Saipan to join in the Flores Point defense.

The Navy had responsibility for the air defense, there were no Army air units in the Marianas. On June 1 the air strength was 420 aircraft divided between Guam, Saipan and Tinian. They were backed-up by more planes in the Carolines and Iwo Jima. By June 15, and the invasion, over one-half of the air strength had been diverted to New Guinea to help in the defense of Biak Island. Many planes were lost in combat and the few surviving air crews fell ill to tropical diseases. The limited number of aircraft remaining in the Marianas were destroyed in aerial battles, or on the ground, prior to the invasion of Saipan. And, as soon as reinforcements arrived they were destroyed by American carrier planes. A small group of pilots were evacuated by submarine, but most were converted to infantry to fight and die in the defense.

The total Navy strength was about 6,200. A combined total for the ground defense of Saipan was about 31,650.

Air reinforcement units had to be coming so the Saipan command continued construction of the Banaderu Field at Marpi, with its 4,380-foot-long runway, and an emergency field at Oleai. Banaderu was scheduled to receive 24 planes and Oleai only eight planes. By mid-June the Banaderu site had only been cleared. While the emergency field at Oleai, a 140-foot wide and 3,875 foot-long runway on a straight stretch of the beach road, was ready for use. Its use was restricted since it was constructed crosswise to the prevailing winds. This poor siting and other construction delays at the new airfields, made little difference since aircraft were so scarce by the time of the American landings.

The 31st Army anticipated an invasion in November 1944, leaving only five months to fortify the Marianas. The 7th, 11th and 16th

Engineers and troop labor could meet this schedule. Engineers and troop laborers followed the manual and tradition as to fortifications and defensive strategy. This was to deploy the troops while the defensive construction was under way. At Saipan the plan was to complete the field positions in one month, and permanent fortifications within three months.[10] In instructions to the 1st Expeditionary Force the stated doctrine, was "that the enemy will be destroyed on the beaches through a policy of tactical command based on aggressiveness, determination, and initiative." The warrior spirit was to prevail; it was more important than steel. It was a concept of war completely outdated by the massive firepower of the Americans, which could most easily reach defenses sited on the shoreline.

This thin linear defense started with offshore underwater obstacles and mines. At the water's edge were mine fields, anti-landing craft obstacles and barbed wire. Material and ordnance shortages at Saipan meant that few of these obstacles were emplaced. On the landward edge of the beach were trenchworks occupied by infantry armed with machine guns and rifles. Along the beaches were pillboxes and blockhouses, with machine guns, 20mm guns, 37mm and 47mm guns. Placed on the ends of the beaches were guns in pillboxes to fire enfilade. On the land edge of the beach, or in cliffs to the rear, were coastal defense guns from 75mm to 200mm, emplaced in casemates, and open positions. Located at the beaches, especially on the more seaward points of land were 200mm antiboat guns. A gun designed to drop plunging fire onto enemy vessels in the bays and inner reef areas. Two infantry defense lines were a key component of the defense. One line was at the beach and the second line of trenches was about 100 to 200 yards to the rear. The second line location varied with terrain features, using inclines, ridges, or cliffs when available.

The defenders received instructions to hold their fire until the landing ships were inside the reef and moving towards the shore. A heavy defensive fire would destroy the landing ships and then beach defenders and artillery would stop the assault forces. Should the enemy get ashore in large numbers they would be counterattacked right away, while they were disorganized. These counterattacks were to drive the enemy into the sea, where the Japanese Navy would destroy the invasion convoys and troops trying to reboard.

General Obata divided Saipan into four defense sectors. The northern sector was the top half of the island, to the north of Flores Point. This included the Banaderu (Marpi) airfield, which was still under construction in June 1944. Defending the northern sector was the 135th Infantry Regiment, 43d Division, commanded by Colonel Eisuke Suzuki. Its 1st Battalion was on Tinian.

The second sector was a naval defense area, a small area around the Flores Point Naval Base, to the south side of Garapan and east to Mount Tapotchau. Within this zone were the naval base, Tanapag Harbor, the Garapan naval stores, and Garapan landing beaches. This sector was defended by the SNLF and 5th Base Force. Occupying the front line was the 1st Battalion of the 136th Regiment.

A third sector was the central area from the southern edge of Garapan to Afetna Point and east to the central mountainous spine. This sector included the Oleai and Susupe beaches (Red and Green), where the 2d Marine Division landed. Assigned to this critical sector was one of the best units on Saipan, the 136th Infantry Regiment. Commanded by Colonel Yukimatsu Ogawa, it was at its full strength of 3,650 soldiers, and had its full quota of equipment. Two companies of the 3d Battalion, 136th Regiment, were in reserve at Chacha, the 1st Battalion was in trenches in the naval sector, and the 2d Battalion reinforced by the remaining company of the 3d Battalion defended the Oleai beaches, the site area with some of the fiercest fighting. Colonel Ogawa established his regimental CP in Oleai on an incline above the beach.

The fourth defense sector was the southern, from Afetna Point to the southern tip, and across the entire island. This sector included potential western landing beaches (Green, Blue and Yellow) and the eastern shore landing beach of Laulau Bay (Magicienne Bay). Assigned to defend this sector was the 47th Independent Mixed Brigade, commanded by Colonel Yoshiro Oka; two companies of the 3d Battalion, 9th Independent Mixed Brigade (IMB); and the 16th Shipping Engineers, commanded by Major Masaichi Tsunekawa.

Four infantry companies, from the 136th Regiment and 9th IMB, were in reserve above Laulau Bay. They could resist a landing at this bay or operate as a mobile force against western landings. Armor support was available from Colonel Takashi Goto's 9th Tank Regiment with 48 tanks in readiness near Chacha village, positioned to respond to landings on either shore.

Aslito Airfield was within the southern sector, but had no ground defenses. To the west of the airfield was a ridge line with troops to block the way to Aslito. On the airfield were the 1st, 2d, and 6th Batteries of the 25th Antiaircraft Regiment, commanded by Lieutenant Colonel Jitsunori Niiho. Like other Saipan antiaircraft units they faced a serious ammunition shortage. Guarding the southeast approach to Aslito was Nafutan Peninsula. Here the 317th Independent Infantry Battalion, 47th IMB, was installed in caves and dugouts. The 316th and 318th Independent Battalions were also stationed in the south. There was also the 47th IMB Engineer Unit, and one battery of light field guns.

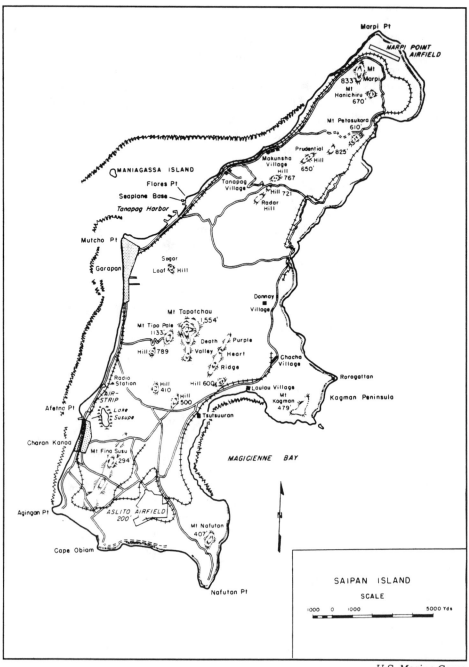

Marpi Pt

MARPI POINT
AIRFIELD

Mt
Marpi
833' Marpi
Mt
Hanichiru
670'

Mt Petosukora
610'

Prudential
Hill 825'
650'

MANIAGASSA ISLAND

Makunsha
Village
Hill
767

Flores Pt

Seaplane Base

Tanapag Harbor

Tanapag
Village

Hill 721

Radar
Hill

Mutcho Pt

Garapan

Sugar
Loaf Hill

Donnay
Village

Mt Tapotchau
1,554'

Mt Tipo Pale
1133'

Death Purple

Hill 789 Valley Heart

Ridge

Chacha
Village

Rarogattan

Radio
Station

Hill
410

Hill 600

Kagman Peninsula

AIR-
STRIP

Hill
500

Laulau Village
Mt
Kagman
479'

Afetna Pt

Lake
Susupe

Tsutsuuran

Charan Kanoa

MAGICIENNE BAY

Mt Fina Susu
294'

Agingan Pt

ASLITO AIRFIELD
200'

Mt Nafutan
407'

Cape Obiam

SAIPAN ISLAND

SCALE

1000 0 1000 5000 Yds

Nafutan Pt

U.S. Marine Corps

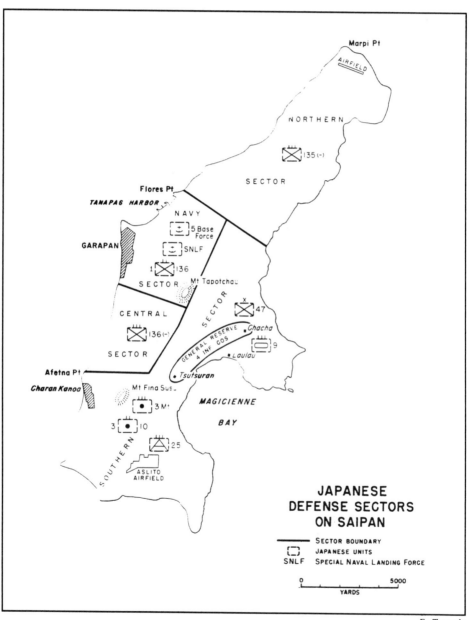

Marpi Pt

AIRFIELD

N O R T H E R N

135 (-)

S E C T O R

Flores Pt

TANAPAG HARBOR

NAVY

5 Base
Force

SNLF

GARAPAN

1 136

S E C T O R   Mt Tapotchau

SECTOR

C E N T R A L

136 (-)

*GENERAL RESERVE
4 INF COS*

X

47

Chacha

9

S E C T O R

Laulau

Afetna Pt

Tsutsuran

Charan Kanoa

Mt Fina Sus

MAGICIENNE

3 M*

BAY

3   10

S O U T H E R N

25

ASLITO
AIRFIELD

JAPANESE
DEFENSE SECTORS
ON SAIPAN

——— SECTOR BOUNDARY

[ ] JAPANESE UNITS

SNLF SPECIAL NAVAL LANDING FORCE

0   5000

YARDS

F. Temple

General Yoshitsugo Saito, commanding general of the 43d Division, had his headquarters at the elementary school on the south edge of Chalan Kanoa. Preinvasion bombardment hit the school encouraging Saito to transfer his command post to a hill cave 500 yards northwest of Hill 500. Saito used six command posts during the defense of Saipan, driven out of each by American bombardment. The staff of the 31st Army Headquarters had their command post in a cave, 1,800 yards east of the Garapan pier. With the absence of General Ogata the 31st Army Headquarters supported General Saito. Colonel Oka, commander of the 47th IMB, had his headquarters in a cave on Hill 500. Admiral Nagumo had his headquarters at Flores Point.

On June 5 when General Obata departed for Belau, many Saipan defenses were unfinished, and others had not received their weapons. For example, on Nafutan Point were empty concrete positions for 127mm dual purpose guns. The guns were in storage at Garapan. Near the empty 127mm positions were three 140mm emplacements with the guns being installed. By the time of the American invasion, there were more guns in storage or not yet installed than were operational. Unavailable were 12 guns at their positions but not operational, another three 140mm coastal defense guns were loaded on a rail car at the Garapan Naval Base, and 42 guns were in storage. The stored weapons included: three 127mm dual purpose guns; one 140mm coastal defense gun; 32 120mm dual purpose guns; and six 200mm antiboat guns. Thirty-two guns were operational, they were: four 200mm antiboat guns; eight 6-inch coastal defense guns; four 120mm coastal defense guns; and 16 120mm dual purpose guns.[11]

Not only was Saipan short of installed guns, there were other serious deficiencies. There was a shortage of materials and time to build beach obstacles or to lay mine fields. One Matsui transport fully loaded with mines was lost to an enemy submarine torpedo. Worse yet, mines in stock had not been installed by invasion day. Despite all the many shortages, a powerful defense was in place. The preinvasion bombardment missed many guns, especially the well-camouflaged artillery, and the Marines paid dearly.

Coastal defenses were ready. In the north, Captain Sanji Takashina's 55th Naval Guard Force gunners manned coastal defenses on the eastern end of Marpi Airfield. Installed here were three 140mm, Type 3 (1914) coastal defense guns in open revetments. The Type 3 designation was part of a standard Japanese equipment numbering system. These numerical designations for weapons, tanks, and aircraft were the year within the reign of an emperor, in which the item was accepted into service. A rifle accepted in 1905 was a Type 38 for the 38th year of the Meiji reign (1868–1912). In late 1912 a rifle coming into service would be a Type 1 for the first year of the Taisho reign. By the end of the 1920s, during the Showa period (1926–1945), this system had become confusing. You had weapons with the same type numbers but from different years. To return order, the calendar year replaced the emperor year. For example, a tank accepted by the Army in the Japanese year 2595 was a Type 95, the year 2595 or 1935 on the Roman calendar.

These north shore 140mm guns were wrapped in burlap and natural vegetation. Nevertheless, they were detected by American intelligence and knocked out in the preinvasion bombardment. While not the case at these guns, Japanese camouflage was very often skillfully done, concealing weapons from observation. Camouflage was an important part of island defense; training manuals stated that camouflage was stronger than concrete.

A battery of three Type 10 (1921), 120mm dual-purpose (DP) guns was also emplaced at the east end of the Marpi runway for antiaircraft and coastal defense fire. The Type 10 120mm DP gun was ubiquitous in the Pacific. In 1941 this naval gun, used on destroyers, was placed in the ground antiaircraft defense role. Production of the 120mm was increased in 1943, with the guns going to the Pacific islands.

A few machine gun and infantry positions were manned along the rugged west coast from Marpi to Flores Point. At Flores Point and to the south were numerous defenses. The most likely landing sites were these western beaches. Defending the Flores Point naval base were three Type 10 80mm antiaircraft guns on the ridge 3,000 yards to the east. This battery was destroyed in the preinvasion attack. This ridge also had two 6-inch Whitworth-Armstrong naval guns. The Japanese purchased these guns from Great Britain in the early 1900s. During the War in the Pacific they were removed from obsolete ships for use as coastal defense guns. This British model, and also a Japanese version produced at the Kure Arsenal, were used throughout the Pacific islands.[12] An impressive camouflage effort saved both guns from detection and they survived the preinvasion bombardment.

At the entrance to Tanapag Harbor is tiny Managaha Island (Maniagassa). Installed on this island were three, Type 3 (1914), 140mm coastal defense guns, in largely unfinished casemates. To protect the harbor and naval base antiaircraft guns, Type 96 (1936), 25mm, in single- and dual-mount versions, were sited on the island. (The 140mm guns and one 25mm gun on this island survive and are described along with other extant fortifications in Chapter XVI.)

Two Type 10 120mm guns were emplaced on the ridge above Flores Point. One of the Type 10s was in an open emplacement and the other in a casemate, still with its forms which were awaiting drying of the cement. A testimony to the unexpected early arrival of the American invasion force.

Sited at Muchot Point on the north side of Garapan was a 120mm coastal defense gun, Type 3 (1914) in a concrete casemate. Around the 120mm gun were machine guns and 20mm pillboxes. On the cliff 1,600 yards east of Muchot Point was a battery of four Type 10 120mm guns, in open emplacements. They fired at American carrier planes during the June raids. American aerial or naval bombardment put them out of commission before invasion day.

Masonry and concrete pillboxes with 20mm guns and trench works were constructed along the Garapan beach front. Sited in the hills behind Garapan were 12mm machine guns and Type 88 (1928) 75mm antiaircraft guns. This was a truck drawn, mobile gun, with outrigger arms for temporary installation. In the Pacific they were most often permanently installed.

A battery of three 140mm, Type 3, coastal defense guns in open emplacements was located 1,500 yards south of Garapan and 1,000 yards inland of the beach. These guns were sited to fire on the sea approaches to Garapan and Chalan Kanoa. At the time of the enemy landings they were mounted on timber platforms but not levelled or the soil compacted around the base to finish the installation.

The beach front from Garapan to Agingan Point was defended by over 30 machine gun positions, trenchworks, and infantry defenses. At the Oleai runway were batteries of 25mm and 75mm (Type 88) antiaircraft guns. Six more 75mm AA guns were emplaced 1,000 yards east of Lake Susupe, to protect the runway and the inter-island radio station.

Afetna Point was heavily fortified as a strongpoint to fire flanking onto the beaches to the north and south. Among the guns were 37mm guns in pillboxes, 20mm, machine guns and howitzers to lay plunging fire on targets as they moved ashore from the reef.

Strong defenses were built at Agingan Point, 5,000 yards south of Afetna Point. Among its defenses was a battery of two 6-inch Whitworth-Armstrong, Model 1900 guns. Both were in casemates, one to fire on the channel between Saipan and Tinian and the other on sea approaches. These casemates were unfinished and destroyed in the preinvasion bombardment. Additional weapons on Agingan Point were 37mm, 20mm, and machine guns.

One of the three 1941-constructed circular blockhouses was southeast of Agingan Point on southern Agingan Beach. Its 20mm guns had been removed and installed in field fortifications. To the rear of the southern beaches were infantry positions. East of the Agingan Beach blockhouse, on Obyan Beach, is a second four-port blockhouse. It was also empty of guns, used instead to store anti-boat mines awaiting beach emplacement.

On the southern plateau was Aslito Airfield. Its antiaircraft defense was two batteries of 120mm guns (Type 10), and six batteries of 25mm and 75mm guns. One 120mm battery was on Cape Obyan, on the southwest side, and the second was on the northeast corner. The gunners of this battery were good marksmen, downing a number of U.S. aircraft. A third 120mm battery, on the east side of Aslito, was not installed. The guns were in storage. During the preinvasion bombardment, two mobile Type 88 75mm guns were hurriedly placed in the larger 120mm gun positions. These 75mm guns put up a terrific resistance and required multiple attacks to be silenced.

Aslito, the main Saipan airfield, had no ground defenses and lacked any demolition plans to prevent it from falling into enemy hands in usable condition. Elsewhere on Saipan was the same failure to have destruction plans to deny bridges, roads, supplies, and weapons to the enemy. The confidence in victory blinded the defenders to these important defensive tools. In some cases captured materials were used against the Japanese. Marines used captured fuel supplies in the invasion of Tinian. Captured food was useful in the feeding of civilian populations.

Still within the southern defense zone was the heavily defended Nafutan Peninsula, guarding the southern sea approach, Laulau Bay, and Aslito field. Sited on the peninsula was a battery of four 1900 Whitworth-Armstrong 6-inch guns, three with armor shields were in open emplacements. The fourth 6-inch gun was in an unfinished reinforced concrete casemate. All were camouflaged and despite extensive bombardment two survived with little damage.

Three 140mm Type 3 (1914) guns, wrapped in canvas and straw for camouflage, were in dugouts on the east slope of Mount Nafutan. These unfinished 140mm positions were the best designed positions on Saipan. The guns were completely below ground and not visible from the sea. For firing, the gun barrel was moved into a notch in the low parapet ground level wall. After firing, the gun barrel was traversed out of the notch and held below ground, invisible to the ships at sea. Nearby, were three empty 127mm positions and a radar on Mount Nafutan.

Laulau (Magicienne) Bay had historical use as a harbor. General Obata anticipated a landing here so he assigned a high priority to its protection. This included extensive trenchworks with supporting machine gun positions, coastal defenses, and antiaircraft guns sited on the ridges to fire dual missions against low flying planes and land targets. Along the beach were trenches with rifle pits and light machine gun positions. In front of some of the trenches was wire entanglement (the only beach on Saipan with wire installed), and a double 200-yard long wire entanglement was located in the grass and brush on the edge of the beach. There were also trenches, rifle and machine gun positions on the hillside to the immediate rear of the beach. The defenses were especially strong at the mid-point of Laulau Bay, where they were tied to the four-gun blockhouse.

American planners considered landings at Laulau Bay. One plan was to land the 1st Battalion, 2d Marines, the night before the main landings on the west coast. This battalion was to rapidly push inland, capturing Mount Tapotchau. They would hold this feature until the 2d Marine Division reached it. Later the Laulau plan was changed to a landing following the main western landings with the battalion attacking enemy positions from the rear. When planners received details of the powerful Japanese defenses at Laulau, the landings here were dropped as too risky.[13] The U.S. Army 27th Infantry Division planners also considered Laulau Bay as an invasion day target. One plan called for the 105th and 165th Regiments to land here and drive northward across the island to the Flores Point navy base. This plan was dropped when the 27th was designated the floating reserve.

Laulau Bay received preinvasion bombardment, evidence that landings might happen here. This bombardment caused little damage to the main defenses. The effectively camouflaged blockhouse and trenchworks were untouched until hit during the landward capture of this area. At that time Japanese soldiers made it a position. This blockhouse was a good example of elaborate efforts to hide defenses. Soil was terraced against the walls of the blockhouse and planted with Arwahal vines and grass. The roof was covered with soil planted with vines growing down the sides of the blockhouse on dried vine lattices. Areas of the blockhouse which might be visible were given a camouflage paint treatment of sand and light green colors.

Along Laulau Bay were pillboxes harmonized into the rock cliffs. Housing 20mm and 37mm guns they were among the most expertly camouflaged positions in the Pacific. The pillboxes built into the slopes have only tiny concrete embrasures, given a texturized finish or rock face to blend them into the natural setting. One of the most impressive was a 20mm pillbox, sited between two emerged limestone sea stacks. Its concrete face was covered with stones making it invisible until you were directly on top of it.

On a small point of land jutting out into the bay to the north of mid-point of Laulau Bay were two 120mm Type 3 guns. One was in a casemate and the second in an open position. Near the guns were a range finder, command post, and barracks area. Both guns were detected and put out of commission by naval bombardment.

Antiboat guns, 200mm high trajectory, to drop plunging fire onto landing vessels, were rushed into service in 1943. During 1944 the Central Pacific islands and especially the Marianas were provided with these Type 3 weapons. Generally, they were put on points of land so they could drop fire into the bays between the points. This created a "devils' horns", interlocking fire on the inner reef area. Four Type 3 200mm antiboat guns were installed on Laulau Bay, on the north and south sides. The guns were in open positions, camouflaged by natural vegetation. They went undetected, but this was not a landing area.

To the north of Laulau Bay is Laulau Kattan Beach (Brown Beach on U.S. invasion maps and today Tank Beach). A battery of three 120mm Type 10 guns was under construction on this potential landing beach. The guns were laying on the ground near the excavations. Work was completed on machine gun positions and two 20mm gun pillboxes. In addition to these fortifications Laulau Kattan had an extensive deception effort. Dummy weapons and facilities were built to deceive and draw fire from the attack forces. These positions included a searchlight tower with mannequin operators. There was also a palm tree log, painted to look like a gun tube. It was even wrapped with canvas camouflage, and nearby was a stack of projectiles, made of wood.

Saipan artillery was well-sited. The 9th Field Heavy Regiment had twelve Type 4 (1915) 150mm howitzers and 30 Type 94 (1934) 75mm mountain guns on the reverse slope of Mount Fina Susa. The 3d Independent Mountain Artillery Regiment and the 47th Independent Mixed Brigade Artillery had emplaced artillery above Laulau Bay and four Type 4 (1915) 150mm howitzers on Hill 500. Altogether, there were 65 artillery pieces, all preregistered on the landing beaches and potential beachheads. Numerous mortars were sited in the high ground just beyond the beaches. The artillery and mortars would prove to be the most effective defenses on Saipan. The artillery laid deadly fire onto the beaches and was not discovered and completely neutralized for two days. While Saito's artillery was effective, it failed to achieve its maximum potential due to two factors. First, was an inability to coordinate the guns for massed fire on one target. Each battery was preregistered on targets in their zone, but not all the guns could be called in on one target. Second, there were no trucks, prime movers, or horses to relocate artillery in danger of being overrun. Artillery was abandoned and lost as the Marines advanced inland.

The most important error made by the Saipan command was to fail to take advantage of the island military geology, with its mountainous terrain. This was terrain which favored the defender. It was ideal for defense-in-depth. Ignoring the terrain, General Obata created a linear defense on the beaches. The plan was standard Army doctrine, to destroy the enemy at the water's edge. If the enemy made it ashore counterattacks were to drive the invasion forces into the sea. This doctrine had already failed in the Kiribati Islands (Gilberts) and the Marshalls. A thin linear defense could not withstand the tremendous American firepower. But at the small, low atolls in the Kiribati and Marshalls, a beachline defense was the only option given their small size. On these islands an airfield occupied the center portion, removing the potential of defense-in-depth. Additionally, the low, flat atolls did not have terrain well-suited to such a defense.

There were recent examples of more innovative island defenses. However, they deviated from tradition. The Marianas commanders, bound by tradition, were unable to innovate. Had they not been so committed to past tactics they could have refined and improved innovative defenses. What was most needed was to create a defense less suspectable to the overpowering American firepower. Two recent examples offering a starting point were the Attu and Biak defenses. Colonel Yasuyo Yamasaki, in the May 1943 Aleutian battle of Attu Island, demonstrated excellent use of the terrain, reducing the American firepower advantage. There were no beach defenses, and his largest guns were 75mm. The U.S. 7th Infantry Division was allowed to land unopposed, while the defenders waited in trenches and foxholes in the hills above the valley routes to the island center. As the 7th Division soldiers struggled walking over the tundra covered valleys preregistered gunfire rained down. When the GIs tried to locate the hill foxholes and dugouts, they had trouble identifying them. Sometimes it was even more difficult for the Americans, when fog hid the hill slopes. During the foggy periods the defenders fired at predetermined targets, while the enemy could only wait for clearer skys. This defense proved costly for the invaders, American losses were about 550 killed, 1,200 wounded and 2,100 non-battle casualties (largely cold weather injuries) from a U.S. Army ground force of 15,000. The anticipated quick U.S. capture of Attu was prolonged, but could not be prevented. Losses for the Japanese garrison were 2,500 killed, and only 29 prisoners.[14]

The second case of a local commander diverting from the thin beach line defense was in the southwest Pacific, at Biak Island. Here, Colonel Naoyuki Kuzume, commanding an island garrison of about 11,400 men, had only light beach defenses. In place of beach

3. **Three 140mm coastal defense guns on a railcar at the time of the American invasion**
National Archives

4. Type 93 13mm machine gun located in hills above Laulau Bay.
National Archives

5. A Type 96 dual-mount 25mm becomes a Marine toy.

National Archives

6. This dummy Type 96 above Laulau Bay failed to attract an attack.

National Archives

7. The range finder for the 120mm battery on Laulau Bay escaped destruction.

National Archives

8. One of the antiaircraft guns for the defense of Flores Point was this Type 88 75mm gun.
National Archives

9. This Type 10 120mm dual purpose gun was only slighty damaged.

National Archives

10. An unfinished 140mm position on Nafutan Peninsula. Note the shelf to hide the barrel and the firing notch.

National Archives

11. A 6-inch gun in open revetment on Nafutan Peninsula

National Archives

12. The casemate for this Nafutan 6-inch gun is only partially completed.

National Archives

defenses the ridges above the airfields were heavily fortified. The plan was to deny the enemy use of the airfields, and therefore denying the island.

Colonel Kuzume's central defense was located in caves, located about 11,000 yards from the Mokmer Airfield. These caves were actually three depressions linked by underground tunnels and caverns. Through the use of stone-filled fuel drums, coral stone walls, and blast walls, these depressions were turned into an awesome defensive network. Additional positions were in a low ridge nearby.[15]

The U.S. Army 41st Division (less one regiment) landed on Biak on May 27, 1944. They encountered little resistance on the beaches but as they neared the first airfield, they ran into heavy fire from Kuzume's ridge line cave positions. To overcome the entrenched defenses the American's needed more troops. The first airfield on Biak was captured in one week, but the escarpment caves remained in Japanese hands. Another two weeks were needed to capture the second airfield. Once both airfields were in U.S. hands, a concerted effort was made to take the caves. They were captured following deadly hand-to-hand combat. It was a defense that delayed the American use of the airfield for one month and had made more costly the assault on Biak.

THREE

Beachline Overrun. A New Defense Line Formed

Saipan's thin linear defense could not stand up to American firepower. Massive naval and air bombardment ripped apart the beach defenses and left the defenders dazed, and unable to regroup. They could not effectively reorganize or carry out quick and effective reactions. Ultimately, the Saipan defenders withdrew to the more defensible interior mountains.

On March 12 the U.S. Joint Chiefs of Staff had issued the directive for the capture of the Marianas by Admiral Chester Nimitz's forces. These islands would be used as advanced naval bases, and more importantly as air bases for B-29 Superfortress bombing of the home islands. Their occupation would block the sea routes and cut off the rescue of bypassed islands such as Chuuk. Over 100,000 military would languish on the bypassed Caroline Islands.

The target date for the assault on Saipan was June 15, 1944, followed by invasions of Guam and Tinian soon after. Admiral Nimitz on March 28 drew up the force structure, while retaining overall command. Under Admiral Nimitz was Vice Admiral Raymond Spruance, commander of the Fifth Fleet. Directly in command of the actual amphibious assault was Vice Admiral Richmond Turner, Joint Expeditionary Force. Admiral Turner also commanded the Northern Attack Force, for the capture of Saipan and Tinian. A Southern Attack Force was commanded by Rear Admiral Richard Conolly. Major General Roy S. Geiger, USMC, commanded the Guam assault forces, comprised of the 3d Marine Division and 1st Provisional Marine Brigade. The floating reserve for the Marianas was the 27th Infantry Division, and in general reserve was the 77th

Infantry Division. Aerial support was provided by Vice Admiral Marc N. Mitscher's Fast Carrier Force. Vice Admiral Charles Lockwood provided submarines for patrol, intercept duty, and to recover downed aircrews.

The ground commander for the northern landings was Lieutenant General Holland M. Smith, USMC. Smith had for the Saipan and Tinian amphibious invasions three combat experienced divisions; the 2d Marine Division, commanded by Major General T. E. Watson; 4th Marine Division, commanded by Major General Harry Schmidt; and as floating reserve the U.S. Army's 27th Infantry Division, commanded by Major General Ralph C. Smith. The total invasion strength was 66,779 marines and soldiers.

Preinvasion air raids began on June 11 when the U.S. Task Force 58 with 15 carriers struck. That afternoon fighter sweeps by 225 aircraft hit Saipan, Tinian and Guam. Japanese losses were 81 planes in the air and 29 on the ground while U.S. losses were 11 planes and 6 crewmen. Antiaircraft guns at Aslito put up resistance and were responsible for some of the 11 losses. The handful of surviving 1st Air Fleet planes could only offer a feeble reaction in the future. Control of the air had passed, this day, to the Americans.

Takeo Yamauchi, in his trench behind Oleai Beach, witnessed the U.S. carrier plane raid of June 11. He recalled that at about

four o'clock the air attack was broken off. Whole sections of the mountains were burned black and the island was dark with smoke. Thirteen or fourteen naval-defense planes had taken to the skies to meet the Americans and were quickly shot down in air-to-air combat. I actually saw them falling. After that, no Japanese planes flew over Saipan. They came back the next morning at four-thirty. The primary ammunition storage depots and anything that stood out were strafed. We tried to shoot at American planes with our rifles. Not many Japanese anti-aircraft guns remained. I saw a few American planes explode in midair, but there was no effective fire from the ground anymore.[1]

On June 12 U.S. carrier aircraft discovered Japanese convoys in the Marianas area. U.S. carrier planes hit hard a convoy headed north, at about 125 miles west of Pagan Island. Convoy losses were nine transports, a torpedo boat, three submarine chasers, and a net tender. That same day U.S. planes destroyed three more transports, two near Saipan, and one in Tanapag Harbor. The next day another convoy was detected escaping to the west of Guam and attacked with one transport destroyed and others damaged.

It was frustrating to observe the unchallenged American attacks. Tokuzo Matsuya, of the 9th Tank Regiment, recorded in his diary the enemy mastery of the air:

> 11 June — At a little after 1300, I was awakened by the air raid alarm and immediately led all men into the trench. Scores of enemy Grumman fighters began strafing and bombing Aslito airfield and Garapan. For about two hours, the enemy planes ran amuck and finally left leisurely amidst the unbelievably inaccurate anti-aircraft fire. All we could do was watch helplessly.
>
> 12 June — With daybreak enemy planes (even more than yesterday) made a sudden attack. The all day strafing and bombing was much heavier. It must have caused great damage at Garapan and Aslito airfield.
>
> 13 June — At 0930, enemy naval guns began firing in addition to the aerial bombing. The enemy holds us in utter contempt. If only we had a hundred planes or so.[2]

A soldier stationed on Tinian, home of the 1st Air Fleet, could only wonder what had happened. He wrote in his diary, on June 12, that:

> of all the tens of Japanese planes one can't see even one during a raid. The planes which cover the sky are all the enemy's. They are far and away more skillful than Japanese planes. Now begins our cave life. Enemy planes overhead all day long — some 230 in number. They completely plastered our airfields. . . Where are our planes? Not one was sent up. Our AA guns spread black smoke where the enemy planes weren't. Not one hit out of a thousand shots. The Naval Air Group has taken to its heels.[3]

On June 13 when the naval close-in preinvasion bombardment task groups appeared offshore, it looked like an invasion force, there were so many ships. However, the heavy naval bombardment precluded spending much time looking to the sea. Naval shells ripped apart the landscape, tearing out trees and man-made features. Those in the beach trenches hugged the ground, and a few were buried alive. Kitchens and food supplies were lost so some units had little food that day or the next. Surprisingly the death toll was not high but it was a horrible experience.

A soldier's diary entry for the June 12 raid recorded that: there was a fierce evening air attack. I have at last come to the place where I will die. I am pleased to think I will die calmly in true samurai style. Naval gunfire supported this attack which was too terrible for words.[4]

Construction workers at Aslito were reported to become very depressed as the base came under heavy naval bombardment. However, the damage was not great and loss of life was limited. Many shore positions remained operational. The extensive shelling of the west coast indicated to General Saito that an invasion was imminent and identified the western beaches as the landing sites. Saito was confident that the enemy would be repulsed at the beach and forced into the sea. Then, Admiral Ozawa would show up with the Mobile Fleet, to destroy the disorganized landing forces in the waters offshore.

Mitscher's carrier planes achieved complete aerial superiority in the first attack. Thereafter, no Japanese planes would contest the American carrier aircraft. However, the antiaircraft guns at Aslito airfield remained a danger. To end this threat the first rocket attack was launched on June 13 against Aslito Airfield. Leading the attack was the commander of VT-16, Commander Robert H. Isely. As Isely lowered his plane to the attack pattern, Type 10 120mm guns opened fire, striking his and a second TBF Avenger, sending both down in flames on the south side of the field. After the capture and rebuilding of Aslito airfield, it was renamed Isely Field in his honor. Base signs and descriptions of the field incorrectly spelled it Isley Field and many histories perpetuate this error.

The U.S. shelling got better on June 14. Men of the 47th Independent Mixed Brigade on Afetna Point came under especially intense naval and air bombardment. A number of the gun positions were destroyed with some personnel casualties. Muchot Point near Garapan also received a heavy attack but the 120mm coastal defense guns survived.

The defenders on Nafutan Point were in their cave shelters for eight hours as U.S. warships shelled the peninsula. Despite this horrible pounding the 6-inch battery was in service and fired on, but missed the cruiser *Montpelier*. Also, the 140mm guns at Marpi had near misses on enemy ships off the north coast. Additional coastal defenses to challenge American warships were the 140mm guns on Managaha Island. They fired on the battleship *Maryland*. This battleship, joined by the *California*, returned fire silencing this battery. Of all the Marianas coastal defenses the most effective was a battery of three 6-inch guns in caves to the south of Tinian Town. They went into action on June 14 straddling the *Cleveland*, and hitting the *California* and the destroyer *Braine*. Casualties on the two ships were four killed and 24 injured.[5]

During the preinvasion bombardment Saito's men remained alert for landings. They could observe American underwater demolition teams searching for obstacles off the western beaches. Beach defenders opened fire on the UDT teams as they worked, killing four and wounding fifteen. Under the cover of a heavy smoke screen UDT 7 was safely recovered. The UDTs had found few obstacles or mines.

The no-show by the Japanese 1st Air Fleet remained perplexing. Tokuzo Matsuya asked in his June 14 diary page "Where are our planes? Are they letting us die without making an effort to save us?" Soldiers also wondered where was the fleet. One rumor had it on its way and all the defenders would have to do is hold on for a short time. The mighty fleet was coming to destroy the American ships.

Even after the battleship pounding of shoreline batteries on June 14, some were still operational. American success had been greater in knocking out the exposed antiaircraft guns. Captain Shimamura, an artillery instructor sent to Saipan to observe artillery operations, learned that:

> Beach positions withstood four days of bombardment. Those observation posts and gun emplacements that were protected by splinter-proof shelters were able to withstand the bombardment. Dummy positions proved very effective. During bombardment, both day and night, movement to alternate positions was very difficult. Communication lines were cut frequently, and the need for repairs and messengers was great.[6]

There were problems on the American side. Two May intelligence estimates of Japanese troop strength had to be revised upwards. And, on June 14, the final estimate was still low. Estimates in the range of 18,000, widely missed the true number of 30,000. The U.S. invasion force of 66,779 was not as overpowering as believed by the planners. Also the U.S. had poor maps, lacked information on terrain features, and confronted defenders with the ultimate responsibility of protecting the home islands from American very long-range bombers.

It is not known if the Saipan commanders believed their optimistic statements, or were engaged in troop morale boosting, or the desire to transmit positive statements. The 31st Army messaged the Imperial General Headquarters that the U.S. "did not carry out large-scale shelling and bombing against the positions on the landing beach. . . . Even though we received fierce bombing and shelling, our positions were completely sound".[7] For the individual soldier, his existence was not so rosy. A tanker in the 9th Tank Regiment witnessed a naval supply warehouse and ammunition dump at Laulau Bay destroyed. He had no way of coping with the explosions. We could do nothing but wait for them to stop.[8]

Afetna Point received a terrific pounding but the dug-in positions survived. On the morning of June 14 the point was shelled by the *Birmingham* and *Indianapolis*. That afternoon, guns of the *Tennessee, California*, and *Birmingham* and aerial bombing and strafing struck. Again on June 15 American ships shelled Afetna. Despite such a pounding, the point would come alive as Marines landed, with its hidden guns firing enfilade on the beaches.

At dawn on June 15 the U.S. bombardment thundered onto the west coast beaches and Aslito Field. A hail of fire was received at Agingan Point, Afetna Point, Muchot Point, and Managaha Island. Incoming rounds included 8-inch, 14-inch, and 16-inch projectiles. The naval bombardment ceased, only to be replaced by air raids. Bombing and strafing runs lasted for thirty minutes, stopped, and naval shelling resumed. It was largely an American show, but battery fire from Ushi Point, Tinian, hit the *Tennessee* killing eight.

Marines loaded into landing craft, headed for the west coast with landings below Garapan, from Oleai south to Agingan Point. To the north soldiers of the 135th Infantry Regiment observed landing craft headed for Tanapag. However, the craft circled in the water and then returned to their ships. It had been a feint. Not knowing if they might return, General Saito ordered the 135th to remain in position. The soldiers waiting at the western beaches were hugging the ground waiting for the bombardment to lift. Naval gunfire continued to rain upon them, even as the landing craft approached. Once the naval bombardment ceased, strafing and rocket attacks struck at shoreline positions.

From a safe distance, Second Lieutenant Rai Imanishi viewed the landing as having a profound importance. The lieutenant wrote that the:

> Combined Fleet is about to engage the enemy in decisive combat . . . in the Marianas sector. The enemy has already begun landing on Saipan. Truly, we are on the threshold of momentous occurrences. Now is the time for me to offer my life for the great cause and be a barrier against the enemy advancing in the Pacific Ocean.[9]

When the landing craft crossed over the reefs, the shoreline weapons and artillery behind the beaches opened up with deadly fire. Thirty-one Landing Vehicle Tracked (LVTs), (amphtracs) carrying the men of the 2d Marine Division, were hit and stopped short of the Oleai-Susupe beaches (Red/Green Beaches). Most of the LVTs made it ashore. But, as they climbed onto the beaches mortar and artillery fire rained down on them. Every beach was chewed up by artillery fire, causing heavy Marine casualties. Heavy casualties did not slow the Marines, who managed to get 700 LVTs and 8,000 troops over the beaches in the first twenty minutes.[10]

The beachline defense, in the early hours, extracted heavy costs from both sides. As an example, all the battalion commanders of the 2d Marine Division were casualties. Quickly Marines stepped forward to lead the men to their objectives. Machine gunners of the Japanese 136th Infantry, in positions on a slight incline behind Oleai (Red Beach), caused high casualties among the 6th Marines. Also, mortars found and hit tempting targets such as the 2d Battalion, 6th Marine, command post.

Effective fire was directed against Marines landing at Susupe (Green Beach). The Afetna Point defenses, harmonized into the terrain, caused death among the landing force until this strongpoint was attacked and destroyed from the rear on the second day, D+1. These defenses held out longer than those at Oleai Beach, which fell during the initial landings. One company in the second Oleai line was ordered to counterattack the Marines in the maneuver area, the land between the two lines. The counterattackers charged the Marine line only to be cut down by machine gun and rifle fire. Japanese soldiers in the second line who remained in the trenches were safe for the moment, as the Marines halted and dug in. These defenders in the second line were instructed to hold their line while other units counterattacked that night. During the night, stragglers from the defeated counterattack passed through the second line headed for the rear. There was little talk, but those who did spoke of a crushed counterattack.[11]

Beachline defenses survived in the south where the 4th Marines landed. Agingan Point defenses had been hurt but not completely destroyed. They joined the fray once the Marines tried to push off the beaches to the north. This heavy fire forced 4th Marine Division LVTs to halt short of their inland debarkation points. Japanese artillery took a heavy toll. Lieutenant Colonel Nakashima's 3d Independent Artillery Regiment was making it a miserable time for the invaders. There were also hidden machine gunners who practiced fire discipline, firing only short bursts when a landing wave first came onto the beach. These machine guns could only fire so long before the Marines pinpointed their locations and knocked them out.[12]

The early Japanese success in slowing the Marine inland movement and causing heavy casualties was followed up with ineffective and wasteful small piecemeal counterattacks. These violated the notion of massive counterattacks to drive the enemy into the sea

13. Marines hug the beach at Oleai; soon they will push inland.

14. A knocked-out Type 95 light tank

before a beachhead could be established. This resulted from an inability at division and higher headquarters to correctly ascertain the situation and develop counterattack plans. The disorganization was much greater among the defenders than the Marines on the beaches.

A small force of 15 to 25 Japanese died in a counterattack against the 6th Marine regimental command post and a nearby aid station. More effective was an abandoned Type 95 light tank on the beach, which came to life with its 37mm gun firing on LVTs bringing up the 6th Marines reserve. This tank, after firing a few rounds, was destroyed by bazookas and grenades.

Ridgeline positions, 900 yards inland of Agingan Point, had escaped destruction. Occupied by soldiers of the 47th Independent Mixed Brigade (IMB), these guns rained intense fire onto the southern beaches. Additional firepower came from the antiaircraft guns at Aslito, now taking on ground targets on the southern beaches. Agingan Point put up a strong defense, but fell at a cost of 150 men.

Surprisingly, Chalan Kanoa was defended by only a handful of snipers. No use was made of the rubble. However, one soldier climbed the sugar mill smokestack and for two days served as a spotter. Hurriedly, infantry of the 47th IMB formed along the road inland of the Chalan Kanoa junction. They were killed by machine gunners on LVTs moving up the road. The U.S. Marines pushed towards Mount Fina Susa and its important artillery positions. As they neared the mountain, heavy artillery fire of the 3d Mountain Artillery Regiment and mortar fire halted their movement.

Colonel Takashi Goto tried to help block the landings. He dispatched his 4th Tank Company to the southwestern beaches, where they took up anti-landing positions. Heavy bombardment drove the tanks off the beach to rear–sheltered positions where they were of little value. Once Marines were ashore, they came out to do battle. These tank actions included two 4th Company tanks striking the 6th Marines at Oleai at noon. Both tanks were blown apart by Marine bazooka and grenade fire. Three more 4th Company tanks unsuccessfully struck at the 6th Marines. During the invasion day 4th Tank Company actions, the unit lost 11 of its 14 tanks. They had not hurt the Marines.

The most effective defenses of the invasion and next day, were skillful ridgeline and mountain artillery positions which had been missed by the American bombardment. On the forward and reverse slopes of ridges and small hills were batteries of 75mm and 150mm artillery. All the guns were preregistered on important target areas.

Artillery observers spotted the American armor coming ashore at noon, over the Susupe beaches (Green). This was a serious threat, which called for immediate reaction. In response a furious artillery barrage was delivered against the Susupe beach. It could not stop the arrival of the armor. Once American armor was on land it would be much more difficult to drive the Marines into the sea. Only a short time later, American infantry-tank actions broke up a southern counterattack.

American artillery was also landed the first afternoon. Again Japanese artillery tried to destroy the landing craft carrying the weapons. Only a few howitzers were hit. The opportunity to drive the Americans into the sea was quickly disappearing. Enemy artillery and armor were ashore and Marines had made some progress in moving inland. By nightfall, there were two American divisions ashore. But, the Marines had suffered about 2,000 casualties and were short of their goals. On the Japanese side a number of beachline defenses remained intact, they included Afetna Point and ridge positions. The most opportune time for counterattacks had passed, but the first night could provide the stealth for powerful counterattacks. During the day the 31st Army radioed Tokyo that the Army this evening will make a night attack with all its forces and expects to annihilate the enemy at one swoop. There was a huge gap between this grandiose message to Tokyo and the actual counterattack. Instead of a massive attack with all the forces, there were small and uncoordinated efforts. The first counterattack was comprised of elements of Colonel Suzuki's 135th Infantry Regiment. This was an evening infantry-tank charge against the 6th Marines, 2d Division. About 200 soldiers of the 135th Regiment marched down the coastal road from the north for a reconnaissance-in-force probe of Marine lines seeking a weak spot or gap. None was found and the 135th Infantry pulled back. The 135th then formed up for a head-on thrust against the 6th Marines.

At 0300 a bugle call and battle screams announced the second counterattack against the 2d Marine Division. Within moments, U.S. destroyers fired 5-inch star shells, turning night into an eerie daylight, robbing the 135th of stealth. The 31st Army reported that "as soon as the night attack units go forward, the enemy points out targets by using the large star shells which practically turn night into day. Thus the maneuvering of units is extremely difficult."[13] Another training manual assertion was now myth, that night is one-million reinforcements.

The upright Japanese soldiers, silhouetted by the star shells, were cut down by automatic fire, rifle fire, and 5-inch shells from the *California.* Most of the counterattack force was destroyed, but a few infiltrated to the regimental command post where they were killed by U.S. armor and infantry. Seven hundred warriors of the 135th Infantry Regiment died in the counterattack.

The third counterattack, a tank-infantry charge from Garapan, hit the 2d Marine Division a few hours before daylight. It got nowhere, halted by a wall of Marine gunfire.

In the south, a heavy artillery and mortar barrage preceded the 0330 counterattack. This time, to achieve surprise, a group of civilians walked in front of the column. For awhile the Marines assumed the column was a civilian surrender party. At the last moment the deception was realized, and artillery called in to destroy the column. Another southern counterattack, one hour later, also failed.

During the night, Japanese artillery and mortar subjected all the occupied beaches to harassing fire. While the firing was in progress, infiltration teams sought out gaps in the American lines. One gap which was effectively exploited was at Chalan Kanoa between the 2d and 4th Marine Divisions. At 0530 about 200 Japanese advanced from Lake Susupe to the Chalan Kanoa Beach and through this gap and onto the sugar dock. They hoped to disrupt the unloading process and to kill Marine shore parties. Killing was in the other direction as Marines and shore party personnel repulsed the charge.

The counterattacks were too late, and too little, to achieve the desired results. General Saito, fearful of losing all his forces, had ordered small piecemeal charges to save troops for future actions. By trying to save men, he instead lost them in too weak counterattacks. These limited attacks had no chance of realizing the defense plan to counterattack in force when the invaders were most disorganized. A great opportunity was lost on invasion day; the Marines had only reached one-half of their first-day objectives with heavy casualties. The ideal time for an all-out counterattack was early in the landings and at the very latest the first evening, but General Saito hesitated.

The morning light of June 16 was bad news. Even if not understood by the Japanese, the night counterattacks had not driven the Marines back even an inch. With daylight, defensive positions could be observed and hit by American planes who had total control of the skies. There was also American artillery, naval gunfire, and American armor. The favorable news for General Saito was his operational artillery in the hills and high ground overlooking the targets below. Time was against Saito, the shortcomings in Japanese artillery use were becoming more critical. Unable to mass fire, the artillery had done poorly against the important U.S. armor and artillery landings. Also, the Marines were advancing on the artillery, which could not be relocated for the want of prime movers.

The warrior spirit was alive and the Saito's men expected the great and powerful Combined Fleet would show up to destroy the logistical support of the invaders. Troop reinforcements must also be on the way. There were no reinforcements and the Mobile Fleet was headed to an area west of Saipan for the decisive sea battle. General Saito, reviewing the situation, planned another and more powerful counterattack. As he developed plans more U.S. troops poured ashore, the 165th Regiment, 27th Infantry Division, landed. Unknown to Saito, this morning, June 16, Admiral Spruance cancelled the invasion of Guam and was landing his floating reserve at Saipan. Submarine contact reports warned Spruance that the Mobile Fleet had left its anchorage and might be headed to the Marianas. Admiral Soemu Toyoda, commander of the Combined Fleet, had given the order for A-Go (the sea battle) on June 15, when he was informed of the landings at Saipan.

Since he had not received reinforcements or Navy help, General Saito, fearful of large losses, refused to consider an all-out counterattack. He did come up with a limited attack, designed to surprise the Marines so as to break into their positions. It was a tank-infantry assault to capture the inter-island radio station at Susupe, occupied by the 6th Marines.

Colonel Takashi Goto provided 37 (Type 95 and Type 97) of his surviving 44 tanks for this operation, the largest tank-infantry battle of the Central Pacific. Colonel Yukimatsu Ogawa, commanding the 136th, teamed up 1,000 soldiers with the tanks. Since the Marines had come to anticipate night counterattacks, this one would be a daytime attack, to achieve surprise. The mission objective was to break through the 6th Marine lines and advance 400 yards to the radio station. Once the radio station was captured the infantry and armor could use it as a base of operations for attacks on Marine lines from the rear and to destroy supply dumps and weapons on the beach.

General Saito's orders read:

> The center force (136th Infantry Regiment) will attack the enemy in the direction of Oleai with its full force. The tank unit (9th Tank Regiment) will advance SW of Hill 164 (a hill, 164 meters high, on Laulau Road) after the attack unit. . . has commenced the attack. The tank unit will charge the transmitting station and throw the enemy into disorder just before the penetration of the attack unit into this sector.[14]

The 9th Tank Regiment was a well–trained unit, with a June 16 strength of: Headquarters Company (6 tanks), 3d and 5th Companies (11 Type 97 and 3 Type 95 tanks each), 4th Company had only three tanks left, and the 6th Company was divided between Guam and Saipan with seven tanks on each island. Saipan and Guam were better equipped with armor than previous Central Pacific battlefields. They had the improved late-model Type 97 (Chi-Ha) medium tanks in addition to the light Type 95 (Ha-Go). A 47mm Type 1 high velocity gun gave the Type 97 more firepower than the Type 95 (1935) with its 37mm gun. There was also heavier armor plate on the Type 97 (1937), 8mm to 25mm thickness, compared to 6 to 12mm on the light tank. While the Type 97 was an improvement over the Type 95 it was no match for the American Sherman, with its 75mm main gun. The M4 Sherman had an armor plate of 12mm to 75mm and welded construction which was stronger than the bolt and rivet design of the Japanese tanks.

Unfortunately for the Susupe mission the island command had poor intelligence data. The planners did not conduct reconnaissance to find a weak spot to penetrate, but ordered the charge against well-organized Marine front lines. Saito's staff incorrectly anticipated that the Marines would be digging in when his forces struck at 1700. They had already completed their lines. The final element, surprise by an early operation, was possible. But, Colonel Goto did not get his tanks out of the forest near Chacha village to Susupe on schedule. It was 0315 before the tanks were on Laulau Road just above the Susupe swamp. As the tanks, divided into seven assault teams, climbed down the slope to the swampy area below, their noise alerted the Marines. A few tanks got bogged down in the swamp. The rest hit the ready Marine lines at 0330. The Marines opened fire with all available weapons, machine guns, mortars, bazooka, artillery, and even naval gunfire was called in. Star shells lighted the battlefield. Then as Japanese tanks were hit and burning, the fires silhouetted other tanks and infantry making them easy targets. Quickly the battlefield turned into a one-sided killing field with Colonel Ogawa and Goto's soldiers dying. They could not escape, reorganize, or find shelter.

Overall it was a poorly planned and executed attack. The tanks had not planned routes or designated targets. They entered battle with no knowledge of the enemy, his positions or strength. It was an uncoordinated assault with crew chiefs standing in open turrets to direct the tanks and accompanying infantry. The tanks moved in no particular order, except in the general direction of the radio station. Their aimless thrust left them open to repeated hits.[15]

Colonel Goto lost about 20 tanks and was probably killed in the counterattack. Descriptions of 24 to 31 tanks destroyed are likely too high, given the number of tanks encountered during the remainder of the campaign. Infantry losses in the 136th were very high. There is no record of a lessons-learned analysis of this flawed operation. Colonel Takuji Suzuki, chief of staff of the 43d Division, did report to higher headquarters that American star shells robbed the attack of cover of darkness.[16]

Colonel Eisuke Suzuki, commanding officer of the 135th Infantry, informed his troops of the attack, optimistically stating that: the main strength of the Marianas force carried out a night attack against the enemy that landed at Oleai during the night of 16 June. Despite the heavy blow we dealt the enemy, he is reinforcing his rear forces in the vicinity of Oleai, although the process is not yet complete.[17]

Saipan had become an exception to the Japanese practice of piecemeal armor attacks. During the night attack, a "mobile mass" was employed; but, in the open, on wet terrain, against American firepower, it was a huge mistake. The only successful Japanese tank attacks in the Marianas would be jabs coming out of jungle cover to hit U.S. troop bivouacs and then rushing back into the jungle.

Japanese artillery had a better night, on June 16, than the armor and infantry. Mortar and artillery fire were directed against U.S. artillery of the 10th Marines. Eight Marine artillery pieces were hit. Unknown to the Japanese, many of these weapons were repaired and back in service by the next afternoon.

At the end of June 16, General Saito, had he had adequate intelligence, would have been aware that the U.S. forces had experienced about 3,500 casualties. The first two days had been costly for the Marines. Yet they were certain that victory was forthcoming. Morale had been greatly lifted by the Marine destruction of the counterattack at Susupe. On the Japanese side this failed counterattack was symbolic of the command leadership weaknesses. Their operations were poorly conceived and miserly in force strength. The only successes were the artillery sited in the hills and the hard fighting by the individual Japanese soldier.

During the night of June 16 there was retreating. Soldiers of the 136th at Oleai Beach, if physically able, escaped. The wounded men committed suicide. Many rushed to the rear in a disorganized exodus, but there was no peace for those on the retreat as American artillery found them. For days retreating soldiers wandered the mountains seeking shelter from American shelling. In this disorganized retreat they were of no value to the defense.

On June 17, Army Chief of Staff Hideki Tojo encouraged the Saipan command to fight harder, imploring that:

Because the fate of the Japanese Empire depends on the result of your operation, inspire the spirit of the officers and men and to the very end continue to destroy the enemy gallantly and persistently; thus alleviate the anxiety of our Emperor.

Major General Keiji Iketa, chief of staff, 31st Army, responded:

Have received your honorable Imperial words and we are grateful for boundless magnanimity of the Imperial favor. By becoming the bulwark of the Pacific with 10,000 deaths we hope to requite the Imperial favor.[18]

On June 17, the U.S. Army 165th Regiment headed for Aslito Field, where defenders waited on a southern ridgeline a few hundred yards before the field. When the Army troops working their way up the ridge were most exposed, the defenders counterattacked and drove them off. The desire to defend this line was strong since Aslito was undefended except for antiaircraft guns, with their barrels depressed to fire antipersonnel. These guns had already fired on the Marines on the north side of the airfield.

Substantial Japanese losses occurred on June 17. All orderly movement was lost. It became increasingly difficult to evacuate the dead and wounded. More worrisome, was the number of good defenses given up. Also, large quantities of supplies were abandoned. In the midst of this disorder, General Saito strove to maintain an offensive posture with night counterattacks. They were small-scale, piecemeal attacks of one or two squads testing weak points in the enemy lines. Some attack teams sought out armor and artillery for destruction by explosives, mines, or grenades they carried for this purpose. While usually unsuccessful, these night missions kept alive the belief of offensive fighting rather than unacceptable static defense.

This day Japanese aircraft using the Rota Field got into the air for bombing raids on U.S. shipping. Landing Ship, Tank (LST) *84* was hit and set ablaze but the fire was contained and extinguished. Another bomb hit and damaged the escort carrier *Fanshaw Bay*. Additional attacks on ships missed their targets. A few of the attacking planes fell to U.S. antiaircraft, most managed to escape. It was a raid of limited proportions, and did nothing to help the Saipan garrison. There would be few future missions, since so few planes were available. Planes from Guam, Peleliu, Iwo Jima, and Chuuk bombed Saipan, rarely hitting anything.

Demonstrating that not all coastal defenses had been destroyed, shore batteries at Muchot Point (120mm) and southeast of Garapan (Type 10 120mm) fired at naval targets on June 18. The gun crews sent shells towards the destroyers *Philip* and *Phelps,* with two shells hitting and damaging the *Phelps.*

A Japanese counterlanding was ordered during the night of June 18 with troops of the 1st Battalion, 18th Infantry, loaded on barges at the Flores Point Base. At 0430 they sailed out of the harbor headed for the beaches. American Landing Craft Infantry (LCI) gunboats detected the landing force, destroying 13 craft and forcing the others to retreat.

American firepower continued to make life hell for the defenders trying to regroup. Wherever the Japanese soldiers moved they came under fire from aircraft, artillery or naval shelling. Existence was a constant terror. In one attack on a retreating group of the 135th Infantry planes came in at low altitude strafing the column, killing about 100 men. Later that night the retreating soldiers were hit by artillery. As they resumed their escape more artillery rained down on them. Finally this small group found a cave where they hid for two and a half days.[19]

On June 18 General Saito recognized that the beach line defense was lost. He drew up a new security line, which ran from a point about 1,000 yards below Garapan, southeast to White Cliff, on the south slopes of Mount Tapotchau to Laulau Bay. With this line the American advance was to be blocked, giving time for the Saipan defense to be bolstered by reinforcements. It was a mobile defense with a line defense combined with strongholds and offensive actions, including infiltration, and sniping, in front of the line. Major General Keiji Iketa, 31st Army chief of staff, on June 18, reported the battle situation to Tokyo. His account indicated a disorganized and collapsing defense. The 43d Division Headquarters had only three companies at its disposal. Also, the 43d command post was shelled with the division commander and some staff killed. Little else was known except that the U.S. was directing fierce naval gunfire, bombing and strafing of all positions.[20] General Iketa was wrong about General Saito being killed. Some of his staff were wounded in the attack, but the general was alive. Recognizing that the island was in danger of being overrun, Saito ordered all secret documents destroyed. Large quantities were destroyed, but tons of papers were captured by the Americans and proved valuable in future Marianas and Carolines' operations.

Mobile defense tactics were employed, while other troops prepared the new line of security. In front of the line were delaying, harassing positions, and from them offensive jabs were made.

One jab was two tanks slashing into the Marine lines, causing 15 Marine casualties before the tanks were stopped by bazooka and artillery fire. Meanwhile to the southeast, machine gun and mortar defenses held up the advance of the 23d Marines to the east of Chalan Kanoa.

In the south, the undefended Aslito Airfield was occupied by the U.S. Army's 165th Infantry on June 18. Fighters were using the field four days later. The American use of this airstrip meant increased air support for the enemy ground forces. It was a serious blow for General Saito. Also on June 18 the 4th Marine Division reached the east coast cutting off the lower portion of the island, except Nafutan Peninsula which was still in Japanese hands.

Saipan received messages from the Imperial General Headquarters insisted that the island be held. One message declared it imperative that the beaches still in friendly hands be preserved so reinforcements could be landed (however, there were no plans to dispatch more troops). The enemy was to be denied the use of Aslito and Banaderu (Marpi) Airfields. A warning from the emperor was enclosed, that the loss of Saipan would open Tokyo to U.S. bombing. "You must hold Saipan" the emperor emphasized.

Units were in place on Saito's new security line by June 19. At the Garapan end was the Yokosuka 1st Special Naval Landing Force and other naval troops. To their east was the 135th Infantry on the west slopes of Mount Tapotchau. Holding the area to the southeast of the 135th was the 118th Infantry, which also could swing towards Laulau Bay to defend against a landing there. General Saito believed that the Americans might still land here. Elements of the 47th Independent Mixed Brigade defended Kagman Peninsula supported by the 9th Expeditionary holding the shore north of Kagman Peninsula. In reserve was the 136th Infantry at Chacha, in the northwest corner of Kagman Peninsula. Finally the 9th Tank Regiment was in reserve to support the 118th Infantry and to guard against a Laulau landing or tank advances up the coast.

Defenders on Nafutan Point were proving to be excellent fighters, making good use of the terrain, some of the most jagged coral anywhere. They placed there weapons to defend the most likely approaches, worrying less about the nearly impassable avenues. Most of the shoreline was too rugged for access. It is broken limestone, with fissures, caves, and rough seas blocking entry. Reaching the point from the west was prevented by a sheer hill mass of nasty sharp coral pinnacles covered by thick jungle growth. Probably the least difficult route was to climb the steep shoreline cliffs on the south coast. This was the route that the 105th Infantry, 27th Division, used to get onto the peninsula. As they climbed these slopes they were most harassed by surrendering civilians and then automatic weapons fire. Once on the peninsula the GIs encountered a strong defense. The 47th Independent Mixed Brigade held tough on Nafutan Point until June 27.

By June 19 the Japanese had experienced horrible losses, gone were three and a half of the eight battalions of the 43d Division. The artillery resources were down to eleven 75mm guns, with four of five artillery battalions destroyed. Only a few tanks remained. The 47th Independent Mixed Brigade was in shambles. Losses in the front line defenses were about 50 percent.

There was still hope, the men on Saipan had not given up on the prospect of the mighty Mobile Fleet or Army reinforcements coming to their aid. Also, the Japanese solider remembered past victories over materially superior forces. They had the advantage of Yamato Damashii, a spirit and fighting ability, which could overcome an enemy numerical advantage. Slowly there was a change in attitudes, with overconfidence giving way to the recognition of impending death and defeat. Tanker Matsuya Tokuzo related this feeling:

> The fierce attacks of the enemy only increase our hostility. Every man is waiting for the assault with all weapons for close quarters fighting readiness. We are waiting with "Molotov cocktails" and hand grenades ready for the word to rush forward recklessly into the enemy ranks with our swords in hands. The only thing that worries me is what will happen to Japan after we die.[21]

FOUR

The Sea Battle of the Marianas

The Imperial Japanese Navy desire for an all-out sea confrontation with the Pacific Fleet was at hand. Finally, near the Marianas the Japanese Navy could slug it out with the enemy. Once the American Navy had been defeated the U.S. would lose its willpower and retreat from the Pacific.

On March 1, 1944 the plans and naval reorganization to realize the decisive sea battle were made. The Combined Fleet was reorganized into a 1st Mobile Fleet which included most of the ships in the Navy except area commands and submarines. Vice Admiral Jisaburo Ozawa, formerly commander of the carrier forces, was named commander. His fleet had the carriers as the central element, with the destroyers, heavy cruisers and battleships as a screen.

Plans for this decisive sea battle were developed in April. On May 3, Admiral Soeumu Toyoda, commander in chief, Combined Fleet, issued the general order for A-Go, the decisive naval confrontation. Admiral Toyoda believed the battle would take place in the Belau area or the Western Carolines near Yap and Woleai. These waters, south of the Woleai-Yap-Belau line were within reach of a number of land airfields. Air commanders had instructions to conduct relentless attacks, to whittle down the American ships as they steamed towards the final battle. Besides the availability of land planes, this region had the advantage of being near fuel oil supplies. Since fuel supplies and transport capabilities were so short, a battle here was convenient. Believing it would happen in this region was influenced by wishful thinking.

The fuel problems were relieved in early May when the decision was made to use unprocessed Borneo petroleum, even though its highly volatile elements increased the danger of fire as well as fouled boilers. Using this fuel the ships at the standby point of Tawi Tawi (in the Sulu Sea off northeast Borneo) were filled to capacity and now able to fight in the Marianas or wherever the U.S. headed.

Privately, some in the Imperial Japanese Navy believed that the decisive battle strategy was an obsession, holding back the fleet and missing opportunities to attack enemy shipping. Admiral Matome Ugaki, commander of the First Battleship Division, recorded in his diary that it was a mistake to wait for the big battle. Avoiding naval actions against smaller groups of American ships, had favored the Pacific Fleet which was growing while the Japanese fleet suffered serious losses.[1]

Private reservations aside, the great battle concept dominated naval strategy. The admiral who would have the opportunity to realize this great sea victory was Admiral Ozawa. Ozawa was, according to the eminent naval historian Morison, a worthy antagonist. He "was one of the ablest admirals in the Imperial Navy; a man with a scientific brain and a flair for trying new expedients, as well as a seaman's innate sense of what can be accomplished with ships. Although not himself an aviator, he was a strategist, and it was he who had initiated the offensive use of aircraft carriers".[2]

In May the sea confrontation in the south seemed at hand when on May 27 when General Douglas MacArthur's forces landed on Biak Island, off the north central coast of New Guinea. Biak assumed great importance with its airfields. Should these fields fall to the enemy the decisive battle plan was in serious danger. The airfields could be used by the Americans to attack the Mobile Fleet. To prevent their loss Japanese aerial reinforcements were sent to Biak on May 29. For troop reinforcement a naval task force, Operation Kon, was dispatched to Biak to land soldiers and destroy enemy shipping. Before Kon could reach the island it was discovered. The force was recalled to try again. A second reinforcement effort was also turned back due to reports of an Allied naval force. On June 10, Admiral Ugaki, the Kon commander, received tremendous firepower when for a third try he was given the super battleships *Yamato* and *Musashi,* a light cruiser, and six more destroyers. While Ugaki was regrouping, Admiral Toyoda received word of the June 11 carrier strike at Saipan, which he read as a signal of the American advance to the Marianas. This was the opening for the final battle, in the seas west of Saipan. On June 12 Toyoda ordered Ugaki to halt Kon and to steam northeast to rendezvous with Ozawa in the Philippine Sea.

Admiral Ozawa led the Mobile Fleet out of Tawi Tawi on June 13. Two days later, A-Go was activated, to annihilate the enemy in the Marianas area. The admiral's message to the fleet repeated Admiral Togo's inspiring message to the fleet, before the Battle of Tsushima, that the "fate of the Empire rests on this one battle. Every man is expected to do his utmost."

Late on the afternoon of June 15, Ozawa had his Mobile Fleet in the Philippine Sea. The next afternoon Admiral Ugaki's force rendezvoused with the Mobile Fleet. On June 17, the ships refueled and headed for the decisive battle area west of the Marianas.

Vice Admiral Kakuji Kakuta, commanding the 1st Air Fleet, Tinian, radioed Admiral Ozawa that his land-based planes were doing their part to whittle down the U.S. carrier airpower. Kakuta reported that U.S. ships and aircraft had been destroyed, realizing the first phase of A-Go. Unfortunately for Ozawa, this was false news. The facts were heavy losses in the 1st Air Fleet, and destruction of the Mariana air bases. The airfields on Guam, Rota, and Tinian had been hard hit, and Aslito field lost. A-Go would not receive help from the 1st Air Fleet, it was up to the carrier planes and Ozawa had fewer of them. Not only was Ozawa facing a numerically superior air enemy, he was also at a strong disadvantage in aircrew training and experience. Admiral Ozawa had aircrews with as little as two months' training and the best only six months, while the U.S. airmen had at least two years training or more and many were combat veterans.

On June 15 the U.S. submarine *Flying Fish* sighted a task force in the central Philippine waters. That evening, the *Seahorse* spotted another task force. Warnings were issued to Admiral Spruance, who considered the potential for battle near the Marianas. The next morning he postponed the Guam landings and ordered Mitscher to take on the Japanese fleet. By June 18, all four U.S. carrier groups were headed to meet the 1st Mobile Fleet.

After these initial submarine sightings Spruance lost contact with the Japanese fleet. Meanwhile, the Japanese had air patrols looking for the American ships. Both sides were searching for each other. Admiral Ozawa had the better luck, locating Task Force 58 during the afternoon of June 18. Once he had determined the U.S. position, he changed course to increase the distance to take advantage of the longer range of his aircraft. Because his planes were lighter, minus armor and self-sealing fuel tanks, they had an attack range of about 300 miles compared to 200 miles for the American planes. Also, Ozawa planned to attack the U.S. ships and then fly on to Guam, land, refuel, and on the return trip to their carriers the planes would again strike the enemy. It was a fine plan, except the Mariana air bases were unavailable.

The decisive battle was near. Admiral Ozawa expected to realize the Japanese Pacific strategy. The battle would begin the next day, June 19. Early in the morning of June 19, over 300 carrier aircraft were ready and Ozawa believed he had hundreds more at Guam, Rota, and Tinian. The admiral was confident of a smashing victory.

Carrier Division 3, in the van force, launched the first raid at 0830. In this raid were 16 Zero fighters, 45 Zeros carrying bombs, and 8 torpedo-carrying Jills. At 1000, the U.S. battle line warship radars detected this incoming flight. By 1038, U.S. fighters were launched to intercept this flight. The raiding planes reached the battle line but could only inflict minor damage to the *South Dakota*, at a cost of 42 planes.

A second attack was launched by Carrier Division 1 at 0856. In this raid were 53 Judy bombers, 27 Jills, and 48 Zero fighters. Late in the launch, Warrant Officer Sakio Komatsu, as he lifted off the *Taiho*, observed the track of a torpedo headed for his carrier. Without hesitation, he crashed his plane into the torpedo. This heroic act was not enough, another torpedo from the *Albacore* struck and damaged the *Taiho*. Meanwhile, the carrier aircraft headed for Task Force 58. They were detected by radar 115 miles short of Task Force 58, and Hellcats off the *Lexington* met them at 60 miles out. Most of the Carrier Division 1 aircraft were shot down, only 31 of 128 returned to their carrier or landed at Guam. These heavy Japanese losses had achieved little. A bomb blast above the *Wasp* killed one sailor, and another bomb killed three on the *Bunker Hill.*

Ozawa's Carrier Division 2 launched 47 planes at 1000. Incorrectly vectored, one group of about 27 planes, found empty seas at the target locations. The remaining 20 aircraft located Task Force 58 and attacked. They failed to inflict any damage. At least this time only 17 planes were lost, with 40 making back to the carrier force.

A fourth Japanese attack was launched at 1130. In this group were 30 fighters, 9 Judys, 27 Vals, 10 Zeros with bombs, and 6 Jills. Misdirected, a number of this raiding team turned to Guam and Rota. Thirty of the 49 aircraft over Guam were destroyed in dogfights with U.S. carrier planes with most of the 19 surviving planes seriously damaged. Aircrews who found Task Force 58 were similarly mauled. The fourth raid had nothing to show for its heavy losses. Four raids had cost one-half of the aircraft put into the air.

Shortly after noon the submarine *Cavalla* torpedoed the carrier *Shokaku*. The carrier started to burn, but the fires were extinguished. However, dangerous fumes filled the ship and soon after 1500 she exploded and sank. Not long afterwards the previously damaged carrier *Taiho*, also filled with fumes, exploded. She sank that evening. With the sinking of the *Taiho* Admiral Ozawa moved his headquarters to the cruiser *Haguro,* and in his new headquarters planned additional raids. Included in his plans were the many planes he assumed at Guam. On June 20 he relocated his flag to the carrier *Zuikaka*, which had better communications. At this time the admiral had ready his plans for missions on June 21.

At 1540 on June 20 American search planes found the Japanese. Quickly Task Force 58 launched 216 aircraft. As the American force neared the Mobile Fleet, Ozawa sent up a screen of 75 planes (he had only about 100 left). His aircraft put up a good fight but were outnumbered. Ozawa lost another 65 planes. The ships fought back with intense antiaircraft fire and maneuvers, but they could not escape the persistent Americans. Torpedo-armed Avenger planes sank the carrier *Hiyo*. Admiral Owaza concluded that it was time to withdraw.

The total Japanese aircraft losses were 395 carrier and 31 float planes out of an original strength of 476. About 445 aviators were lost. U.S. losses were 130 planes (80 splashed during the night recovery on June 20) and 76 aircrew. Extreme losses among the Japanese planes reminded one American sailor of a "turkey shoot." For the victorious Americans this battle became known as the Great Marianas Turkey Shoot. The Japanese named it the Battle of the Marianas. Whatever its name, it was a decisive battle, but completely opposite the Japanese expectation. With the defeat the Imperial Japanese Navy was unable to support the defenders in the Marianas. The fall of the Marianas was now certain, and the Japanese home islands would be within reach of the very heavy B-29 bombers.

Submarines made a huge contribution to American success in the Marianas. They sank numerous transports, created disorganization among the survivors, sent weapons and equipment to the bottom, and sounded the alarm that Admiral Ozawa's ships were on the move, and then sank two carriers in the Battle of the Marianas.

The Japanese 6th Fleet, the submarine fleet was near worthless. They failed to sink or even damage one U.S. ship while losing 17 of their own during the Marianas campaign. Not that they were absent, Vice Admiral Takeo Takagi moved his submarine fleet to Saipan in the spring of 1944 to support its defense and A-Go. Takagi assigned three I-boats (I-10, I-185 and I-5) to intercept the U.S. Fifth Fleet in June, but all three I-boats were lost without inflicting any damage. The submarines served as transports to bring supplies to the Marianas and evacuate pilots who no longer had aircraft. Admiral Takagi was to leave on one of the evacuation submarines but it was sunk before reaching Saipan. Unable to get off Saipan, he remained to fight and die in the final mass attack.[3]

FIVE

Collapse of the New Line. Pull Back to a Central Defense

The new defense line across the island, from below Garapan to the east shore, was too late. As the line fell, surviving Japanese troops pulled back to central mountain positions.

General Saito's troops were in a tough battle. They had fought well, but had no means of negating the superior American firepower. On June 19, Marine artillery drove Saito from his cave headquarters near Hill 500 to new headquarters in a depression cave above Chacha Village on the neck of Kagman Peninsula. The 47th IMB also moved its headquarters from Hill 500 to Chacha, leaving behind only a delaying force. On June 20, following an intense rocket attack, Marines overran this Hill 500 force. Inspecting the hill the Marines discovered numerous caves, including the 47th IMB headquarters, and an observation post with excellent views of the battlefields below. From the Hill 500 observation post American advances were apparent, Aslito Airfield was being fixed, and artillerymen were installing 155mm guns on Agingan Point, to fire on Tinian. Any possibility of support from Tinian was greatly reduced once this island was subject to regular land-based artillery barrages.

On June 20, survivors of the 136th Regiment formed up the east slope of Mount Tapotchau. This regiment was down to 400 men from 3,200. All its officers were dead. These terrific losses and great suffering had not destroyed the will and warrior spirit of the 136th Regiment and other Saipan units. Tokuzo Matsuya, 9th Tank Regiment, wrote that his tank regiment:

> now had six Type 97 and six Type 95 tanks. . . Even if there
> are no tanks, we will fight hand to hand. . . I have resolved

69

that, if I see the enemy, I will take out my sword and slash, slash, slash at him as long as I last, thus ending my life of twenty-four years.[1]

Bypassed defenders in the Susupe and Hill 500 areas harassed the supply parties at the beaches. One bypassed rifleman hit a U.S. ammunition stockpile on Oleai Beach and set it afire. While a Marine detail was fighting the fire it exploded a second time killing a number of Marines. That night 12 Japanese bombers attacked ships in the anchorage, but did not hit any.

General Saito desperately needed new troops. He turned to the other Mariana Islands but the commanders on Rota and Tinian demurred, realizing that they were the next targets. Guam was too far distant, given American patrols, to send reinforcements.

The huge losses in the sea Battle of the Marianas had not caused the naval general staff to give up the Marianas. On June 21 proposals for the recapture of Saipan were considered. One plan was a naval task force created from the Mobile Fleet with air reinforcements coming from naval training groups and the Army. The Army pilots, not trained in carrier operations, would take off from the carriers, but not land on them. A ground force of one division was included to assault the three U.S. divisions at Saipan. This plan also included another try at the decisive sea battle. Two serious flaws made it a pipe dream. First, the use of Army pilots untrained in carrier takeoffs would have made a mess of the operation. Second, one division was too few soldiers to take on the three U.S. divisions. The plan died when the Army refused to support it. Another plan, never tried, was a naval bombardment of American forces on Saipan. The battleships *Fuso* and *Yamashiro* were to blast away at important targets.[2]

Facing great manpower shortages, Saito pulled back his defenses and consolidated them at hill and terrain feature strongpoints in the central area. They were on the south of Garapan, at Mount Tipo Pale, Mount Tapotchau, "Death Valley," the central massif, Hill 600, and across to Kagman Peninsula. Machine guns and mortars were installed in natural fissures, caves, and on reverse slopes. As the machine gun crews were positioning themselves on June 22, they could observe Marines edging towards Mount Tipo Pale where excellent defenses were ready. The narrow approach to the southeastern slopes of Tipo Pale was ideal for defense. Riflemen and machine gunners took up positions in a small finger ravine on its lower approach. The Marines, however, found an undefended path to the top and bypassed the defended routes. Later, a Marine Scout-Sniper

Platoon, attempting to clear the well-defended approach was driven back. Defenders in cliff holes laid a deadly fusillade on the Marines.[3]

The defenders at Tipo Pale held on for two days and then withdrew to set a trap on the descending north slope of the mountain. Marines climbing down the only trail on the steep north side walked into the trap. Machine guns and rifles opened fire on the Marines struggling down the mountain side. A fierce fight ensued, finally Marines freed themselves from the trap.

While Hill 500, with its fine observation post, was in American hands, the main island observation post, on the summit of Mount Tapotchau, was held. Observers in this post spotted targets during the day. At night, the guns fired, hidden by darkness. The first week of the Saipan battle had cost the command structure dearly. General Iketa listed the status of unit commanders:

> Colonel Oka (47th IMB) is believed to have died in breakthrough at Chalan Kanoa, dawn of the 18th. Colonel Arima (commander 9th Expeditionary Unit) wounded in battle, hospitalized. Colonel Goto (Commander 9th Tank Regiment), whereabouts unknown since night of 16th. Believed to have died in battle. Colonel Koganezawa (Commander 7th Engineers) missing since morning of 19th, believed to have died in battle. Lieutenant Colonel Nakajima (Commander 3d Independent Mountain Artillery) wounded, hospitalized.[4]

The Saipan defense was now only a shell of its former self. The 43d Division was down to four battalions. There were no combat forces left in the 47th IMB, and only one-half infantry battalion in the former Expeditionary Force. Saito had an artillery strength of only 13 pieces, and one battery of antiaircraft guns. His total personnel strength was 15,000, but many of them lacked weapons.[5]

General Iketa sent instructions to the 50th Infantry Regiment on Tinian to shell Aslito Airfield when enemy planes were present. Tinian was also asked to send reinforcements by barge, under the cover of darkness, ignoring the American patrols. Certainly the observers on Mount Tapotchau had reported these patrols to headquarters. Iketa was grasping for help, in a situation where nothing was working. His assessment of the battle remained encouraging, on the evening of June 22, he recorded that:

> The enemy [6th Marines] in vicinity of Hill 230 (west of Tipo Pale) has attacked our positions on the east side of the same hill. This has been repulsed. The enemy [8th Marines] south of Hill 343 (1,200 yards south of Tapotchau) is infiltrating through our positions accompanied by tanks and it is not

known at present whether we can hold this hill. Division contemplates smashing the aforesaid enemy tonight.[6]

By June 22 the new line of security had been penetrated, forcing the defenders back into the central spine. From the observation post on Mount Tapotchau, the Japanese observed P-47s, launched from the *Natoma Bay* and the *Manila Bay*, landing at Aslito field. The Japanese artillery on Tinian stayed silent, the gunners feared that shelling Aslito would bring American counterbattery fire. The key to the defense of Saipan was now the dominating Mount Tapotchau with its observation post, the primary source of data on American activities. Apart from reports from this observation post Saito knew little about American capabilities. He knew little about the Marines, their tactics or traditions.

On June 23, Admiral Nagumo began to offer advice and take a more active, but ignored role. He was a Navy officer with a meaningless paper fleet, and the Army did not listen to naval officers concerning land operations. Now that the Army and Navy were compressed into a small pocket, the two services made some effort to consult each other. A more involved Nagumo signed a joint order of the Central Pacific Area Fleet and the 31st Army. It was a remarkably vague order to reinforce Saipan with troops from Rota, Tinian, and Yap. The order was absent specific units or detailed instructions leaving the door open for noncompliance. Nagumo suggested that barges might be able to reach Saipan from Tinian, traveling in the southeast waters. This area, noted Nagumo, was patrolled by two or three destroyers, but he gave no advice of how to avoid the patrols. Once safely in these waters the barges were to land troops above Laulau Bay, the river at Mount Hanachiru.[7]

Additional troops never arrived. With each new General Iketa summary, it became clearer that communications were cut off between the headquarters and the field. U.S. artillery had severed the wire, and now even runners were having trouble finding units. All this was isolating the chief of staff from the battle facts.[8] On the front lines conditions were almost intolerable. Morale may have weakened but the willingness to die an honorable death remained strong. One Noncommissioned Officer (NCO) said to his diary, "I heard the Japanese radio news with stories of great victories. We haven't heard of any victories lately. What will we do until the day of our annihilation? I wish my mother could know about the life we are leading."[9]

One of Saito's staff officers recorded that he was "groggy from intense bombardment and naval shelling—our forces have been continually caught in a concentration of naval gunfire and the dead and wounded continue to increase." The naval shells with instantaneous fuses were causing many deaths and terror.

On June 24, when General Iketa reviewed the battle situation, he found that the Mount Tapotchau defenses were doomed. Iketa indicated the deterioration of the defense, writing that in the 43d Division area the enemy had infiltrated and broken through our positions. The Marines had also overrun Chacha on Kagman Peninsula, and the battle was closing in on the command post near Chacha. It was now impossible to hold on without reinforcements. Again the call went out to Tinian or anywhere for fresh troops.[10]

As the battle neared Saito's headquarters and artillery rained down around it, the time for a new location had arrived. On June 24 General Saito transferred his command post to a cave in the rocky northeast slope of Mount Tapotchau. It was his best Command Post (CP), with a communications center and staff chamber. Saito had only a few days to use it when again he moved, on June 27, when naval gunfire pounded these slopes.

As the defense compressed into the central spine it became stronger, despite the fact that Saito had many fewer troops. Defensible locales were found and used to their fullest. One was Mount Tapotchau, which was strongly defended. On the west slope strongpoints were created in the foothills and small knobs. While the east slopes and a 1,000-yard wide valley at the base were a powerful barrier. Movement on the valley floor was subject to interlocking fire from the slopes above and ridge lines to the east. When soldiers of the U.S. 27th Infantry Division attempted to use the valley as an approach to Mount Tapotchau, they were blocked. Soon they named this bloody route, Death Valley. The eastern ridges became known as Purple Heart Ridge, for the bloody task of neutralizing them.

The Japanese defenses of Death Valley were awesome. Machine guns, mortars, and a few 75mm mountain guns were placed in caves on the ridges and Mount Tapotchau east slopes. Brush was laid in front of the firing ports, hiding the positions from observation. All the gun crews displayed great patience, limiting fire so as not to give away their locations. When a target was well within range, the gunners would fire a round or two, kill or wound an American, and cease fire before they were detected.

Despite great suffering the defenders in this area, the 118th, and the 136th in the center, fought well. The 118th Infantry Regiment had the defense line from Mount Tapotchau to Laulau Bay. They fought hard, surprising since this regiment had lost so much in convoy sinkings. While the 136th had started the Saipan campaign in good condition, it had seen some of the toughest fighting on the island. They were hard hit at Oleai and in the withdrawal inland. Now the regiment was only one-third of its original strength, down to less than 1,000 men.[11]

On June 23 the Death Valley defenders gave the soldiers of the 27th Division a rude welcome. Accurate fire from the hidden caves halted the U.S. advance. Next, the GIs called up a heavy bombardment of the ridge caves. When the bombardment was lifted, the 27th soldiers resumed their forward march only to come under more deadly fire. This first day, the U.S. infantry was held to a negligible advance.

Failure of the 27th Division to advance into Death Valley was for Saipan's ground commander, Lieutenant General Holland Smith, USMC, further evidence of the lack of leadership in the Army division. General "Howlin Mad" Smith, who had enough, decided to relieve the 27th Division commander, Major General Ralph Smith. General H. M. Smith took his ideas to Admiral Richmond Turner who agreed, and together, they visited Admiral Spruance, who authorized and directed the relief of General Ralph Smith on June 24. Major General Sanderford Jarmon, who was scheduled to be island commander once Saipan was secured, temporarily replaced Smith. General Ralph Smith was one of five generals sacked in the Pacific, the most controversial. This was a Marine general firing an Army general. There was little doubt that the 27th Division had been slow, and it was General Ralph Smith's responsibility to get better results. In defense of the division, it had the bad luck of encountering some of the toughest terrain and best Japanese defenses.

General Saito was unaware of command issues among the Americans. He had his own problems, he was tired, frustrated, and seeking explanations for his failures. In one message he blamed poor commanders and loss of control of the air, stating that:

> Having lost the influence of the Emperor due to the weakness of our representatives, we are not able to work at our best here. Please apologize deeply to the Emperor that we cannot do better than we are doing.
>
> However, the right hand men of the Emperor are rejoicing because they are not in places of death during the fight. The Governor General of the South Seas, a non-combatant, will retreat to the north end of Saipan. However, because of the units sunk at sea, the various forces have no fighting strength, though they do have large numbers; it is regrettable that there has been considerable disturbance in time of battle from the points of view of control and of code books and other secret documents.

There is no hope for victory in places where we do not have control of the air and we are still hoping here for aerial reinforcements.

Biggest obstacle to our forces, according to one unit commander, is lack of care in the selection of battalion commanders and above.

Praying for the good health of the Emperor, we all cry, 'Banzai'.[12]

Saito had a few viable strongholds, but not enough troops to turn them into victories. At best they could only slow the American onslaught. Death Valley and to the east on Kagman Peninsula, the 47th IMB on Hill 600, were holding tough. At night, the eastern units made counterattacks, employing many of the remaining tanks. On the evening of June 23, a counterattack of six tanks struck down the boundary between the 105th and 106th Infantry. Five tanks were stopped by 37mm guns and bazooka fire, but a sixth tank escaped. One hour later, a five tank-infantry counterattack advanced down the road in the middle of Death Valley. Four tanks were quickly knocked out, but the fifth broke through U.S. lines to machine gun the battalion aid station and set an ammunition dump ablaze. From the dump, the tank turned to the east where it was destroyed by the 23d Marines. Meanwhile the large explosion at the dump threw fragments into the American lines, forcing a withdrawal. While the flames lighted up the area, artillery on Mount Tapotchau laid down a barrage. Once the fire had burned out, the Americans returned.

On the west shore the once neat and orderly Garapan was now rubble. The Americans who had spared the city for use as a headquarters changed their plans. Instead it was destroyed by artillery and naval bombardment. Its rubble created plentiful opportunities for a slow building-by-building battle. When the 2d Marines came to town on June 24, no use had been made of the debris. Garapan's only defenses were a few pillboxes, a ridge on the southeast side, and hills on its east side.

The defended southeast ridge could not hold out long against Marine firepower. After the ridge was lost, the survivors counterattacked, trying to climb its steep face. They were easily killed by Marines on top. It was a wasteful counterattack, probably attempted for a quick death in a warrior manner. The defenders at this stage of the island battle were exhausted, hungry, thirsty, and many ready to die. Shortly after the ridgeline charge, a second counterattack struck the 2d Marines. This time it was seven Japanese tanks rushing down the beach road to strike head-on the Marines.

Six tanks were destroyed with no serious damage to the Marines, but one tank got away.

Well-hidden and sheltered locations in the western ridgeline north of Garapan were exploited by the 1st Yokosuka SNLF. The U.S. 8th Marines fighting here, later described them as "nightmarish," a wall of terror which stopping the Marines on June 23. The next day when the Marines resumed moving, the Japanese in this honeycomb of hidden underground fought back.[13] Despite their "nightmarish" character, this exploitation of the natural assets, above Garapan barely slowed the 8th Marines. They were old hands at neutralizing caves; it had become a science. Infantry and engineers worked as a team to hit the caves with flame-thrower blasts and demolitions. One by one the caves and their occupants were destroyed.

On the east side of Saipan the Death Valley defenses were still intact on June 24. The 27th Infantry Division had been slowed. Elsewhere, the Americans kept coming. Kagman Peninsula, which had been largely abandoned, fell quickly to the 23d and 24th Marines. As these defenses collapsed, new orders went to the 50th Infantry Regiment on Tinian to send one company with attached machine guns and rapid fire guns. Another request was sent to Guam, asking that men be staged through Tinian. Given the complete American blockade, it would be remarkable to get any troop boats to Saipan. This day it was attempted. Eleven barges with reinforcements crept out of the Tinian Town Harbor at midnight, and headed for Saipan. Hardly had they gotten out of Tinian Harbor, when they were observed by the destroyer *Bancroft* and destroyer escort *Elden*. The American ships opened fire, sinking one barge and turning back the others.

Heavy artillery and tank gunfire slammed into Mount Tapotchau on June 25, driving off the Japanese. Once the barrage lifted and the Marines reached the summit, a counterattack was launched. The Marines could not be dislodged.

A desperate situation was reached by June 25 when General Saito's armed frontline strength was only 2,000:

Approximate
<u>Strength</u>

118th Infantry Regiment	300
135th Infantry Regiment (exclusive of the 1st Battalion, which was on Tinian)	350
136th Infantry Regiment	300
47th Independent Mixed Brigade	100
7th Independent Engineers	70
3d Independent Mountain Artillery Regiment	(No weapons)
9th Tank Regiment	3 tanks[14]

There were additional units, but they lacked weapons and a fighting ability. Many units faced serious water and food shortages. A long message, and more realistic than usual message, described the American superiority in the air and naval firepower:

> The fight on Saipan as things stand now is progressing one-sidedly since, along with the tremendous power of his barrages, the enemy holds control of sea and air. In daytime even the deployment of units is very difficult, and at night the enemy can make out our movements with ease by using illumination shells. Moreover, our communications are becoming disrupted, and liaison is becoming increasingly difficult. Due to our serious lack of weapons and equipment, activity and control is hindered considerably. Moreover, we are menaced by brazenly low-flying planes, and the enemy blasts at us from all sides with fierce naval and artillery cross fire. As a result even if we remove units from the front lines and send them to the rear their fighting strength is cut down every day. Also the enemy attacks with fierce concentration of bombs and artillery. Step by step he comes toward us and concentrates his fire on us as we withdraw, so that wherever we go we're quickly surrounded by fire.[15]

On June 26, Japanese defenses continued to collapse, except in Death Valley and on Nafutan Peninsula. At Nafutan, the U.S. 105th Infantry had been stymied by soldiers of the 317th Independent Infantry Battalion, 47th Independent Mixed Brigade. The 317th was nearly out of food and water. The time had come to take action. Instead of piecemeal counterattacks or a wild charge into American lines, the commander, Captain Sasaki, developed a fighting withdrawal to get to the 47th IMB headquarters at Hill 500 (he was unaware that the brigade had been driven off the hill). On June 26, Captain Sasaki issued his orders for the breakout and raids en route to the 47th headquarters on Hill 500:

> The Battalion will carry out an attack at midnight tonight. After causing confusion at the airfield, we will advance to Brigade Headquarters in the Field (Hill 500). The C. O. of the Ikeda Company will command the first attack unit. Under his command will be: 3d Company, the Hira Company, and the Murone Platoon. C. O. of the Koshiro Company will be C. O. of the second attack unit and will have under his command the Inoue unit, the Engineers, the remaining Naval units. Units will assemble at 1930 in areas to be designated separately. You must carry out the attack from the designated places. Casualties will remain in their present

positions and defend Mount Nafutan. Those who cannot participate in combat must commit suicide. We will carry the maximum of weapons and supplies. The password for tonight will be "Shichi Sei Hokoku" (Seven lives for one's country).

> Bn C. O.
> Capt. Sasaki.[16]

Captain Sasaki's troops slipped through the 105th lines at about 0100. Their first contact was when one group walked into the 105th command post area. A fire fight ensued with 27 Japanese killed, but most kept moving towards their initial objective, Aslito Airfield. They reached the airfield at 0230 and torched a P-47, "Hed Up N Locked" of the 73d Squadron, 7th Air Force, and damaged three more. Fighting at Aslito lasted over one hour and then the Sasaki force headed for Colonel Oka's Hill 500 headquarters, where they would get new orders. The first unit reaching Hill 500, at 0520, encountered Marines, not the 47th IMB. Both sides were surprised, but after a few moments of confusion, a close-in battle broke out, with the total loss of Sasaki's force.

A second element ran into artillery positions of the 14th Marines between Aslito and Hill 500. A hot battle ensued at the 14th Marines camp with 33 Marine casualties and 143 Japanese killed. Japanese survivors tried to escape into the jungle, but were pursued and killed by Marines. By the end of the day, the Sasaki raids were defeated. Five hundred dead Japanese lay on the ground at Aslito, Hill 500, and the 14th Marines camp. Despite the uneven numbers to the opposite of "Shichi Sei Hokoku" (seven lives for one's country), this was one of the more effective counterattacks. Its accomplishments included penetration of the American lines, damage to aircraft, and fighting with a plan.

At the Saipan headquarters General Saito and his staff had not given up on the idea of finding fresh troops. General Iketa sent another order to the 50th Infantry, at Tinian, to barge men to Saipan. When finally attempted on July 2 it was a complete failure.

Japanese light bombers struck the American anchorage and Aslito Airfield. One bomber crashed into the boom of the cargo ship *Mercury* but caused only slight damage. Aslito was unsuccessfully bombed. To reduce the chance of more bombing raids, U.S. carrier planes struck at any airfield which might launch planes to interfere with the Marianas operations. The airfields at Pagan, Rota, Tinian, and Iwo Jima were revisited and neutralized again.

15. Aslito Field under new management on June 26, 1944

U.S. Air Force

The naval shelling of Mount Tapotchau was unrelenting. General Saito was reaching a point of desperation. He could not escape the shelling. Caves and shelters were little help. Major Takashi Hiragushi, 43d Division intelligence officer, agreed, stating that he most feared the naval shelling. A captured Japanese lieutenant stated that the greatest single factor of the American success was naval gunfire. "Perhaps the highest testimonial of the efficacy of this particular weapon came from General Saito himself when he wrote on 27 June, 'If there just were no naval gunfire, we feel with determination that we could fight it out with the enemy in a decisive battle.'"[17]

Six

The Final Strategy and Last Battle

General Saito had no respite from the shelling. As soon as he moved to a new command post, it came under attack. This relentless shelling must have had an impact on them as they considered the final defense. They concluded that the best defense was a line across the narrow waist of the island. However, only on the west coast could troops complete the line before Marines arrived. When this northern line collapsed, General Saito decided upon a final all-out counterattack, with soldiers dying an honorable death.

On June 27 Saito moved to a new cave command post, in an overgrown depression, 2,200 yards north of Mount Tapotchau. At his new headquarters a tired and frustrated General Saito called a conference to establish the final strategy. A number of officers proposed a final charge to die gloriously in battle. However, General Saito stated that: "Because there are many military units which were left scattered on the field of battle, gather these all together and construct positions from here toward the north in the narrowest portion of Saipan Island. Here they were to 'chew the American forces to pieces.'"

At this point the staff determined the best positions on maps. They fell in a line running from north of Tanapag through Hill 221 (Radar Hill) to Tarahoho on the east coast. It would require rapid construction, but all the picks and shovels were at the Banaderu Airfield site. These building tools had to be obtained and distributed to the soldiers constructing the final line.

General Saito had lost communications with his units, finding himself isolated from the battlefield situation. He still had hopes of aerial reinforcement, stating his case to Guam:

> Because the enemy planes which have appeared in the air are only carrier bound bombers and reconnaissance planes the situation is such that our large fighter formations could seize good opportunity for daylight sinking of enemy destroyers, etc.
>
> However as the fate of the Empire will be decided in this one section, we trust you (Guam) will decide to send fighters to Tinian.[1]

Unaware of the destruction of the 1st Air Fleet, Saito planned for the arrival of planes. He kept workers building the runway at Banaderu. He ordered it be ready to receive planes on July 10, believing that the Saipan garrison could hold out until that date. Then the 1st Air Fleet could fly in fighters to attack American ships and ground logistics. Meanwhile, his land defense was a gradual withdrawal to the final defense line. As some units pulled north, others continued work on delaying positions in the central area. Delaying defenses in caves on the ridge north of Mount Tipo Pale produced the desired result, delaying the Marines to June 28. Four small hills (called the Pimples by Marines) with well-hidden machine guns and riflemen also held up the Marine advance. The hidden guns in the ridgeline defenses of Death Valley caused heavy U.S. casualties this day. On June 28 there was a more successful than usual counterattack in Death Valley as two tanks were able to sneak up on a 3d Battalion, 106th Infantry, command post during a staff meeting of the 2d and 3d Battalions. As quickly as the tanks arrived they escaped unscathed, leaving behind 12 dead officers and men of the 106th.

More messages asking for fresh troops were sent to Tinian. Colonel Takashi Ogata, the Tinian commander, was not eager to comply. There was the American naval blockade of Tinian, and regular artillery and air attacks on his installations making it obvious that Tinian was next.

By June 29, the defense of Death Valley was down to Hill Able, on the north edge of Purple Heart Ridge. This last stronghold prevented an American advance. An American attack this day could not dislodge the Hill defenders. During the night, Hill Able men pulled out, leaving behind a delaying force. The next day the delaying positions fell to the 27th Division.

Also, on June 29, mortar shells falling near Saito's headquarters suggested it was time to find a new facility. General Saito set up a new command post on June 30, in a cave in the Valley of Hell (Paradise Valley) about 1,000 yards east of Makunsha Village. This was his last command post.

More delaying detachments fell on July 2 and 3. Garapan was defended by only a few snipers and machine guns when it was captured on July 3. A lone machine gunner on the grounds of Admiral Nagumo's estate on the northern edge of Garapan harassed Marines as they traveled through the northern district of the town. A surviving Type 10 120mm gun above Tanapag Harbor caused trouble for Marines as they moved to Muchot Point.

Hunger and thirst in the central area was commonplace. Many were reduced to eating tree leaves and snails. Nevertheless, the central strongpoints did not give up. They fought to their death, trying to give troops headed north as much time as possible. With the broken communications an orderly withdrawal was impossible. The 135th Infantry drew back to their new positions, in the center, one day ahead of schedule, disrupting the plan. This premature move left the naval and 135th Infantry units on the west and the 136th Infantry on the east, isolated.

The Valley of Hell was terror filled. There was no good news and on July 4, the 165th Infantry attacked the valley and a fierce naval bombardment hit the command post area, wounding Saito. Shrapnel ripped into the general's arm. Saito, who had not eaten or slept well in days, was at the end of his rope. He was wearing a long beard and was a pitiful sight. His mental attitude probably matched his physical appearance.[2] Already, the final defense line was collapsing in the center and east. The final defense was in danger. A conference was called to review the desperate situation, and to decide on the final phase of the battle. Discussions at the conference centered on two options. One choice was to retreat to the north tip and fight to the end. Admiral Nagumo favored this option, the fleet might yet appear. Saito responded that food and water supplies were exhausted, to continue would bring a slow and painful death. Surrender was not mentioned, since it would bring shame and disgrace. Saito concluded that the most honorable and heroic option was an all-out counterattack. This would realize death in true Japanese military fashion. This would be a gyokusai attack, which roughly translates to "breaking the jewels", an expression from a sixth-century Chinese work, describing the principled man as one who would rather smash his precious jade, than compromise to save the roof tiles of his home. The term became a national symbol of heroic warfare following the 1,000-man all-out counterattack at Attu Island on May 29, 1943.

Saito faced some problems in realizing the gyokusai. First, his units were dispersed and communications were broken. His staff estimated that it would take two days to assemble all the men. Second, many soldiers were weaponless. It was decided that they should arm themselves with spears, bayonets tied to poles or sticks. While the central element of the counterattack was to achieve a heroic death, the gyokusai was given a theoretical objective, to reach deep beyond the frontlines to the supply depots and destroy the logistical support for the American forces. At Attu, it had been to reach the American artillery and turn it against the GIs.

Orders were issued to all Army troops to assemble in the Matansa area 900 yards north of the Valley of Hell. Navy men waited at an assembly area, at Matoisu, on the northwest approach to Mount Petosukara. All were ordered to participate in the counterattack, scheduled for the night of July 6.

Delaying positions and sections of the defense line, across the narrowest portion of the island, were still intact. Naval personnel of the 1st Yokosuka SNLF and the 54th Guard Force were in place at the south entrance to the Flores Point Naval Base. There was also supporting fire for the naval defenses, from troops on the ridgeline only 100 yards to the east. Together these positions turned the southern approach to Tanapag into a choke point. However, the 27th Division arrived over the hills from the east, avoiding the choke point. With tank infantry teams the 27th overran the ridgeline defense to capture the Flores Point Naval Base on July 4.

On July 3–4 strongpoints in the central area and east coast were lost to Marines. A number of central hill positions were destroyed, including Hill 721, Hill 767, and Fourth of July Hill. When the defenders were able to stop the Marines, it was usually short-lived success. Artillery was brought forward, and its heavy fire forced the defenders to retreat. Marines climbing the central hills on July 4 found the foxholes empty.

That day, Colonel Ogawa leading a group of soldiers north, walked into a U.S. 165th Infantry command post. Both sides were surprised, but opened fire almost immediately. Twenty-seven Japanese were killed, including Colonel Ogawa, commander of the 136th Infantry Regiment. Found on Ogawa's body was a July 2 order to withdraw to the final line. His assignment was a hill, 500 yards east of Radar Hill, where he was to establish his command post. The remnants of the 136th Regiment and attached stragglers were to form up on the new line, in the vicinity of Radar Hill.

Men of the 136th, who reached their assigned areas east of Radar Hill, got there about the same time as the Marines. They had no time to dig in, and found themselves chewed up and destroyed by the more powerful Marines of the 4th Division. Only on the west was the final line taking shape. Anchoring the west edge of the line on the 450-yard wide coastal flats above Tanapag were pillboxes left from the anti-landing role. Since they fired to the ocean their value was limited but were manned to thwart landings behind the line. Inland of the beach 40 yards was the coastal road and the junction with a cross-island road heading east. Another 20 yards to the east of the coastal road was a narrow gauge railroad from the sugar days. An eastern border was formed by ridges, broken with valleys. The most important was a 80-yard wide gulch, later nick-named Harakiri by the Americans, which had a dry stream bed running down its floor to the sea. Another significant feature was a coconut grove just south of the cross-island road.

Mobility offered by this flat terrain, with roads heading north and east, favored the armor-supported Americans. To mitigate this advantage the north-south coastal road was mined with upended 250-pound aerial bombs, and a minefield, 250-yards deep, blocked overland movement. The 1st Yokosuka SNLF and 135th Infantry Regiment fell back from Flores Point, taking up positions on this the west end of the final line. Since the line was only a short distance from Flores Point, and they had a road, it was an easy move. It gave them time to get into place. An integrated defense was developed, with snipers in trees, and infantry on the ground of the coconut grove. The broken, jagged cliffs of the 80-yard wide gulch held machine guns, mortars, and riflemen. Infantry defenses were also established on the floor of the gulch. And, the length of the dry stream bed from the gulch entrance to the ocean was a ready-made trenchworks, with over one hundred machine gunners and riflemen. A small knoll in front of the stream bed was converted into a machine gun stronghold.

Especially important in protecting the coastal plain were the ridges and Harakiri Gulch. Guns at the western entrance to the canyon fired on the coastal plain. They had their first test on July 5 when the 165th Infantry tried to climb down into the gulch from the southeast. The defenders stopped the American soldiers with withering machine gunfire forcing an immediate retreat. Next, two tanks tried to enter the gulch from the cross-island road. Japanese soldiers placed mines on the tanks, disabling both. Three tanks were sent to recover the two disabled armored fighting vehicles. Only one tank could be recovered, the second tank was abandoned. Defenders in the gulch blocked all 165th Infantry efforts to enter the gulch.

An advance above the cross-island road was stopped by mines in this area.

Before they could be readied, defenses in the east central area at Mount Petosukara, were struck by Marines, who demolished this line on July 6. A large group of civilians, 700 to 800, surrendered near the mountain that night. Also, defenders on the east rim of the Valley of Hell came under Marine attack. Guns and mortars stopped the 25th Marines; they dug in for the night.

Japanese machine gunners and infantry on the western coastal plain waited for the American infantry to resume its northern push on July 6. The waiting gunners practiced fire discipline, firing only when they could hit a target, and their favorite target was the engineer crew clearing the mines. A hail of fire was not enough to stop the engineers. Once the mines were neutralized, tanks were brought forward. Upon their arrival, they were greeted by 47mm antitank fire. The first two American tanks were damaged and retreated with others to safety. Heavy U.S. fire was then directed at the entrance to Harakiri Gulch. It was so intense that the entrance positions had to be abandoned. When the fire lifted the defenders returned, but in getting back they exploded a minefield. Many were blown to pieces and orderly movement disrupted. The blast was so great that it sent Americans in search of shelter. The 3d Battalion, 105th, waited for the dust to settle and then resumed its efforts to penetrate the gulch. A couple of defenders used the confusion to climb into the abandoned American tank and turn its guns against the invaders.

Next, the U.S. infantry launched an all-out attack on the gulch. For unknown reasons, about 60 Japanese soldiers committed suicide. Thereafter, Americans called this Harakiri Gulch. Defenders who decided to keep fighting opened up with intense and accurate gunfire. A terrific fire fight followed with Americans caught in cross fire on the canyon floor, again driving them back.

During the afternoon, three American tanks attempted to fire on the Japanese in the dry stream gully. These soldiers had no weapons to stop the armor, the tanks moved along the trench, firing point blank into it. Over 100 men died in the trench. Once this dry stream bed was neutralized the GIs could walk unmolested to their objective 600 yards north. Scattered sniper posts were neutralized as the Americans pushed north. Guns in the ridges to the east fired a few rounds at the American formations causing some casualties. With collapse of the western portion of the final line, the north defense line was no more.

General Saito had finished his defense. Too exhausted to lead the gyokusai, he decided on suicide before the all-out counterattack.

Joining him would be Admiral Nagumo and his chief of staff, Rear Admiral Hideo Yano, and General Iketa. The four set a time, 1000 hours, July 6, for their suicides. They accepted full responsibility for having failed their emperor. The night before, a simple farewell feast of canned crab meat and sake, was celebrated. The four officers talked of better days.

The next morning, at 0600, Master Sergeant Toshio Kitani, of the 135th Infantry, had the opportunity to observe General Saito as he concluded his role as island commander. Toshio Kitani:

> was shocked by his appearance. Frail and gaunt, the commander of all army forces on Saipan was obviously near the point of exhaustion. The sleeve of his shirt was blood-soaked and torn where a bandage had been applied to a shrapnel wound. But he was on his feet and, in a weak but authoritative voice, was ordering his staff to assemble all unit commanders for a conference. Kitani, feeling it important that he, too, know what was to happen, took a place with officers who, in the gloom of the cavern, failed to see the stars of his rank. Gradually the large cave became filled with men, many of whom wore fresh bandages.
>
> A hush fell over the cave as Saito stepped onto a small platform. In a voice that occasionally trembled with emotion, the aged warrior began to deliver the most difficult speech of his life. Two candles, mounted on the wall of the cave behind him, cast a flickering light upon the paper from which he read and silhouetted the defeated general, catching highlights in his graying hair. His hands were steady, and his eyes burned with the determination for which he was famous.[3]

General Saito, had read his final message, which was also mimeographed and distributed to his units:

MESSAGE TO OFFICERS AND MEN DEFENDING SAIPAN

I am addressing the officers and men of the Imperial Army on Saipan.

For more than twenty days since the American Devils attacked, the officers, men, and civilian employees of the Imperial Army and Navy on this island have fought well and bravely. Everywhere they have demonstrated the honor and glory of the Imperial Forces. I expected that every man would do his duty.

Heaven has not given us an opportunity. We have not been able to utilize fully the terrain. We have fought in unison up to the present time but now we have no materials with which to fight and our artillery for attack has been completely destroyed. Our comrades have fallen one after another. Despite the bitterness of defeat, we pledge, "Seven lives to repay our country".

The barbarous attack of the enemy is being continued. Even though the enemy has occupied only a corner of Saipan, we are dying without avail under the violent shelling and bombing. Whether we attack or whether we stay where we are, there is only death. However, in death there is life. We must utilize this opportunity to exalt true Japanese manhood. I will advance with those who remain to deliver still another blow to the American Devils, and leave my bones on Saipan as a bulwark of the Pacific.

As it says in the "SENJINKUM" [Battle Ethics], "I will never suffer the disgrace of being taken alive," and "I will offer up the courage of my soul and calmly rejoice in living by the eternal principle".

Here I pray with you for the eternal life of the Emperor and the welfare of the country and I advance to seek out the enemy.

Follow me.[4]

General Saito transferred command to his chief of staff, Colonel Takuji Suzuki, who completed the final gyokusai preparations. Suzuki sent out reconnaissance patrols to locate gaps or weak points in the American lines. They found a huge, 500-yard wide gap and this information was passed onto the assault forces. With this data Suzuki directed some units to pass through the gap and rush to Tanapag. At Tanapag, they were to reassemble for an attack on the supply dumps in the Garapan area. Other units were to use the gaps to swing behind the U.S. lines and attack them from the rear. There would also be headlong charges against the American lines. Operations were limited to the western west, with its flat ground suitable for a rapid thrust. This type of terrain fit the combat training of these troops, operations on a large maneuver area. The counterattack was scheduled for 0200 on July 7.

Japanese survivors of Saipan have created various images of the last moments of the four senior officers and their suicides. However, no witnesses lived to give the exact details, so the descriptions draw upon traditional ceremonial traditions. This included facing to the northeast in the direction of the Imperial Palace, and bowing reverently. In their headquarters' caves the officers, next kneeled, made a ceremonial cut of the stomach, and called out "Tenno Heika! Banzai!" (Hurrah for the Emperor) before being shot in the head by aides standing behind them.

General Saito's body was only partially cremated when concerns over the smoke attracting U.S. artillery halted the process. His remains were covered with soil. Meanwhile, Admiral Nagumo, Admiral Yano and General Iketa were buried at secret locations in the Valley of Hell. After the battle, Marine General H. M. Smith ordered General Saito buried at Tanapag with full military honors.[5]

Captain Sakae Oba who arrived at the Matansa assembly area late on the afternoon of July 5, described it as chaotic. Men were milling about, looking for their units. Many had no weapons, but tied bayonets or spears to poles. Oba and his eighty soldiers were relatively well armed, but were hungry. Sergeant Kato, an engineer, was sent out to locate food for one meal before the next day's attack. Having assigned this important duty Oba laid down to rest.

The next morning he was awakened by someone reading a document. It was Sergeant Kato, who was reading orders, to the assembled group. They directed that: "the Imperial forces, whether navy or army, are therefore ordered, by the authority of Vice Admiral Chuichi Nagumo's headquarters, to continue fighting and to avoid participation in an obvious suicide attack. Only by continued resistance can we provide assistance to our naval forces that are even now en route to this area to drive out the invading American devils and to retake the island."[6] Oba inspected the orders, noting that they were signed by Commander Onodera for Admiral Nagumo. They countermanded the gyokusai orders of General Saito.

Nagumo's orders created a dilemma, Was the fleet coming? Oba had Army orders to follow, and what did a Navy commander know about ground battle? No one paid attention to these orders, nearly all the men were ready to die in the all-out counterattack. One exception was Captain Oba, who believed that staying alive to fight on was important. He recalled the string of Japanese victories, and believed that the war could be won. The gyokusai would be nothing more than suicide and insuring an American victory. This was a minority view, most of the men had already made their choice to die fighting the enemy, reminding themselves that in death there is life. The counterattack was an opportunity to exalt true Japanese manhood.

Captain Oba planned to infiltrate the American lines, and swing left to the foothills of Mount Tapotchau. Many more Japanese readied for the gyokusai. Some groups were loose collections of stragglers and others were the few survivors of formal units. One example of a straggler formation was 32 men led by Master Sergeant Kitani, who named his group the 1st Platoon, Saipan Infantry. Addressing his platoon, he told them that this attack would turn the tide of battle. It would cut the enemy's supply line from the sea and deprive him of the superiority of firepower that has given the Americans a temporary advantage.

The gyokusai was a roll call of the original Saipan units, but now remnants. Included in this all-out effort were the 118th Infantry, 135th Infantry, 136th Infantry, 43d Division Headquarters, 43d Field Hospital, 3d Independent Mountain Regiment, 16th Shipping Engineer Regiment, 9th Tank Regiment, 55th Naval Guard Force, 1st Yokusuka Special Naval Landing Force, and various other remnants. A few civilian workers and at least one civilian woman joined the battle (she was identified among the dead).

The American frontline, above the village of Tanapag, on the west shore, was occupied by the 105th Infantry. Westernmost was the 2d Battalion, on a narrow front near the shoreline. To the east and across the railroad tracks was the 1st Battalion with a 250-yard wide front. East of the 1st Battalion was 500 yards of undefended ground, all the way to the 3d Battalion in positions at the entrance to Harakiri Gulch. There were antitank guns sited to fire on this gap, but it left considerable room for Japanese to pass through undetected.

During the night of July 6–7 the 105th was notified of an impending all-out counterattack. A captured seaman of the 55th Naval Guard Force told of the attack. With receipt of the warning the 105th asked for reinforcements, but were informed that none were available. The regiment took no other action to improve their frontline, which might have included trip-wire forward outposts or outposts in the undefended gap.

Last minute problems in organizing the attack groups delayed the time of the gyokusai from 0200 to 0400. Finally at 0400 following further delays, the attackers supported by two Type 95 tanks moved out of the point of departure. They reached the American front lines at about 0510. Immediately a large force poured through the gap to strike at the 3d Battalion, 105th, at the entrance of Harakiri Gulch, while other elements swung around to hit the 1st Battalion, 105th from the rear. Yet more soldiers bypassed the 3d Battalion to get quickly to the Marine artillery near Tanapag village. The remainder of the counterattack went toe to toe with the frontlines of the 1st and 2d Battalions, 105th, one American:

Sergeant Eugene "Mac" McCandless, Company E, 2d Battalion, was asleep when the Japanese hit and I had no warning that the attack was coming. Someone in my platoon was yelling "Mac" wake up. There was great confusion and disorder with firing coming from all directions it seemed. Mortar fire was falling into our positions from the hills to the east.[7]

The 2d Battalion put up a terrific resistance, but was overrun, with survivors pulling back to Tanapag. Furious fighting was everywhere along the front lines. Colonel William O'Brian, commander of the 1st Battalion on the east flank of the line, fought back with his .45 caliber pistol until he was out of ammunition. Then he jumped on a jeep to fire its mounted machine gun. The next day his body was found at the jeep and around it many Japanese dead. Colonel O'Brian was posthumously awarded the Medal of Honor. His brave stand had given his men time to pull back to Tanapag village where a new defense perimeter was established. At this point they held out until afternoon when Sherman tanks arrived to bolster their defense.

There was intense fighting at Harakiri Gulch where the 3d Battalion, 105th, received a punishing attack. Forward elements had by now struck at the 3d Battalion, 10th Marines artillery encampment above Tanapag village. The Marine artillerymen fought the Japanese in hand-to-hand combat. Nevertheless, the Marines were overrun, at a cost of 136 casualties. Reporter Robert Sherrod would write in a July 19, 1944 *Time* article of Marines firing their artillery point-blank at the attackers. However, in the post-battle clean up, their 105mm ammunition was found neatly stacked and unused. Over 300 Japanese dead were counted near the artillery.

Army and Marine survivors withdrew to Tanapag village to hold on until reinforcements showed up. These reinforcements were slow in getting to the battlefield and by the time they were on the scene the gyokusai had exhausted itself. Heavy losses among the Japanese and regrouping of the Americans to form a new perimeter had turned the tide. Marine tank reinforcements and 27th Division reinforcements regained control of the Tanapag area during the afternoon. By evening most of the lost ground had been recaptured.

Politics have clouded the record of this counterattack. There are questions regarding: the numbers of Japanese involved, the 27th Division reaction to warnings, fighting worth of the 27th Infantry Division, and what happened at the Marine artillery. Influencing the account of this event was General Holland Smith's negative view of the 27th Division, that it lacked a fighting spirit. Therefore, he readily accepted his staff estimates of a Japanese force of 300 to 400 soldiers and two tanks, routing two U.S. Army battalions, and inflicting on them casualties of 406 killed and 512 wounded. The dead included most of the frontline senior officers and company commanders.

Of course, General Smith's account made the 27th Division furious. The division had fought hard and died, only to be portrayed as overrun by a small collection of Japanese. To correct the record, the division conducted a systematic body count locating 4,311 Japanese dead; 2,295 of them at the 1st and 2d Battalion battle areas, 322 at the Marine artillery area, and 1,694 around Tanapag village. Faced with these higher figures General Smith's staff reconsidered their estimate. General Smith then estimated 1,500, a figure he thought liberal. After the war, in his book *Coral and Brass*, he revised it upward to 3,000. A Korean laborer, Mamoru Iwaya, who participated in the counterattack estimated 3,000 attackers. Major Takashi Hiragushi, another captured participant, initially stated that it was 1,500 but later changed his estimate to 3,000. With the chaos at the two assembly areas no one really knew how many were involved. A special board appointed to investigate the counterattack concluded that 2,500 to 3,000 Japanese charged the American lines. This is probably the closest we can get to the true number.[8]

Captain Oba, who decided to live, led his men southeast towards Mount Tapotchau. Along the way they encountered American encampments, but kept moving, avoiding combat. In the distance they could hear the sounds of the fighting at Tanapag. They did not hesitate, firmly committed to reaching shelter in the mountain foothills.

A few survivors of the gyokusai and others who stayed back in the assembly areas, escaped to the northern jungle. Some remained in the Valley of Hell, and fought here on July 8. Marines routed the Japanese and continued north. A few feeble counterattacks were attempted that night. Marines reached the north tip, the next day. This left only Managaha Island in Tanapag Harbor which fell on July 13, and remnants of the island defense hiding in northern caves, the central and Mount Tapotchau areas.

Soldiers and civilians hiding in caves, crevices, and dense undergrowth in the broken terrain in the north could hear loudspeaker broadcasts urging them to surrender. Instead, hundreds jumped off the Marpi cliffs to their deaths on jagged coral or the ocean below. Mothers clutched their children as they jumped. Death was preferred over dishonor and the horrible fate they expected at the hands of the Americans. Propaganda that they would be subjected

16. Japanese soldier, armed with a bayonet tied to a stick, killed in the all-out counterattack.

17. Civilian woman who joined the gyokusai dies in battle.

National Archives

18. **General Saito, the Saipan Island commander, was buried by the American Marines, with full military honors.**

National Archives

to hideous torture, raped, and killed had been effective. Some elected to stay in hiding and fight as small groups or individuals.

Many soldiers and civilians hid in the coastal caves in the north. That Admiral Turner declared Saipan secured at 1615, July 9, 1944, made no difference. These hideouts would make the mopping up operation a dangerous activity, but American offers of food and water were hard to resist. Despite thirst, many still refused to surrender.

On July 10, an official flag raising ceremony was held at General Holland M. Smith's headquarters in a sugar company duplex in Chalan Kanoa. Seabees were already hard at work to convert Saipan into a forward base for the B-29 Superfortresses to bomb the home islands and to build bases to support future operations.

More Japanese surrendered or were captured on Saipan than in previous Central Pacific battles. The total military prisoner count was 1,780. In this group were 17 officers, 904 enlisted, 838 Korean laborers, and 21 unidentified. More would be captured over the next year. Three factors account for this larger POW count. First, there were the U.S. loudspeaker broadcasts and safe passage pamphlets dropped from the air which encouraged many to surrender. Second, disorder and disruption of unit cohesion left individuals freed from military bonds and the code to never surrender. Third, there was recognition among many that the war was lost and death here would not change that fact.

While the civilian suicides were dramatic and captured on film, they were actually a small percent. Most civilian deaths were battle related. The civilian death toll from bombing, shelling, disease and suicide was less than one-third of the population.[9]

By the end of August 1945, the internment camp at Susupe held:

13,373	Japanese
2,426	Chamorros
1,365	Koreans
810	Carolinians
17,974	Total

A huge medical crisis existed. Many of the people in the camps were sick or injured, with untreated wounds, malnutrition, exposure, and dysentery. The first and most critical needs were medical care, food, and developing sanitary living conditions. By the fall of 1944 the immediate health problems had been treated. Attention then shifted to employment and establishing social order. A fishing fleet, farming and schooling were established. In 1946, the Japanese and Koreans were returned to their homelands.

About 28,500 Japanese died in the defense of Saipan. The American losses were 3,471 killed, and 13,160 wounded. This was a casualty rate of twenty percent, about the same as other tough battles at Attu, Tarawa, and Peleliu. In terms of ratios of dead, Japanese losses at Saipan were greater. At Saipan about nine Japanese died for every American death. In the battle of Attu it was less than five.

It was late in the War in the Pacific, but finally the Japanese paid attention to lessons learned during the Saipan campaign. They had a significant impact on future operations. The defenses created at Iwo Jima and Okinawa had depth. Defenders were burrowed in and had to be dislodged. Also, there would be no more wasteful mass counterattacks.

The end of the War in the Pacific was not the end of the straggler problem in the Marianas. While Saipan stragglers spent most of their time engaged in gathering food, they remained a danger. These stragglers always had the potential for violence, especially when encountered. Captain Oba led the best organized group. Soon after Japan surrendered the Oba camp in the Mount Tapotchau foothills was hit with leaflets telling of the end of the war. Written in Japanese, they urged all stragglers to lay down their weapons and surrender, under order of the emperor. Captain Oba told his men that the leaflets were a trick. Over time as American patrols subsided Oba considered the possibility of Japan's defeat. He learned from contacts in the Susupe internment camp that the unthinkable was true, Japan had surrendered. Captain Oba concluded that it was appropriate to surrender his group, so he initiated discussions with the Americans to bring in his group. On December 1, 1945, Captain Sakae Oba and fifty men walked out of the jungle to surrender to Major Herman Lewis, USMC.

SEVEN

Failures

The terrible Japanese defeat in the Marianas was their own undoing. Victory was not possible, but a much better defense was available. Had the Marianas commanders employed defenses similar to those at Iwo Jima the American casualty figure might have been four or five times higher. Iwo Jima was the only major battle in the Pacific where the Marines suffered greater casualties than they inflicted.

A summary of failures at Saipan indicates how the value system created inappropriate battle strategies. Central to the defeat was the excessive importance placed on spirit. Victory was the anticipated outcome of individual bravery. Hand-to-hand fighting could overcome numerical weakness. But, what was the Japanese soldier to do, under bombardment from an unseen enemy. What good was the sword in this situation? Spirit in this situation could never hope to defeat the Americans with their enormous firepower.[1]

On a societal level there was an overconfidence in victory, a product of the cultural belief in Yamato Damashii, the spirit of old Japan. This was a divine power, an esprit-de-corps on the broadest level, making Japanese better soldiers. Japan could expect to defeat numerically stronger enemies because of this common honor. The Japanese had special individual qualities as warriors, while belittling the enemy as soft and corrupt. Since Americans were soft the United States would not be up to a fight. Given the weakness of the opponents, individual bravery and aggressive actions guaranteed victory. Fitting this notion of fighting spirit was the offense, counterattack, and overpowering the enemy with the sword. These

98

values were encased in a highly bureaucratic military with obedience to authority and tradition.[2] Easy victories during the first six months confirmed this belief. When the victories stopped in 1942 there was no counterbalancing critique, since that would have meant a rejection of this central cultural belief. Instead the "victory disease", an expectation of victory and blind faith provided the will to rush headlong to total destruction.

This overconfidence and belittling of the enemy also caused a lack of interest in intelligence gathering. When you are confident of victory and have little fear of your enemy, it is less important to know him. Admiral Ugaki wrote in his diary of the failures of reconnaissance. He argued that an "operation starts with knowing its enemy...an enemy suddenly attacked Saipan on the morning of the 11th. What loose reconnaissance!...the lack of a sense of reconnaissance must be the cancer of our system."[3] The Marianas campaign exhibited a remarkable absence of knowledge regarding the U.S. forces, their training, experience, and equipment.

Another factor in defeat was the obsession with the decisive sea battle, allowing American freedom of naval movement. As the Americans steamed to the Pacific islands, the Japanese saved ships, held back to engage in the big battle. To wait was to miss opportunities to inflict damage on the Pacific Fleet. Smaller sea fights could have reduced the American fleet, and contributed valuable experience. While the Combined Fleet waited for the all-out sea confrontation, the unmolested Fifth Fleet reached Saipan.

Poor Japanese submarine tactics in the Marianas, and in the larger War in the Pacific, added to their grief. This is in sharp contrast with the substantial contribution of American submarines. They played a central role in the victory in the Philippine Sea and isolation of the home islands. One reason for the Japanese failure was the obsession with the decisive sea battle, which diverted submarines from attacks on American transports, to save them for the big battle. Japanese submarines were also diverted to a supply role, to bring food to bypassed garrisons such as Chuuk (Truk). Japanese submarine deployment was too rigid, there were orders to stay at an ambush point, not to leave it, even in hot pursuit.

The concentration on the decisive battle left other sea services neglected. There were serious shortages in the transport service and its protection. These weaknesses meant that not enough men or materials got to the Marianas. Had all the troops and building supplies reached Saipan and the Marianas its defense would have been much stronger.

Another serious shortcoming was engineering. Rapid airfield construction was never possible. The labor intensive construction battalions struggled to build airfields with hand labor. Meanwhile American Seabees and Army engineers quickly built runways with heavy equipment. In the Marianas construction delays held back the 1944 airfield expansion program. However, this was not a great disaster since the 1st Air Fleet lost its planes during the preinvasion period.

Added to these general inadequacies were shortcomings specific to the Marianas.[4] The most crucial was the failure to realize the potential of the topography. Island commanders stuck with the linear, beachline defense, easily destroyed by the overpowering American naval and aerial bombardment. Contesting the enemy on the beach placed the troops and coastal defenses in the most exposed and least sheltered positions. Had there been a defense in depth, the guns could have been placed in the central mountain spine, in caves to obtain cover and concealment. An island plan employing the central hills could have exploited the defensive value of these mountains. However, to sit and wait for the enemy was unacceptable for the offensive-minded warrior. It did not fulfill the notion of spirit, to attack, to win by aggressive actions. When the Saipan defense fell back into the central spine, with greatly reduced forces, it extracted heavier casualties among the American forces.

The Japanese commanders in the Marianas refused to study and learn from previous errors. The island defenders held the course, even when it was clearly a defective plan. Commanders displayed an absurd persistence to stay with doctrine. Finally, with the defeat in the Marianas attention was directed at lessons learned. Meanwhile the Marianas commanders engaged in wishful thinking, and face-saving messages to Tokyo. Also, the level of intelligence was deficient, the assault arrived about four months earlier than anticipated. Never in the defense of Saipan did the Army know much about the enemy he opposed. They knew nothing about the Marines, their tactics and traditions. Worse yet, they did not recommend to Guam and Tinian better ways to defend.

Delays in sending reinforcements to the Marianas and the unexpected early arrival of the Americans made impossible the completion of defenses. At Saipan, only 32 of 89 coastal defense guns were available. The 1st Air Fleet arrived to defend the islands, but was quickly destroyed. By the time of the invasion, Americans had total air mastery.

Japanese artillery was effectively preregistered on potential targets. During the landings and initial landward push this artillery caused many American casualties. Two shortcomings kept this artillery from being more efficient. First, the guns could not mass fire against targets. A second mistake was not to have prime movers, tracked vehicles or horses, to move the artillery when positions were in danger of being overrun. Not only was artillery abandoned, but huge quantities of supplies, ordnance (one 15-ton cache of mortar rounds was fired back at the Japanese by Marines), aircraft, airfields, roads, bridges, and water supplies were surrendered intact. Mines, barbed wire, and obstacles were little used. Many of the deployed mines were so deteriorated as to be ineffectual.

Armor use was ineffective and failed to exhibit creative reactions. The tank-infantry counterattacks were poorly planned and executed. Given the inferiority of Japanese armor, an innovative employment was necessary, but did not happen. Late in the battle, hit-and-run tank tactics achieved some success.

Interservice conflict caused the loss of valuable time and energy in arguments over control and decision making, instead of working together to create a strong defense. In the field the result was competing and conflicting orders.

On an individual level, the soldier and sailors defending the Marianas were outstanding. Often the Japanese soldier displayed exceptional fire discipline, holding their fire to the right moment, and then firing only one or two rounds, and stopping before their detection. The defenders made good use of cover and concealment in the central defense zone. Failure was with the military bureaucracy that placed "too much reliance...on precedents. Relying upon precedent is an easy way of avoiding serious conflict and of reaching decisions when strong leadership is lacking... Military organization must have appropriate goals and must respond flexibly to changing realities."[5]

EIGHT

Tinian: From Prehistory to American Invasion

For most of its history the natural resources of Tinian were not fully exploited. Both the Spanish and German administrations failed to develop its cattle and farming potential. The Japanese were the first to make effective use of its flat terrain and good soil. Large areas were cleared for sugarcane fields, and later airfields. In 1939 Ushi Airfield was built on the north end of the island, and five years later it had the significant role of the Imperial Navy's 1st Air Fleet headquarters.

Only three miles of sea separate Tinian Island from Saipan, but the islands are very different. Tinian is flatter and smaller, at twelve miles long and six miles wide at its widest point. In prehistoric times there were two main settlements, one at Sunhalom, (today San Jose), and Marpo. Impressive prehistoric remains in San Jose's Taga latte stone park recall early life on Tinian. This park contains a prehistoric latte stone foundation of 12 pillars, each 15 feet tall and five feet in diameter. Only one column is standing, yet the resting stones suggest a building of about 54 feet long and ten feet wide. Legend describes these remains as the house of Chief Taga, who cut and carried the huge stones from a nearby beach.

Spanish missionaries from Guam visited Tinian. Padre San Vitores, when he arrived in 1668, found the island torn apart by warfare. The Marpo and Sunhalom districts were locked in combat. The padre unsuccessfully tried to bring peace. Unable to stop the war, the padre sailed back to Guam to get help. He returned with Father Luis de Medina, lay assistants, and soldiers. This Spanish contingent talked with both sides and reached a peace accord.[1]

102

Two years later a rebellion broke out on Guam. The Spanish had a tough fight on their hands, stopping the revolt was made harder by rebels escaping to Tinian to hide out. Therefore in 1671 the Spanish established an office on Tinian, to locate and capture rebels. The Chamorro rebellion dominated the Spanish administration. There was no thought given to the economic development of Tinian. For the Chamorros, the rebellion was costly, their numbers were decimated by warfare and disease. In response to the population decline the Spanish removed many residents of Tinian and Saipan in 1681 to farm deserted lands. Two years after the end of the rebellion, in 1695, all the remaining Chamorros on Tinian were relocated to Guam. Tinian was largely abandoned except for cattle running wild. On a regular basis, work parties were dispatched to the island to slaughter and process the beef for Guam consumption. Tinian was in this wild state when Englishman Lord George Anson, on a raiding expedition against Spanish possessions, discovered the island on August 27, 1742. Lord Anson had lost most of his crew to scurvy and his ships to storms. They had gone months without fresh meat and vegetables, the raiders needed fresh food more than battle. The Anson mission found the island a bounty of food, water, and few Spanish to challenge them.

Anson discovered cattle, hogs, and chickens running wild. There were abundant fruits—sweet and sour oranges, limes, lemons, and coconuts. Also there was breadfruit, to take the place of bread. All this in a beautiful setting.[2] Anson remained at Tinian for nearly two months, while his crew recovered. He wanted to capture the Marianas, but his contingent was too small to overrun the Spanish in Guam. Recognizing his impotence, the expedition sailed for Macao on October 21, 1742. Tinian returned to the wild, except for Guam slaughter parties. As Guam's population rebounded, there was a limited resettlement of Tinian.

By 1818, the population of Tinian was one Spanish administrator and 15 residents to manage the herd and farm. In 1853, a leper colony was established with the lepers taking care of the cattle and growing tobacco. Two years later a smallpox epidemic killed the 20 lepers and the other residents of Tinian, leaving alive only two laborers who escaped. Following the epidemic 21 Spanish prisoners were dispatched to the island to take over the cattle operation and prepare the leper colony for reopening.

In June 1869, the Spanish leased the entire island to H. G. Johnston, a local resident. Johnston hired 230 Carolinians as ranch hands to salt and dry beef, slaughter hogs, and grow farm products. It was a successful operation cut short by Johnston's death in an 1875 boat accident. His wife took over but failed. The government then assumed control, employing the Carolinians from the Johnston ranch. Little interest was shown in the ranch, and neglect set in. By 1888 the village of Medina (San Jose) was in terrible condition. The next year, Tinian's 235 Carolinians sought better conditions on Saipan, establishing the village of Tanapag.[3]

The German administration encouraged migration to Saipan and Tinian. This policy had no immediate impact on Tinian. A census in 1902 found only 36 Chamorros and 59 Carolinians on the island. During this year the cattle ranch as a small operation provided meat for local consumption.

During the Japanese administration, Tinian was again abandoned. Left behind on the island were Pedro "Lasso" Dela Cruz (known for his rope traps to capture cattle) and a few workers capturing and slaughtering the wild cattle and hogs. All this changed dramatically in 1926 when the entire island was leased by the NKK (Nanyo Kohatsu Kabushiki Kaisha) to grow and process sugarcane. The first sugar mill was in operation in 1930. To accommodate the mill workers, a Japanese-designed town with rows of Japanese buildings replaced Medina (San Jose), the traditional village at the harbor. A sugar mill was built on the north side of Medina, and connected to the sugarcane fields by 49 miles of narrow gauge railroad. The town was renamed Tinian Town.

Sugarcane was grown on over 15,000 hectacres, and brought 6,000 people to Tinian in 1930–1931. Four years later, the population was 15,380 Japanese, 31 Koreans, and 26 Chamorros. A Japanese economic boom had come to the island, from the export of over 42,000 metric tons of sugar a year. Over one-half of the sugar produced in the Marianas came from Tinian. Sugar was not the only product, sugar by-products were also successful. Liquors, with names such as "Genuine Old Scotch Whiskey", were produced for sale in Japan.

In 1939–1940 Tinian had its first military project, the construction of a naval airfield at Puntan Tahgong (Ushi). Naval construction battalions and convict labor built, in 1939–1940, a 4,750-foot runway (more than 1,000 feet longer than Aslito), steel hangars, operations building, air headquarters, bomb-proof power plant, barracks, and air raid shelters at a cost of over two million dollars. Ushi was designed as a depot and airfield to launch attacks against the U.S. Pacific Fleet as it steamed towards the decisive sea battle, to whittle it down. Ushi also served as a staging field for planes bound for Chuuk (Truk) and other Central Pacific bases. This base was the only military facility on Tinian until the 1944 build-up. In February 1944, the field was designated the 1st Air Fleet Headquarters, under the command of Vice Admiral Kakuji Kakuta.

Admiral Kakuta, a Navy line officer and not an airman, turned out to be a terrible choice for this crucial assignment. He made a substantial contribution to the Japanese defeat by wasteful air missions and even more by misleading status reports during the Battle of the Marianas (Battle of the Philippine Sea). Kakuta's grossly over-optimistic reports of aerial victories and failure to truthfully report the destruction of his airfields contributed to the failure of the sea Battle of the Marianas.

As part of the 1944 air base expansion program, three new airfields were constructed on Tinian. One field was constructed on the southwest edge of the Ushi Field. A second field was located near Gurguan Point on the west coast; and the third, east of Tinian Town. Two were ready by the invasion (but not really needed since so few planes were available) and the third was almost completed.

The main ground defense unit was the 50th Infantry Regiment, commanded by Colonel Takashi Ogata, who was also the island commander. He had the good fortune of having fully equipped units. Ogata had no straggler units, short of weapons and disorganized. His core unit, the 50th, was a cohesive force, under his command since August 1940, serving in Mukden, Manchuria, from 1941 until its orders to the Marianas in early 1944. The regiment arrived at Tinian in March 1944, containing three battalions. Commanding the 1st Battalion was Captain Matsuda; in command of the 2nd Battalion was Captain Kamityama; and Captain Yamamoto commanded the 3d Battalion. Also in the regiment was one 75mm mountain artillery battalion with three four-gun batteries, a tank company, an engineer company, a supply company, a signal company, and a medical company. A regimental antitank gun platoon added six 37mm guns.[4]

Additional infantry was supplied by the 1st Battalion, 135th Infantry, commanded by Captain Izumi. This 900-man battalion was on temporary duty from Saipan when the Marines landed there. The 1st Battalion was unable to return to Saipan, blocked by American sea patrols.

At Ushi Field was Vice Admiral Kakuta's 1st Air Fleet air units. Additional naval troops included the 1,400-strong 56th Naval Guard Force, commanded by Captain Goichi Oya, which manned the coastal defenses and antiaircraft guns. Its antiaircraft weapons were 24 25mm, six 75mm, and three 120mm Type 10 guns. Attached to the 56th was a Coastal Security Force which laid beach mines and maintained small boat patrols.

Four construction battalions, the 233d, the 523d Air Group, the 833d Construction Battalion, and the 116th Construction, were engaged in airfield construction and defense projects. With the

invasion, they were pressed into combat. Of the 1,300 Korean laborers in the four battalions, only 150 survived. The total Tinian
troop strength was 9,000 divided equally between the Army and
Navy.

Colonel Ogata had his main defenses at the expected landing
areas of Unai Dunkalo (Asiga Bay) and Sunhalom Harbor. Three
defense sectors were established, a northern, western, and southern. The northern sector comprised the northeastern top of the island, which included Asiga Bay. Defending this sector was the 2nd
Battalion, 50th Infantry Regiment, one engineer platoon, and about
1,000 naval forces at Ushi. The western sector was the northwestern section from Gurguan Point (above Tinian Town) to the western
boundary of Ushi Field. Defending this sector was the 3d Company,
1st Battalion, 50th Regiment, reinforced with one antitank squad,
and just south of Mount Lasso was the rest of the 1st Battalion, in
reserve. Landings were not anticipated in this sector, especially at
the pocket beaches in the northwest corner. The third defense sector was the southern, or lower one-half of the island. It contained
Tinian Town, and it was here that an invasion was expected. Assigned to the southern sector was the 3d Battalion, 50th Regiment,
gun crews of the 56th Naval Guard Force, and west of Masalog was
the 1st Battalion, 135th Regiment, as a mobile counterattack force.

A battery of four 75mm guns was attached to each battalion of
the 50th Infantry. This enhanced mobility since the guns moved
with the battalions. Additional battalion artillery came from 70mm
gun units attached to the battalions. What was gained in mobility
was lost in coordinated artillery attacks. Colonel Ogata failed to
realize massed artillery fire, despite a suitable artillery site in the
island center, about one mile south of Mount Lasso. Artillery at this
location could hit almost every area of the island.

Armor support was the Tank Company, 18th Infantry, with
nine Type 95 tanks and three two-ton, four-wheel drive, Toyota "Suki"
amphibian trucks in reserve south of Mount Lasso. The remaining
army support units were to the east and southeast of Mount Lasso.

On June 28, Colonel Ogata issued the same unrealistic defense orders as had General Saito. Ogata instructed the Tinian forces
to destroy the enemy at the beach and to be ready to shift forces to
various points to block an enemy beachhead. How this could be
accomplished in the face of total American air and naval superiority
was left unconsidered. Again, it was blind adherence to doctrine,
ignoring the results of the defeat at Saipan and lessons from its fall.
Where Ogata took account of the battle on Saipan, was to have a
prepared redoubt in the south, which was to be defended to the last
man.

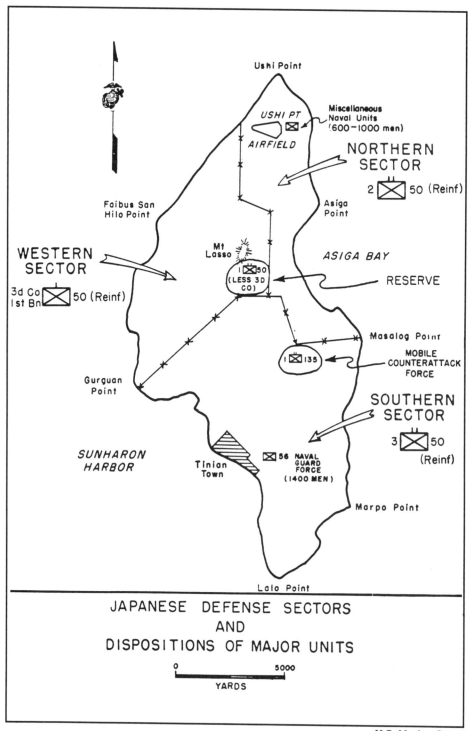

JAPANESE DEFENSE SECTORS
AND
DISPOSITIONS OF MAJOR UNITS

0   5000
YARDS

U.S. Marine Corps

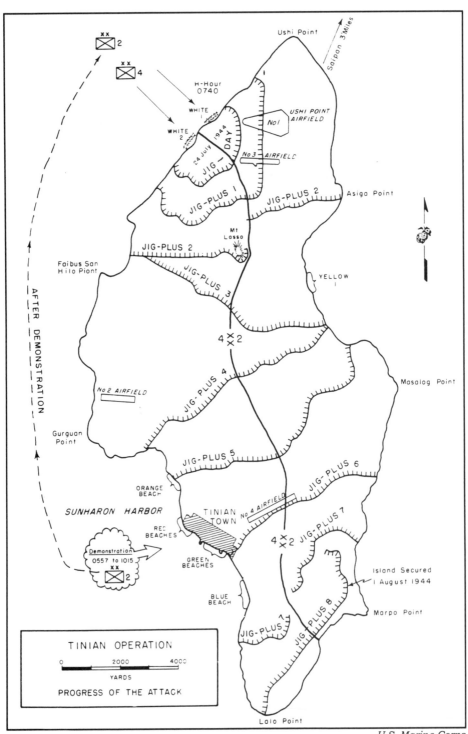

TINIAN OPERATION

0   2000   4000
YARDS

PROGRESS OF THE ATTACK

U.S. Marine Corps

Around the Ushi Airfield were 31 antiaircraft and dual purpose guns including six 13mm machine guns, four 20mm guns, fifteen 25mm Type 96 guns, six 75mm Type 88 guns, and seven searchlights.

On the northwest corner, at White Beach One were infantry defenses, two 75mm guns, and offshore were twelve horned mines. White Beach Two, the next small beach south, had on its top end a pillbox with a 37mm Type 94 gun. Pillboxes at the opposite end, to join in firing up and down the beach, had two heavy machine guns, 7.7mm Type 92. Over one hundred mines were installed off shore, and also the land exits from the beach were mined. There were even booby-trapped souvenirs of watches and liquor.

Six hundred yards to the rear of White Two were three empty 120mm Type 10 emplacements, the guns sitting in a Saipan warehouse. South of the empty emplacements, 300 yards distant, was a coastal road strongpoint, containing 37mm Type 94 and 47mm Type 1 antitank guns.

In the center of the island, below Ushi Airfield and southeast of Beach White Two, there are cliffs rising up to the Mount Lasso massif. Emplaced on the central highlands were three 75mm Type 94 mountain guns, two 70mm howitzers, and mortars.

To the south and above Faibus San Hilo Point were two Type 94 mountain guns for plunging fire on the White beaches and the coastal road. At Faibus San Hilo Point were three 140mm Type 3 coastal defense guns. One fired on the northwest (White beaches) and two guns protected the sea approach from the south. Completely hidden from American observation was a 140mm gun in a cave at Peipeinigul, about mid-point on the west coast.

The six miles of rugged coastline from Faibus San Hilo Point to the north edge of Tinian Town did not require shoreline defenses. There were antiaircraft and dual purpose guns at the Gurguan Point Airfield. Antiaircraft defenses included four 25mm Type 96 dual mounts on the north side of the field, and five dual mount Type 96 guns on the south and east areas. Twelve hundred yards southeast of the runway was a battery of three 120mm Type 10 guns, sited to fire AA and coastal defense against targets at Tinian Town Harbor.

Coastal defenses resumed at Tinian Town, and they included the largest guns on the island. On the beach, on the north side of the town, was a reinforced concrete 75mm pillbox. In the town itself were: two Type 94 75mm guns, six Type 96 dual-mount guns in antiaircraft and anti-landing roles, machine guns, and infantry. A battery of three Whitworth-Armstrong 1905 6-inch guns was in caves south of Tinian Town. On June 14 these guns fired on the *Cleveland, California,* and the destroyer *Braine,* as they bombarded Tinian.

The gunners found their targets, hitting the *California* and *Braine*, killing four crewmen. South of the harbor, steep cliffs and rough seas prevented landings here. This region included the Marpo area, where the final southern redoubt was located. At the redoubt were prepared defenses, which included machine gun, antitank gun strongpoints with carefully established fields of fire, and mortars on reverse slopes.

The east air approach to Tinian Town was defended by a battery of four 120mm Type 10 guns on the south central plateau, 2,000 yards northeast of Marpo Point. Nearby was an advance warning radar.

No beach defenses were needed on the east coast from Lalo Point in the south to Asiga Bay in the north. Asiga Bay, a prime landing site, was heavily defended. On its south end were four 140mm Type 3 coastal defense guns. Along the rocky cliffline above the sandy beach were 23 pillboxes holding machine guns and 20mm to 37mm guns. At the beach ends were two 37mm guns to fire enfilade, and three 75mm Type 10 guns in anti-landing roles. Infantry defenses were placed along the entire length of the beach. Machine guns (13mm) and 75mm antiaircraft guns, on the east side of Ushi field, defended the runway and could fire on Asiga Bay. Protecting the sea lanes on the north and east approaches to Asiga Bay were three 140mm Type 3 defense guns, in camouflaged emplacements, 1,300 yards southeast of Puntan Tahgong Point (Ushi Point). They were in open but camouflaged positions.

All the weapons at Tinian were operational before the invasion, the coastal defenses were: three 6-inch guns; ten 140mm coastal defense guns; ten 120mm dual purpose; six 75mm antiaircraft guns; and twelve 75mm mountain guns.

Tinian was the same as other commands, disrupted by Army/Navy conflict. Colonel Ogata and Captain Oya commanded their individual forces ignoring each other. Of course, this absence of unified command caused disorganized responses and prevented strong joint actions. Interservice hostility was from top to bottom. Sailors had contempt for soldiers. The soldiers noted the absence of aerial reactions, a naval responsibility. An artilleryman of the 50th Infantry Regiment told in his diary of these disappointments and bad feelings towards the Navy:

9 March — The Navy stays in barracks buildings and has liberty every night with liquor to drink and makes a great row. We, on the other hand, bivouac in the rain and never get out on pass. What a difference in discipline!

12 June — Our AA guns spread black smoke where the enemy planes weren't. Not one hit out of a thousand shots. The Naval Air Group has taken to its heels.

15 June — The naval aviators are robbers. . . When they ran off to the mountains, they stole Army provisions. . .

18 June — Admiral Toyoda, CinC Combined Fleet, reported 'We have the enemy just where we want him.' Where is the fleet?

25 June — Sailors have stolen our provisions. . .

6 July — Did Vice Admiral Kakuta (Commander in Chief 1st Air Fleet) when he heard that the enemy had entered our area (Marianas) go to sleep with joy?[6]

On July 22–23, the island received intensified naval bombardment. Most coastal defenses survived, but a significant loss was the battery of 140mm guns at Faibus San Hilo Point, destroyed by 16-inch shells from the *Colorado*. Colonel Ogata reviewing this loss did not realize its importance, since he did not expect landings on the northwest shore. There was nothing in the shelling to indicate a reason to alter his defense plan. The landings were anticipated at Tinian Town and/or Asiga Bay.

The warrior spirit readied the Japanese soldiers for the battle. One soldier of the 2d Battalion, 50th Infantry Regiment, expressed this:

30 June — We have spent twenty days under unceasing enemy bombardment and air raids, but have suffered only minor losses. Everyone from the Commanding Officer to the lowest private is full of fighting spirit.

10 July — When I thought of the desperate fight of the...Saipan Garrison Force, who carried out the final charge on the anniversary of the China Incident, the desire to destroy the enemy once again filled my whole body.

19 July — How exalted are the gallant figures of the Force Commander, the Battalion Commander and their subordinates, who have endured the violent artillery and air bombardment.[7]

On July 22 a terrible new weapon fell on Ogata's troops, napalm fire bombs. These bombs were delivered by P-47s flying out of Aslito Airfield. In this initial mission they dropped 15 fire bombs on possible trenchworks. The fire stripped away cover, removing camouflage. The loss of camouflage robbed the Japanese of an important element of their defense.

Tinian suffered in another way, the island was subjected to 155mm artillery fire from Agingan Point, Saipan. Night and day, artillery barrages ripped through the bomb-proof structures at Ushi Field and other targets. Even the thick, reinforced-concrete naval air raid shelters were not safe.

Despite the heavy U.S. bombardment, Takayoshi Yamazaki, a soldier in the 1st Battalion, 135th Infantry Regiment, was optimistic:

24 July — We heard the story about the shift in the Cabinet (Premier Hideki Tojo and his entire staff resigned on July 18, 1944) and an order to complete the 4th Airfield (inland from Tinian Town. . .) by the 28th. It raised our morale to expect our planes. All the platoon rejoiced to the news.[8]

1. One of the three 6-inch guns above Tinian Town. This battery caused considerable damage to the *Colorado*.

2. A 6-inch of the three gun battery south of Tinian Town

3. Aerial bombardment of Tinian Town base

NINE

The Battle for Tinian

The American landings on two pocket beaches on the north-west end of the island surprised Colonel Ogata. Still, he quickly responded, shifting defenses to meet the situation. During the first night counterattacks hit the Marines. Surprise, an important element of the night counterattack, was impossible. The invading marines were experienced in island warfare, they expected first night counterattacks and were ready. As a result the counterattacks failed, producing heavy losses for Colonel Ogata, forcing him to his southern defense very early. Well prepared positions in the south were unable to hold back the powerful American assault with its superior firepower.

At 0530 on July 24, the island was shaken by a furious bombardment of naval gunfire, artillery from Saipan, and aerial attacks. An awesome bombardment of northern Tinian struck at 0700. Shells from the battleships *California* and *Tennessee*, the heavy cruiser *Louisville*, four destroyers and projectiles from 156 artillery pieces rained down.

The battleship *Colorado*, light cruiser *Cleveland*, and destroyers *Remey* and *Norman Scott* shelled and destroyed Tinian Town. Captain Oya, commander of the 56th Naval Guard Force, in his command post near the 6-inch battery, south of town, spotted seven transports with the bombardment ships. At 0600 the enemy could be seen loading into landing craft, and then form up in a rendezvous area four miles offshore. By 0730, the assault craft were organized and headed for the beaches. As they neared the beaches, mortars opened fire on the landing boats but failed to hit any. Next, the 6-inch battery took on the ships bombarding Tinian, and the landing forces were in retreat. It was a great victory. The Tinian Town defenses had driven off the landing. In fact, it had been a feint. However, the 6-inch shore battery made it real for the U.S. warships, taking on the destroyer *Norman Scott*, 1,800 yards offshore, and the battleship *Colorado*, some 3000 yards from shore. During a 15-minute shelling the guns hit the *Norman Scott* six times. Killed on the destroyer were her commanding officer, Commander Seymour D. Owens, and 18 crew. The *Colorado* took 22 hits, killing 43 men.[1]

The *Colorado* fired back and with help from the *Cleveland* and destroyer *Remey,* the battery was silenced. It was not destroyed until July 28, when the *Tennessee* hit the cave gun positions with 70 rounds of 14-inch projectiles and 150 rounds of 5-inch.

Colonel Ogata, in his Mount Lasso command post, was pleased to hear of the rejection of the Tinian Town landings. At the time he was probably hunkered down, since this area was under heavy bombardment. Even, if he tried to observe the activity offshore, smoke and dust from the bombardment so filled the sky as to deny seeing anything off shore.

On the morning of July 24, at 0750, the 24th and 25th Marines hit the tiny White Beaches. White One was only 50 yards wide, and 1,000 yards to the south was White Two of only 160 yards width. Since a battalion needs 500 yards for a landing, neither beach was adequate. Because major landings were not possible here, Colonel Ogata had only limited infantry defenses. Guns elsewhere quickly responded, artillery at the airfield and Mount Lasso targeted the Marines on the beaches.

The better defended White Two offered the strongest resistance. Three landing craft (LVTs) were destroyed by mines while approaching the beach. As the Marines hit White Two Beach, the two pillboxes, holding 37mm guns, at both ends laid a deadly lane of interlocking fire. From the rear of the beach came machine gun and rifle fire. The Marines sprinted past the pillboxes, and swung back to attack and destroy them from the rear. Fifty Japanese died at these two strongpoints.

By late morning, American armor was ashore, dooming the nine light tanks at Ogata's disposal. That afternoon, U.S. artillery was in action, taking any possibility of preventing a Marine beachhead. By darkness, 15,614 Marines were on Tinian confronting 9,000 Japanese, dispersed and short on unity. Many of the troops were of questionable value. There were 1,500 Korean laborers, and it was not their war. The fighting ability of airmen and naval headquarters' staff was suspect.

The Marines rapidly thrust almost one mile inland in the center to create a sizeable beachhead. Their quick movement gave them time to stop early in the day and lay barbed wire. They would be ready for any night counterattacks. Japanese tactics were predictable and therefore more easily negated.

Colonel Ogata was not certain if these northwestern landings were the only assaults so he could not move all his troops here. The 1st Battalion, 135th Infantry, designated the Mobile Counterattack Force, had standing orders to move to any landings and counterattack. With the White Beach landings, they cleared their southern encampment at Marpo to meet and destroy the enemy on the northwest beaches. Getting to the beaches was difficult. American planes controlled the air so the 135th had to walk along the cliffs and the tree borders of the sugarcane fields to avoid detection and aerial attacks. As the mobile counterattack force headed to the northwest beaches Colonel Ogata sent out small reconnaissance teams to determine U.S. dispositions. They were to bring back data regarding weak points and how best to attack the enemy. With this information, Colonel Ogata decided upon three counterattacks: naval personnel striking the landing beaches from the north, a second team to hit the center, at the boundary of the 24th and 25th Marines, and a third group coming up the coast road, from the south, with five tanks and infantry. Prior to the counterattacks Ogata had his artillery lay down a heavy barrage, starting at 2400, followed by the assaults at 0200.[2]

Naval personnel from the Ushi Airfield were ordered to the north flank of the American landings. They also avoided detection by moving among the trees on the west side of the airfield. This northern naval group of 600, mainly former aircrews and headquarters' men, some carrying machine guns removed from planes, advanced to the lines of the 1st Battalion, 24th Marines. They were detected moments before reaching the Marine positions. Immediately, Marines opened fire with everything they had. Blistering fire mowed down the naval men but did not stop them. These airmen fought well, staying their ground until Sherman tanks came up, at dawn, to finish them. That morning, 476 Japanese bodies laid on this battlefield.

The center counterattack was also discovered early. Marine outposts observed it forming up two hours before the attack. Marines in the center were waiting with a powerful defense when the Japanese struck at 0225. Elements of the 1st and 2nd Battalions, 50th Infantry, and 1st Battalion, 135th, were pushed back. They reorganized and again rushed the Marine lines, this time breaking through. Some 200 Japanese ran through the Marine lines before they could be closed. Behind the lines the attackers broke into two groups. One group went to the artillery, and the second group swung around to fire on the Marine lines from the rear. As this second force attempted its sweep they ran into a Marine strongpoint, and were wiped out, leaving 91 Japanese dead. Success was also denied those trying to take out the artillery of the 2d Battalion, 14th Marines (75mm howitzers). They were stopped by an infantry ring around the guns. One hundred attackers died trying to break through to the howitzers. At the Marine frontline, a frontal attack was under way, but here in a number of charges, the Japanese could not penetrate the lines. At first light, Marine tanks were used to destroy what was left of the center counterattack. About 500 Japanese died in this assault.

One-half of the entire armor strength at Tinian, five tanks, was devoted to the southern assault. The noisy tanks gave the Marines adequate warning. They were ready when, at 0330, the southern force was within 400 yards. As the five tanks showed up at the lines, Marine artillery opened fire and naval illumination shells lighted up the battlefield. Marines then had visible targets for their antitank weapons, bazookas, 75mm guns on half-tracks, and 37mm guns.

The three lead tanks continued through the barrage, into the Marine front lines, firing the entire time. Marines closed in and destroyed them. Bazooka rounds knocked out a fourth tank as it came forward. By then, the Marines also had the fifth tank in range and set it afire with bazooka hits.[3]

Infantry following the tanks did not hesitate to come forward. These soldiers charged the Marine lines, only to be cut down. A few broke through to be killed before they could cause any damage. The losses in the southern counterattack was five Japanese tanks and 267 dead. American readiness and illumination shells turned Colonel Ogata's operations into costly failures.

The Tinian garrison had taken a brutal beating, losing 1,241 troops and five tanks. Lost was the 1st Battalion, 135th, the mobile force, and most of the 1st Battalion, 50th Infantry. The Marines were still in place, having had light losses of less than 100 killed and wounded.

To make matters worse, the second day more Marines were landed. Japanese artillery challenged the waves of 2d Marine Division landing craft, but failed to halt even one. The Marines easily established a beachhead. As this happened, Colonel Ogata developed plans for a defense line from Gurguan Point to the inter-island radio station, then to the center of Asiga Bay. Delaying troops would occupy positions in front of the line to give troops time to prepare defenses. Colonel Ogata moved his command post to a cave on the outskirts of Tinian Town, below the planned line. Before this line was established, Colonel Ogata had decided to withdraw to the redoubt in the southeast corner of the island.

Ogata left blocking positions in the north. One was at Mount Maga, 2,000 yards southeast of Beach White Two. All approaches to this hill were defended by riflemen and machine guns in caves or natural features. At its base were three 47mm Type 1 artillery guns. Additional firepower was delivered by on a plateau on an adjacent ridge. The Maga defenders were ready when the Marines headed towards their strongpoint. But, the Marine tank gunfire, naval gunfire, mortars, and strafing were too much. The Maga defenders left the mountain. Once Marines were on Mount Maga, guns on the plateau to the south opened fire on them. These guns were silenced by Marine artillery.

Much of the Tinian battlefield was open sugarcane fields where Marine tank-infantry assaults made large gains. Ogata's troops were retreating in a disorganized fashion, offering only light resistance. They managed a few infiltration and jabbing attacks. In the north, survivors fought from caves in the cliffs on the northwest tip and caused some problems for Marines.

On July 26, Mount Lasso was a Marine target. With its steep cliffsides, armed caves, and excellent observation, it had the potential to strongly resist the attack, but it would not be tested. Colonel Ogata had ordered it abandoned. There was no fight on this dominating northern mountain. All of the north had been abandoned, including the important Ushi Airfield, with its little damaged and excellent runway. Admiral Kakuta and his airmen joined in the withdrawal to the south. Giving up this little-damaged runway, opened it for American observation planes and surely doomed the island defenders. On July 28, a P-47 landed on the cleaned up runway. Then the runway was used for observation planes and infantry support missions. Ushi Field would be built into the huge North Field, a B-29 base for the bombing of the home islands. It was from this base that the B-29 atomic bomb missions to Japan lifted off.

Marines made huge gains on July 27 and 28 against light resistance. They pushed south, with a line across the entire island, towards Tinian Town. On July 29, guns in well-camouflaged caves on the west shore put up some resistance. There was also a short, but stubborn battle on the east side. That day Colonel Ogata's command post cave came under attack, so he moved to his third and final CP, at a shrine in a Marpo Point cave.

Only delaying units were left in the north and central Tinian, while frantic efforts were under way to occupy the final southern

TINIAN USMC Photo 10-8

4. *Top and bottom,* debris litters Ushi Field at its capture, but the runway was little damaged.

TINIAN USMC PHOTO #1-14

5. 1st Air Fleet headquarters and radio station at Ushi Field

National Archives

defense. Even Tinian Town, with its heavy defenses, was abandoned since the guns were sited to defend against a seaborne assault or had already been destroyed. Some 75mm guns in caves north of town and guns south of the town were manned. With the movement to the southern redoubt, the northern portion of the island fell quickly. On July 30, Marines were at Tinian Town where they were briefly halted by artillery fire. Marine tank fire silenced these guns, and the town fell uncontested that afternoon. No effort had been made to employ the concrete rubble of the town for an urban stand.

Delaying positions on the east side of the island fought for a short time and then were abandoned, with Ogata's men headed south. On July 30, defenders at Masalog Point laid down a deadly barrage of artillery, mortar, and machine gunfire slowing the Marines. Marine tanks, half-tracks with 75mm guns, and mortars eliminated this delaying position. At the end of the day, the Japanese were compressed into the southern end of the island.

A prisoner from the 56th Naval Guard Force, Warrant Officer Akiyama, estimated that the southern redoubt held as many as 6,000 survivors. The principal units were the 50th Infantry, with about 1,800 men, 500 men of the 56th Naval Guard Force, other units and laborers. They occupied strongpoints on the forward edge, cliffline gun positions, and infantry works on the plateau above. On July 30, Admiral Kakuta set up headquarters in Marpo, near Ogata's command post. This day Kakuta sent his last message to Tokyo. He was probably killed in battle on July 31.[4]

On July 31 the southern defenses came under a tremendous bombardment. It was a barrage of about 615 tons of naval-fired shells and 69 tons of bombs. Following the bombardment, the Marines attacked. In the west, south of Tinian Town, the 24th Marines encountered little resistance. More delaying success was achieved in the center of the final line, at the cliffs below the Sabanettan Carolinas plateau.

An impressive 47mm gun and infantry strongpoint on the south defense line waited. The 47mm gun was enclosed by a concrete wall and roof placed against the cliff. On its firing wall was a tiny aperture, so small as to limit its field of fire, but giving it good protection. First, coming into its target area were two Marine tanks. The 47mm gunners hit both tanks, damaging them. Once the damaged tanks pinpointed the Japanese position they opened fire, destroying it and machine gunning 20 men attempting to flee.[5]

Marines of the 4th Division overcame road mines and minefields on the route to the cliffline of the redoubt, some Marines were able to climb the northwestern cliff. Meanwhile, on the east side, the 2d Marine Division troops could not get past defenders in these jagged limestone cliffs. This time, Ogata's southern strategy was work-ing—the 8th Marines on a road climbing up the cliff were driven back by intense gunfire. Late that afternoon, one company was able to rush to the cliffline and climb through thick underbrush to the plateau on top of the cliff. From here to the south tip of the island it was a flat run. With Marines on the plateau the entire southern strategy was in grave danger.

Quickly, the Japanese reaction, recognizing that Marines on the plateau had a clear run to the southern tip of the island. An immediate counterattack drove one portion of the Marine line off the plateau. Then, machine gun and mortar fire were directed at the Marines to prevent them from securing the plateau, but the defenders could not muster enough firepower. That night at 2300, a counterattack was launched against the Marines who were wait-ing, and stopped it cold.

A strong counterattack was tried at 0515 to push the Ma-rines off the plateau. The attackers made a frontal charge at the Marine lines, expecting to overpower them. Immediately with the charge, illumination shells turned the dark night into eerie day-light. Two U.S. 37mm guns firing canister rounds plus machine gun fire stopped the counterattack. The few survivors of the charge withdrew just before daylight and the appearance of American planes. This lodgement on the plateau doomed Colonel Ogata's final defense.

The next day, August 1, more Marines and tanks were on the plateau. As Marines expanded their plateau hold, the defenders could not reorganize to create new lines. Marines made it to the southern tip this day. Lieutenant General Harry Schmidt, com-manding the Northern Troops and Landing Force, declared the island secured on August 1, at 1855 hours.

Many Japanese were hiding in these southern shoreline cliff caves. They were capable of organizing counterattacks and so re-mained a threat to the U.S. island command. During the night of August 1–2, three counterattacks were launched, the fiercest struck the 3d Battalion, 6th Marines command post. It was a tough battle, again the Japanese paid dearly. The next morning, 119 Japanese dead were counted on the battlefield. During the night of August 2–3 a counterattack of about 150 soldiers struck the 6th Marines. In the battlefield clean-up that morning 124 dead were counted in front of the 6th Marines line. According to prisoners captured fol-lowing this attack, Colonel Ogata was killed in this action. He was seen draped over barbed wire, a victim of machine gun fire. If he died in this action, he was buried in a shallow grave with his troops.

6. Marines push across the southern plateau to final victory. *National Archives*

7. Japanese dead are quickly buried by bulldozers.

National Archives

The actions of August 1–2 and 2–3 were the last strong attacks, but small group assaults continued. Many Japanese elected to hide in caves to wait for the Marines to arrive and then fight. Men hiding in these caves stayed silent, waited in the dark recesses, to shot at the Marines silhouetted at the sunlight entrances. Only a few Marines were shot before they changed their tactics. They stood outside the caves calling for occupants to surrender. If there was no response, the cave was sealed.

Thousands of surrender and safe passage leaflets were air dropped in the southern area. Also, loudspeakers and captured prominent Japanese, such as the superintendent of the sugar mill and his wife, tried to talk out those hiding in caves. The broadcasts and pleas achieved success in getting many civilians and a few soldiers to surrender. Like Saipan, some selected suicide over surrender, jumping off the southern cliffs to their deaths. One group tied themselves together and then detonated explosives.

American patrols remained on Tinian to search out stragglers. By the end of 1944, another 542 Japanese were killed and 400 captured at a Marine cost of 38 killed. This brought the final toll of Japanese killed to 8,000. Additionally, 652 military prisoners were captured and 13,000 civilians interned. U.S. losses, including losses on the *Colorado* and *Norman Scott*, were 389 killed and 1,816 wounded.

General H. M. Smith called the Tinian campaign the "perfect amphibious operation." The American actions were well planned and carried out. It was an operation employing experience and brilliant organization.

Ten

Rota and Anatahan, Bypassed Islands

Two Japanese occupied Mariana Islands, Rota and Pagan, were bypassed by the Americans, and neutralized by regular air attacks. Rota is noteworthy for its elaborate and unique cliff-side defenses above the airfield. A third unoccupied island, Anatahan, was the locale of a remarkable castaway story.

Rota Island lies between Guam and Saipan, 32 miles northeast of Guam. It is the fourth largest island of the Mariana Archipelago, twelve miles long and about four miles wide. It was not an important military base for the Japanese. Military construction was limited to a fighter strip built during the 1944 airfield expansion program. The American plans did not include the capture of Rota, since it had limited airfield space and an inadequate harbor.

During the Spanish and German eras, the island was sparsely populated. A 1790 census showed 300 residents. In the late 1800s 75 Carolinians migrated to the island, and the entire population lived in the village of Songsong. The Spanish missionaries visited, but otherwise ignored the island. During the German administration coconut production and farming were encouraged. Rice and taro were the main farm crops, but farming was largely subsistence oriented. Just before the Japanese acquisition in 1914, the population was 480.

Rota witnessed a Japanese population explosion in the 1930s with the arrival of the sugar industry. Fields on the northeast plateau were cleared and a sugar mill was built in Songsong Village. By 1935 the population had grown to over 5,000, and two years later it was 7,621, but only 793 Chamorros and Carolinians. The sugar company converted the native village into a Japanese town in 1936, relocating the Chamorros and Carolinians to a new village named Tatacho.

Rota proved disappointing as a sugar growing island. Its soil was less suitable than Saipan or Tinian. Therefore, the Rota operation was cut back to alcohol production. A smaller work force was needed, with surplus workers sent to Saipan.

A fighter strip was built on the northeast plateau in 1944, and above it on the higher southwest plateau were a few defenses. Where Rota was unique, was the elaborate defenses on the cliff line border of these two plateaus. These works are similar to the defended cave at Biak Island. Both, were intended to deny their airfields to an enemy. A third plateau of much less area was the headland on the southwest end of the island. Located here is Rota (Songsong) Village and Sosanjaya Bay, a bay with only limited anchorage, but adequate to meet the sugar industry needs. Above the bay were two 140mm coastal defense guns in cliff cavities. There was a third 140mm gun, four 120mm Type 10 guns, five 75mm mountain guns, 34 25mm antiaircraft guns, and 74 machine guns. There were ten pillboxes on the south coast and 12 on the north shore.

Major Shigeo Imagawa commanded the Rota garrison of 2,655 from his headquarters at As Manila, Sabana (the southwest plateau). His army garrison was comprised of:

2d Battalion, 1st Infantry Regiment; Captain Akira Tokunaga
1st Battalion, 10th Independent Brigade
One Battery, 3d Battalion, 11th Mountain Artillery with 75mm
    guns
3d Company, 1st Engineer Regiment
One rapid-fire gun platoon[1]

Major Imagawa stationed the 600 soldiers of the 2d Battalion, 1st Regiment, on the north shore. He also had Army units at Rota Village, a radio station at Tatacho, Taruga, and the 1st Battalion, 10th, at As Manila. The Navy forces, commanded by Lieutenant Onizuka, defended Ginalangan, Rota Village and its harbor. There were no ships at Rota, but naval personnel were salvaging material from the *Shoun Maru*, sunk by American bombs and resting in 60 feet of water in Sosanjaya Bay.

American air attacks kept the Rota Airfield neutralized, at a cost. The main threat of Rota were its skilled AA gun crews. Efforts to knock out the 120mm Type 10 and 25mm AA guns on the Sabana and cliff caves were never fully successful.

The most impressive feature of Rota was the cliff defenses on the border of the northeast and southwest plateaus. The 54th Naval

1. The Rota Airfield under attack

Guard Force and engineers were constructing these works, when the Americans landed in the Marianas. One portion of the cliff line complex, the Ginalangan area, has been studied in recent years, and since none of the cliff defenses were assaulted, they are intact.[2] The one-mile long complex is an integrated system of gun caves, barracks, power plants, and medical facilities, located at the 150-foot elevation of the 200-foot high sheer cliff.

Constructed in front of the caves were terraces protected by a concrete and stone firing wall. Between the cliff side and the wall was a narrow communications path, which also served as a water runoff collection system. The water was diverted to concrete-lined basins in caves and to water tanks in a barracks area at the bottom of the cliff. Great care was taken to blend the wall and everything else into the natural setting.

Pillboxes guarded the flank ends of the complex. They had apertures to fire on approaches to the cliff and down the communications path, in case the enemy invaded the complex. In addition to water storage the network of caves had its own power sources. Generators were installed in two caves, one near each end. Command and control was accomplished in a command post on the south end, built into a natural fissure, with three to six-feet thick stone walls to enclose it. Continuing to the north is a generator cave. About forty feet from the generator cave is the southern pillbox, protecting the flank. It is a two-embrasure unit to hold heavy machine guns, and is attached to the firing line, which starts at this point. Next is an ammunition storage cave, with blast walls, in front of each of the U-shaped cave entrances. The water supply for the caves at this section is a few steps to the north in a concrete water tank built into a balcony cavity. Next, is a kitchen facility in another balcony cavity with a stone wall for added protection. The kitchen floors and walls were covered with wood to reduce dampness and make it more liveable.

About 45 feet to the north is the second reinforced concrete pillbox. This one held a 37mm gun to fire on the airfield and the approach to the cliffs. Water for the defenders in this section was stored in a cave tank, twenty-five feet north of the pillbox. Nearby, to the north, is a U-shaped gun ammo cave, with blast walls. All along the complex is the heavy duty stone and concrete firing and defense wall. Beyond the U-shaped cave is a sniper cave, with a bump at its opening, so the sniper could slide down and away from enemy fire. A barracks cave with water storage tank is located 35 feet past the sniper cave. The next cave held a 75mm mountain gun. Just beyond the 75mm position is a large firing position in the wall so the gun could place grazing fire onto the slope below. Within a few feet of the wall firing port is a 120mm Type 10 gun cave. Finally, a pillbox guards the flank at this end. Additional cliff defenses on either side of this one-mile long complex have not been surveyed.

The capture of this defense would have been tough, but it could not withstand American naval and air bombardment, and Marines or Army infantry backed up by tanks and artillery. These defenses went untested, Rota was bypassed and on August 26, 1945, the *Currier* and *Osmus* anchored off the island to effect its surrender. Major Imagawa had already received a radio message to disarm his troops, in readiness for the arrival of U.S. forces. On September 1, a detachment of Company B, 48th Naval Construction Battalion, cleared the harbor in preparation for the landing of the Marine 9th AAA Battalion, to collect the Japanese prisoners. The next day, Major Imagawa officially surrendered Rota to Colonel H. N. Stent, USMC, aboard the *Heyliger*.

The 9th AAA Battalion counted 2,655 military, 5,701 civilians, and 790 Chamorros. The military were removed to the Prisoner of War (POW) camp on Guam. Over the next three days the Marines searched the island and found 13 more Japanese soldiers. Seabees repaired the airfield for local use, the island was not included in the American military plans.[3]

Another bypassed island was Anatahan, 60 miles north of Saipan. Until June 1944 the island was removed from the dangers of war. Forty-three Carolinians and an Okinawan couple lived a subsistence life. The Japanese had seen no reason to occupy the island. Japanese convoys sailed past the island, inbound or outbound from Saipan. On June 10 a convoy of about 17 transports, fishing boats, and escorts, steamed south past the island, headed for Chuuk, with a stop at Saipan. Fishing boats were desperately needed at Chuuk to catch fish and keep this bypassed island alive. Submarine resupply efforts were unable to deliver enough food. When the convoy reached Saipan that evening they received orders to return to Yokohama. The waters between Saipan and Chuuk were too dangerous.

Early the next morning the convoy departed Saipan. At a point about 160 miles northwest of Saipan the convoy was discovered by U.S. carrier aircraft. The planes made repeated attacks over two days, sinking the torpedo boat *Otori*, three subchasers, ten transports, and three fishing boats. Eight crewmen from transports, two Army privates, and 21 fisherman, floated on debris to Anatahan Island.

The castaways, with the help of Carolinians, learned how to gather breadfruit, papaya, and other foods. They were also taught

2. Prisoners of war from Rota listen to the announcement of the surrender of Japan.
National Archives

how to make tuba, an alcoholic drink from coconut trees. However, it was a troubled existence, marred by considerable violence, as the men fought for the attention of the Okinawan woman, Mrs. Kaazuko Higa. While she was married, her husband had left for Pagan Island a few days earlier. This seemed to imply that she was available.

American bombers rarely came over the island, dropping a few bombs. These raids were not serious, since shelters were available. An American landing party came ashore on February 21, 1945, removing the Carolinians, but the Japanese were hidden. With the departure of the Carolinians the bombing of the island was intensified with the goal of encouraging the holdouts to surrender. After a few raids, the bombing was deemed to be of little value so it was stopped.

The Americans returned on September 15, 1945, circling the island and broadcasting in Japanese that the war was over, and that they should surrender. The castaways listened in disbelief, considering it a propaganda announcement. No one surrendered. In October, air–dropped letters from Japan instructed the men to give up; these were also viewed as a trick and ignored. On the island attention turned to finding food and fighting over the one woman. The situation appeared to improve in September 1946 when the group discovered a crashed B-29 on its central mountain. It was a survival gold mine, but also introduced two .45 caliber pistols into the charged setting. On November 13, during a fight over Mrs. Higa, Yoshito Naito used one of the pistols to kill fisherman Taneo Goto.

More American ships steamed off shore during 1946 and 1947 to broadcast surrender announcements. Teams also landed to search for the holdouts. For four years, 1947–1950, the Anatahan group spent most of its time gathering food and making tuba. In 1950, the American command at Saipan was about ready to give up on the idea of bringing back the group alive. Before a military assault, the Americans involved relatives in the attempt to safely recover the castaways. With a list of names provided by the Carolinians, relatives in Japan wrote letters pleading for their loved ones on Anatahan to come home. Then the letters were placed in packages with newspapers, food, beer, and cigarettes, and left on the beach. While the packages were being placed on the beach, Kazuko Higa came out of the woods to surrender. She told of hiding for twelve days from her current abusive husband. Once the ship departed the holdouts ran out to pick up the packages. They were moved by the personal pleas, for example the father-in-law of Chief Petty Officer Junji Inoue, a *Kaiho Maru* survivor wrote:

Earnestly waiting for five years since surrender in vain. We finished your funeral service on the day when we received an official notice of your death. Still could not help thinking that you were among those who survived in a remote island in the South. Just at that time we were informed you were living to our greatest pleasure. Understanding well your state of mind as a warrior, I beg to tell you that Japan was completely defeated. Still this defeated nation is not maltreated and is living its peaceful life thanks to America.[4]

Kazuko Higa supplied the Saipan command with a complete list of names. From this list a second and larger letter campaign, of more than 200 letters, was launched. They were delivered in June 1951, and when the landing group brought the packages ashore, they were greeted by Junji Inoue, who had decided to give up. Once the landing party departed, the remaining holdouts read their letters, discussed surrender, and agreed that it was time to go home. Eighteen men were waiting on the beach, on the designated arrival of the ship, June 30, 1951. The Anatahan holdouts were taken to the U.S. Naval Hospital, Guam, for check-ups, and one week later repatriated to Japan. Five found their wives remarried and Kazuko Higa discovered that her legal husband had remarried and was the father of two children.

The *Guam News* on July 2, 1951, summarized the violence experienced by the holdouts. Of the original 31 castaways, three had drowned, six were killed, one died from American bomb wounds, one was accidently killed, and one executed. Six of the deaths were linked to jealousy over Mrs. Higa. She was "married" to four different men and had affairs with others. None of her husbands left the island alive.

ELEVEN

Guam: Spanish and American Rule

The people of Guam are not strangers to foreign rule and war-fare. During the Spanish era there was a lengthy native rebellion. This warfare and diseases nearly wiped out the native population. Following over 300 years of Spanish rule was a short American occu-pation, starting in 1898. In December 1941 the Japanese captured the island.

Guam is the southernmost and largest of the Mariana Islands. This lush tropical island is about 34 miles long, five miles wide at its narrow waist, and nine miles east to west at its widest point. In 1940 its population was 22,290.

Carbon dating suggests the prehistoric settlement of Guam by 1500 B.C. Archaeologists divide the prehistoric period into two phases: pre-latte and latte. During the pre-latte time the Chamorro people, settlers who arrived from Southeast Asia, lived on the coast. They had a diet rich in fish, gathered foods, and cultivated rice. The later phase, or latte period, is characterized by the stone pillars or latte. These latte are believed to have been house and community building foundations. Latte remains in the Marianas are the cultural symbol of the Chamorro people.

On March 6, 1521 Ferdinand Magellan, the Portuguese explorer sailing under the authority of King Charles I of Spain, arrived at Guam (or Guahan, its Chamorro name). Magellan spent little time at Guahan, departing for the Philippines on March 9.[1] Spain did not take formal possession of Guahan until January 26, 1565. That day, Governor Lopez de Lagazpi stepped ashore to read, in Spanish, the proclamation declaring the islands for Spain. The ceremony was a mystery for the Chamorros who did not understand Spanish. Guahan became a resupply stop for galleons sailing from Acapulco to the Philippines. There was no effort to expand the minor trade between the Chamorros and Spanish or to develop the islands. Contact and relationships were friendly and free of conflict. In 1668 the Spanish got more involved, a Jesuit mission came to the island. Initially the missionaries received a warm reception. This encouraged mission leader, Father Diego Luis de Sanvitories, to drop the negative island name, Ladrones. He renamed the islands, the Marianas, in honor of Queen Marian, who had backed the mission.

Over time, Christianity came into conflict with the native culture, with its strictly ranked social structure and belief in spirits. Violent clashes erupted in late 1668. On July 23, 1670, a Chamorro rebellion erupted with open warfare. A long war followed, with the Chamorros not subdued until 1693. It was a horrible war for the Chamorros who suffered many casualties and the introduction of diseases, reducing the population to an estimated 4,000. Slowly the population rebounded to over 8,500 in the 1890s.

On June 20, 1898 the cruiser USS *Charleston* and troopships under the command of Captain Henry Glass reached Guam, with orders to capture the island. Following this quick operation, Glass was to sail to the Philippines to reinforce Commodore George Dewey's fleet at Manila Bay. While Dewey had destroyed the Spanish fleet, he needed reinforcements to complete the conquest.

To capture Guam, Glass sailed the *Charleston* into Apra Harbor, leaving his troopships safely outside the harbor. Captain Glass expected cannon fire from Fort Santiago on the tip of Orote Peninsula, and from the inner harbor fortress of Fort Santa Cruz. The fortress guns were silent as Captain Glass inched his way into Apra Harbor. When he was well within the harbor and in range of Fort Santa Cruz, Glass fired ten rounds against the fort before it fired on him. Unknown to Glass, there could be no Spanish reaction, the forts were empty.

Instead of hostile cannon fire a small boat came out to meet the Americans. No mail had been received in months, so the Spanish were unaware that they were at war with the United States. According to legend, the Spanish considered the American gunfire a salute. Obviously, the surrender message surprised Governor Jacoba Marina. He had little choice, with a military force of only 54 regulars and a few Chamorro reserves, capitulation was the appropriate response. Following discussions, the governor turned over the island to Captain Glass.

The American flag was raised at Fort Santa Cruz at 1445 on June 21, 1898. It was then lowered and returned to the *Charleston*, since Glass was not leaving behind an American presence to protect the flag. The Spanish governor, his staff, and troops boarded the American ships for their voyage, as prisoners, to the Philippines. Nearly two months later, on August 12, the war ended with Guam becoming an American possession, while Spain retained and sold the rest of the Marianas to Germany. Guam, located on the shipping route to the Philippines and Asia, was retained for use as a coaling station. The U.S. Navy became responsible for its administration since its main activity was fleet support.

President William McKinley appointed Captain Richard P. Leary, USN, the first governor of Guam. Leary had a dual role as governor and commandant of the U.S. Naval Station, Guam, and complete authority over all aspects of island life, civil and military. The new governor arrived on August 7, 1899 aboard the USS *Yosemite*. Among his very first duties were the formulation of laws and regulations concerning the civilian population. There was little in the way of military activity, only the maintenance of a pile of coal dumped in the open. The Navy considered expansion of its role in Guam. A study was launched to identify an effective defense for the island. Captain John Merry, USN, inspected Guam in 1901 and recommended an ambitious defense plan. His plan employed the defensible terrain and included 6-inch, 9-inch and 10-inch guns, to convert the island into a Pacific fortress. This plan never happened. A limited local defense came with the debarkation of a Marine Detachment, later expanded to a Marine Barracks. A Commercial Pacific Cable station opened at Sumay in 1905, linking Guam with Asia and the United States. Marines installed two 6-inch guns at Sumay to guard Apra Harbor and the Sumay facilities.

Over the next few years tensions worsened between Japan and the United States. Japan viewed with growing apprehension the racial discrimination against Asians in America. Simultaneously, the U.S. worried over Japanese military goals following its victory over Russia. America reacted by strengthening its Pacific defenses. In 1909, four 6-inch guns off the *Concord* were sited on Orote Peninsula to replace the two temporary 6-inch guns at Sumay.

A Joint Army-Navy Board studied Guam in February–March 1914, developing a defense plan. This plan included a seacoast and Apra Harbor defense, a second line in the hills, a strongpoint on Orote Peninsula, and a redoubt at Mount Tenjo. The general plan was to have a seacoast defense supported by mobile land defense. Coastal defense guns would be placed on Orote Peninsula to deny Apra Harbor. Troops would be positioned in the hills above the beaches, along maneuver routes, with reserves and a last ditch defense in the redoubt on Mount Tenjo.

In May 1914 Marines started building the defenses. Supervising the program was one of the Army-Navy board members, who remained at Guam. This was the brilliant young Marine officer, Captain "Pete" Earl Ellis. Ellis had prepared a paper outlining the advanced base forces for Guam, Hawaii and the Philippines, while at the Naval War College. He would become renowned for his 1921, Operations Plan 712, "Advanced Base Operations in Micronesia", a plan describing the amphibious assault across the Pacific. This plan was a forecast of the forces needed, landing craft, and many elements of the World War II amphibious operations.

Captain Ellis, during his Guam tour as military secretary and aide to Governor William Maxwell, displayed the troubled behavior that characterized his life. However, his superior planning abilities gained him considerable tolerance. When Colonel John A. Lejuene, Assistant Commandant of the Marine Corps, formed a staff in 1915, he selected three of the best junior officers in the Corps for the positions, one of them was Captain Ellis. During World War I Major General Lejuene, division commander of the 2d Army-Navy Division (today the U.S. Army's 2d Infantry Division) had Lieutenant Colonel Pete Ellis on his staff to prepare operational plans. In an unusual event, his planning excellence, not heroism, earned Ellis the Navy Cross.

Following World War I Ellis returned to his main interest, Japanese military activity in the Pacific. To learn what the Japanese were doing, Ellis embarked on a spying mission. With the approval of General Lejuene, Commandant, U.S. Marine Corps, he went to the Japanese Mandates to gather military intelligence. In October 1922 he embarked on his spying career, using the cover of a trading agent, he stopped in the Marshall Islands. Next he visited the Carolines, and then to Koror, Belau (Palau), where he suspected a major military build-up. At Koror his troubled behavior worsened and dominated his life. He drank heavily and behaved strangely, all observed by the Japanese who had him under constant surveillance. On May 12, 1923, Ellis died at Koror, probably from alcohol-related health problems. There was little to discover, the military build-up in Micronesia did not occur until the 1930s. That Ellis or Lejuene believed that the Japanese would be fooled by his flimsy cover, demonstrates the poor state of American intelligence before World War II.[2]

Meanwhile, in Guam the Marines had made progress in fortifying the island. By 1915, completed fortifications included: two 6-inch guns on southern Orote Peninsula at Tipalao, four 6-inch guns at Orote Point, and two 6-inch guns on Cabras Island in Apra Harbor. Work was under way to turn Mount Tenjo into a redoubt. However, this was all of the 1914 plan to be realized, no additional weapons were received. Finally in 1921, guns became available for the 1914 plan, and later recommendations of a December 18, 1919 joint Army-Navy Board plan included: 7-inch pedestal, 8-inch howitzers, and 3-inch antiaircraft guns. The 7-inch guns were to replace the 6-inchers on Orote Peninsula, Cabras Island, and Mount Tenjo. Three 7-inch guns were received and emplaced at Orote Point, but no more arrived. Unavailable were the 13,500 troops, and naval facilities as recommended in the 1919 plan.

In 1922 the additional guns were on order, but this was the year of the Washington Naval Limitations Treaty. Article 19 of the treaty forbid new fortifications in the Pacific west of Hawaii. Guam received no more guns. Guns already installed, remained until 1931 when they were removed, leaving the island demilitarized. When the Japanese attacked in 1941, the largest guns were two 3-inch antiaircraft guns on the USS *Penguin*.

A Marine Corps seaplane observation squadron established an air station at Sumay in 1921. Flight L (later named Scouting Squadron One), with assistance from the Marine Barracks, constructed squad housing, a shop and hangar on the west side of the village. Scouting Squadron One, except for temporary duty in China, served at Guam until 1931, when it returned to the U.S. mainland as an economy measure. Aviation returned to Guam in October 13, 1935 with the Apra Harbor landing of the first Pan American Airways (PAA) Clipper flight. A few months later mail and passenger service was in place, at the former Sumay Marine Corps Air Station. PAA built new facilities including a hangar, shop, warehouse, terminal building, and hotel. Also, the U.S. improved Apra Harbor to accommodate the Clipper flights. The Japanese protested these improvements, claiming that they were military projects. While they were civilian, the harbor improvements had potential military value. To reduce tensions the Navy cut back the scope of its 1935 Pacific naval maneuvers, restricting them to waters east of 180°, keeping ships out of the western Aleutians, Wake and Guam areas.

In May 1938, the U.S. Congress directed the Secretary of the Navy to appoint a board to study naval base needs. The board, which took the name of its respected chair, Rear Admiral A. J. Hepburn, had little time to study the issues. A final report was due at the end of the year. However, the combined experiences and knowledge of the board made possible this rapid assessment. In its December 1 report the board recommended construction of naval bases at Sitka, Kodiak, and Dutch Harbor, Alaska. The board urged expansion of

Ford Island Air Base, a new airfield at Kaneohe, Hawaii, and patrol plane and ship refueling bases at Midway and Wake Islands. With respect to Guam the Hepburn Report spoke of its present defenselessness, that it had great potential, and was well suited for development as a major advanced fleet base. Additionally, a fortified Guam would make "hostile operations against the Philippines a precarious undertaking." A base here would be a countermeasure to the Japanese on Saipan, and a threat to Japanese bases to the west and east.[3]

When it came time to ask for money for Guam, the Navy cut its requests. It was avoidance, the Navy did not wish to offend members of Congress opposed to the Guam build-up, who feared that the Japanese would view it as provocative. Instead funding was provided for Alaska, Hawaii, Midway and Wake military projects. On February 23, 1939, the House defeated a modest request for Apra Harbor improvements. Finally in March 1941, $4.7 million was authorized for Apra Harbor improvement and fuel tanks on Cabras Island, in Apra Harbor.

Chicago Bridge and Iron Company received the contract for the five steel fuel tanks on Cabras Island. They started construction in May 1941 and completed them just in time for the Japanese to use them. In July, Pomeroy contractors started the harbor improvement work and limited building project at the Piti Navy Yard. Pomeroy surveyors also inspected the island for airfield sites. A favorable site was the flat land to the west of the Marine Barracks golf course on Orote Peninsula. Governor Captain George McMillin, in August 1941, recommended building an airfield at this location. Work had not started when the Japanese invaded. An airfield at this site was the first Japanese military project.

While limited U.S. military construction was in progress at Guam, the Japanese developed their Pacific plans. Their war plan was to exhaust the American and British resolve, believing that both nations would quickly tire of battle and accept Japan's control of Asia and the Pacific. An expected Allied defeat in Europe would further exhaust the Allied will since the Americans and British were "soft and did not have much of a fighting spirit". It was to be a limited war to establish a Japanese empire in China and dominance in the Pacific. On September 6, 1941, these general ideas were turned into specific objectives at an Imperial Conference. By the end of October, the final war plans were finished. This included capture of American, British, and Dutch bases in the South Seas. This included occupation of Guam, the Philippines, Hong Kong, British

Malaya, Burma, Java, Sumatra, the Celebes, Borneo, the Bismarcks, and Dutch Timor.

Operations would begin with the occupations of Guam, Hong Kong, and British Borneo. Thailand and Vietnam (Indo-China) would be controlled while the Philippines were subjected to aerial attacks, followed by landings in the Philippines and Malaya. Soon afterwards, the Bismarcks, Dutch Borneo, and the Celebes were to be captured, occupation of southern Sumatra, and capture of Java. Once the Japanese had Singapore, they would capture northern Sumatra and Burma. These operations would create a defensive perimeter from Burma to the Kurile Islands. In response, the American Pacific Fleet was expected to advance into the Central Pacific. During this advance Japanese air and submarine attacks would deplete the Pacific Fleet. Therefore, at an inevitable confrontation the Japanese Combined Fleet would be numerically equal, and given the perceived superiority of the Imperial ships and crews, have the advantage.

Admiral Isoroku Yamamoto, commander of the Combined Fleet, and his staff created another plan to enhance this decisive battle scenario. This was the surprise attack on Pearl Harbor to destroy much of the Pacific Fleet. Such destruction would delay the American counteroffensive, weaken the Pacific Fleet and demoralize the U.S. Navy. The final battle plans were available in early November with the opening attack scheduled for December 8, 1941 (Tokyo time).

Guam's capture was in the initial operations, to follow soon after the attack on Pearl Harbor. In October and November 1941, seaplanes based at Flores Point, Saipan, carried out intelligence overflights of Guam. These photographic flights took place in October and November 1941. In November, Japanese embassy officials heading for Washington collected data on Guam, flying on the PAA Clipper. This flight included the chance to view Apra Harbor and check for coastal defenses. The embassy personnel sent a report to the Navy vice minister outlining their impressions on the state of American readiness. Unlike Hawaii there is no evidence of spies operating in Guam. After the war, there were accusations that local Japanese had been spies, especially, Samuel Takekuna Shinohara, owner of the Rooster Bar in Agana. He strongly denied these accusations. Evidence indicates his innocence. His best defense was the intelligence gaps evident in the Japanese operations, not having crucial information easily acquired by Shinohara. The Japanese did not have correct numbers regarding military strength, accurate information on the road network, and coastal defenses. On all counts Japanese intelligence was lacking. For example, their estimate of fighting men on Guam was way off, they anticipated 300 U.S. military and 1,500 Guamanian militia. In fact, there were 153 Marines, 271 Navy, 134 construction workers, and an Insular Guard Force of 80.

TWELVE

Japanese Capture and Occupation

Guam in American hands was a threat to the security of the Japanese Mandates. American planes and ships stationed here could disrupt the sea lanes and launch raids against the Japanese in the Marianas. Guam was critical in the overall war objectives, to support the decisive sea battle. Submarines and planes operating out of Guam would whittle down the Pacific Fleet.

A South Seas detachment was formed in November 1941 to carry out the landings at Guam, the Bismarcks and Kiribati (Gilberts). The detachment had three infantry battalions from the 144th Infantry Regiment plus supporting elements drawn from the 55th Infantry Division. For the Guam landings, there was also a 500-man strong Special Naval Landing Force (SNLF) (naval personnel trained at an Army Infantry School) from Saipan. The SNLF brought the total invasion force to 5,500, under the command of Major General Tomitaro Horii:

The South Seas Detachment included:

> 55th Infantry Headquarters Group
> 144th Infantry Regiment (three battalions)
> 3d Company, 55th Cavalry
> 1st Battalion, 55th Mountain Artillery Regiment
> 1st Company, 55th Engineer Regiment
> A Detachment of 55th Division Signal
> 2d Company, 55th Transportation Regiment
> Detachment, 55th Medical Unit
> One Company, 47th Field Artillery

1st Field Hospital, 55th Division
Elements of 55th Horse Depot
Elements of 55th Field Water Unit

A task force commanded by Rear Admiral Aritono Goto provided naval transport and bombardment. This naval task force included the heavy cruiser's *Aoba, Kako, Furataka,* and *Kinugasa* from the 6th Cruiser Division. There were also the light cruisers *Tatsuta* and *Tenrya* from the 18th Cruiser Division. The 6th Flotilla provided the destroyer's *Kikuzuki, Yuzuki, Uzuki,* and *Oboro.* Additional elements were submarines, four gunboats, the mine layer *Tsugaru,* and nine transports to carry the assault troops.

On November 8, the Imperial General Headquarters ordered General Horii to prepare for the capture of Guam. To work out the details General Horii met with Vice Admiral Shigeyoshi Inouye, Commander of the Fourth Fleet, which had general responsibility for naval operations in the Central Pacific. During their November 14 and 15 meetings, at Iwakuni Naval Air Base, they discussed bombardment and landings.

The South Seas Detachment boarded its nine transports, on November 20, at Sakaide, Shikoku Island. From Shikoku they sailed to Oki Harbor, Hahajima in Ogasawara Jima (Bonins). While at Hahajima, on December 2, they received their orders for the capture of Guam. On December 4 the South Seas Detachment sailed for the Marianas.[1]

Meanwhile, the war clouds in the fall of 1941 changed life in Guam. By October 17, all military dependents had departed, except Mrs. J. A. Hellmers, wife of John Hellmers, chief commissary steward. She was too far pregnant to travel to San Francisco on the evacuation ship *Henderson.* Mrs. Hellmers and her newborn daughter became prisoners when Guam fell. They were among civilians and five Navy nurses captured at Guam, who were repatriated in the summer of 1942.

Captain George McMillin, governor and naval station commander, received a war warning message on December 4. Two days later he ordered all classified documents burned. During these tense days the Navy and Marine personnel at the Guam bases and ships anxiously waited for news of the ongoing negotiations between America and Japan. Meanwhile, the South Seas Detachment was steaming toward the Marianas. At sea soldiers of the South Seas Detachment received a pamphlet telling them that they were embarking on a great crusade of liberation, to "free a hundred million Asians tyrannized" by a few whites.

In a radio message from the commander in chief, Asiatic Fleet, on December 8, at 0545, the Guam Naval Station received word of the Pearl Harbor attack. Captain McMillin ordered his emergency defense plan put into effect. As governor he ordered all civilians out of Agana, but this was impossible as people in Agana were headed to the Feast of the Immaculate Conception, High Mass, in Agana's Cathedral. The captain was able to accomplish one part of the plan, to arrest and jail local Japanese. Locked up were: Jose Shimizu, Mrs. Kaneki Sawada, Samuel Shinohara, Jesus Sayama, F. H. Ishizaki and Luis San Nicolas Takano.[2]

The former minesweeper, *Penguin*, which had been on night patrol outside Apra Harbor, was ordered to remain outside the harbor, where it had more maneuver room. Two patrol craft, the converted fishing boats *YP-16* and *YP-17*, stayed docked at the tiny Piti Navy Yard.

Captain McMillin could do little to prepare for war. The island commander had no coastal defenses or large caliber weapons. As Guam braced for war, 18 planes of the 18th Naval Air Unit at Aslito Field prepared for the preassault bombing of Guam. Air crews had been briefed on targets: the ships, fuel tanks, Piti Navy Yard, radio stations, military headquarters in Agana, and the Marine Barracks on Orote Peninsula. On the morning of December 8 they lifted off the Aslito runway, taking an indirect southwest course to avoid Guam's northern, Ritidian Point lookout. When they were west of Apra Harbor the planes turned sharply to the east, dividing into two attack groups.

One group struck Orote Peninsula targets at 0827, bombing and strafing the Marine Barracks. A string of bombs fell to the west of the Barracks striking the golf course and the Pan American Airways Skyway Hotel in Sumay. Four Marines running from the Barracks were injured (later, one of them, Corporal Harry E. Anderson, died). Two Chamorro kitchen workers, Teddy Flores Cruz and Lorenzo Lujan Pangelinan, were killed by a bomb blast in the hotel kitchen, they were the first to die in the battle for Guam. The attackers then bombed the Standard Oil fuel tank farm at Sumay, hitting and destroying one tank.

As the first flight bombed Orote Peninsula, the second group attacked shipping, strafing and bombing the *Penguin*. The bombs were near misses, but close enough to damage the ship. On the second strafing, machine gun fire raked the deck, killing Ensign Robert Gabriel White at an antiaircraft gun, and wounding the ship's captain, Lieutenant James W. Haviland, III. Realizing that the *Penguin* had no chance, he gave the order to scuttle the ship, and for the crew to escape to Sumay. They climbed into life rafts carrying the body of Ensign White. As they rowed to Sumay they watched the *Penguin* sink in deep waters one-and-a-half miles off Orote Point. Now, above Apra Harbor the two flights joined to strike at inner harbor berths. Their first target was the *R. L. Barnes*, an old fuel tanker converted into a mess attendants' training ship. Strafing and bombing failed to sink this ship, semi-permanently moored at a buoy. After the capture of Guam, she was repaired, and served as a Japanese transport. She survived the war, was recaptured, and sold to a British shipping firm, sailing a few more years and then scrapped.

The attackers now turned their attention to the Piti Navy Yard, bombing and strafing *YP-16* and *YP-17* at the dock. One bomb hit the *YP-16*, setting it afire, with flames spreading to the *YP-17*, destroying both. Now the Guam "Navy" was out of service. One Guam ship, the station ship, USS *Gold Star,* in the Philippines escaped destruction. She served out the war as a transport.

During the morning of December 8, a police watch at Finaguayac, in north Guam, spotted a canoe headed for shore. The police and Marines rushed to Machanao Point, and intercepted a landing party of three. Under interrogation, the men confessed that they came from Saipan to act as Chamorro interpreters for the Japanese occupation of Guam. They had an exciting tale to tell, relating to their captors, that a landing would occur the next day at Dungcas Beach (East Agana). While they were correct as to the landing location, they were wrong on the schedule, the invasion was one day later. Captain McMillin, when informed of the Dungcas Beach landing, believed it to be a ruse to remove Marines from their positions defending Apra Harbor. The landings were expected at Apra Harbor, where Marine defenses blocked the road leading from Sumay to Agana and Agat.

That afternoon six planes from Flores Point retraced the morning flight route, arriving over Guam at 1445. They resumed the attack on the Piti Navy Yard, releasing bombs destroying two buildings. From the Piti Navy Yard the planes flew over the Piti rice fields to bomb and strafe the radio direction finder station at Libugon (today Nimitz Hill). Next, they came over Agana to bomb the administrative area around the Plaza de Espana. Hit and destroyed was a house on an alley off San Ramon Street, destroying the upstairs apartment of Radioman George Tweed (his wife and son had departed on the *Henderson*). When the bomb hit, Tweed was on duty in the radio station behind Government House. That night he slept at the radio station.

While Saipan airpower was softening-up Guam, the South Seas Detachment sailed into Rota Harbor to pick up the Special Naval

Landing Force, commanded by Commander H. Hayashi. The SNLF boarded two transports for the short voyage to Guam.

Twelve aircraft of the 18th Naval Air Group returned to Guam on December 9, over their targets at 0845. Targets this time were: the Standard Oil fuel tank farm, the Marine Barracks, Piti Navy Yard, and the Libugon radio facility. Agana was struck again with bombs intended for the Agana Boat Yard shops and the administration area. Bombs dropped on the Government House struck a home 100 yards away, across from the jail. Fragments of the blown-up masonry house sprayed the jail and frightened the Japanese civilian prisoners. They unsuccessfully pleaded for their release. Their freedom came the next day, when the invasion forces released them. Another bomb destroyed a second house near the plaza, and bombs damaged two more buildings. One bomb landed in the garden at Government House, but did no damage to the administration center. The Government House, hospital, and Agana radio station remained undamaged.

Apart from a furious but brief antiaircraft fire from the *Penguin*, and Marines firing .30 caliber machine guns, the attacking aircraft went unchallenged. In blocking positions on the Marine Barracks golf course above Sumay were 122 Marines, armed with rifles and a few machine guns. Thirty-one more Marines were at duty stations scattered around the island. This tiny force was facing 5,500 landing troops of the South Seas Detachment, backed up by a naval task force with shipboard guns.

The South Seas Detachment contained three landing forces, each entering their assigned anchorages between 2400 and 0100 hours on December 10. In the north was the Tsukamoto Force, offloaded from their transports to six barges and four small landing boats in Tumon Bay. They hit the Tumon Beach unopposed at 0225, and started the march to Agana. The second and smallest force, the SNLF, boarded onto six landing craft in Agana Bay to come ashore at Dungcas Beach at 0400 hours. Once ashore they headed west on the shore road to nearby Agana. A third landing group, the Kusunose Force, landed in the south at Merizo at 0230, but found no road to Agat Village and Orote Peninsula, their objectives, so they reboarded and landed at Agat that afternoon.

At 0400, Captain McMillin received word of the landing at Dungcas Beach, but he had no defenses there to challenge the landings. The Insular Guard Force, on alert in their headquarters on the Plaza de Espana, took up positions in Agana. As the Insular Force moved to defense positions, Captain McMillin learned of the Tumon Bay landings.

The SNLF moved rapidly down the shore road toward Agana, Guam's population center with 12,000 residents and the U.S. military administration area. On the east edge of the city near the San Antonio Bridge, the SNLF machine-gunned a truckload of civilians fleeing the city. Fourteen people on the truck died, but three managed to escape to the heavily wooded cliffs alongside the road. The SNLF continued towards Agana, crossing the bridge and heading in the direction of the Dulce Nombre de Maria Cathedral, on the Plaza de Espana.

Near the plaza, the SNLF ran into fierce machine gun fire. Pedro G. Cruz and Vicente Cruz Chargualaf of the Insular Guard Force had set up their .30 caliber machine gun between the tennis courts and the cathedral where the streets became narrow. Their heavy fire halted the SNLF. The attackers regrouped and fought back. Chargualaf was wounded, and put out of action (he died later of injuries), but Cruz kept on firing the weapon, forcing the SNLF to seek cover. The fire fight continued a few more minutes to 0545 when three blasts of an automobile horn sounded a cease fire.

Captain McMillin, aware of two landings, concluded that further resistance would lead to heavy civilian casualties. He directed Chief Boatswains' Mate Robert Bruce Lane to go out onto the plaza and effect a cease fire. Without any prearranged signal, Lane tried three truck horn blasts. Surprisingly, both sides quickly understood the signal. An officer of the SNLF stepped onto the plaza motioning for the island commander to come out of Government House. Commander Donald T. Giles, the civil affairs officer, and Chief Lane came out to meet with the victors. They were escorted to Commander Hayashi's command post near the San Antonio Bridge, where they acknowledged surrender. They returned to Government House with Commander Hayashi, where inpatient frontline troops had already taken Captain McMillin prisoner, at 0615.

Commander Hayashi, Captain McMillin, and Commander Giles sat down in the Government House to discuss the surrender. Unable to communicate, since none spoke the other's language, the talks got nowhere. Captain McMillin motioned in sign language that English-speaking Japanese civilian prisoners were in the jail across the plaza. Chief Lane walked over to the jail, returning with Shinohara, Shimizu, and Mrs. Sawada to act as translators. Shinohara did most of the interpreting. Captain McMillin agreed to the surrender while demanding fair treatment of his troops and civilians. Then, the captain prepared a surrender document, transferring responsibility for Guam's civil government. The document also indicated that the Japanese commander assured civil and prisoner rights. [3] McMillin called Colonel McNulty, the Marine Barracks commander, telling him to disarm his Marines and be ready to surrender. Commander Hayashi thanked the disposed governor and escorted him outside for a flag-raising ceremony. At the flagpole, in front of Government House, the American flag was lowered to be replaced by the flag of Japan. This ceremony completed, Commander Hayashi took the governor's staff car and two trucks, to get to the Marine Barracks ahead of the Army. Hayashi had a second flag raising at the Marine Barracks, requiring the Marines to stand at attention to witness the Japanese ceremony. Guam had been captured by the 500-man SNLF, while 5,000 Army troops were slowly making their way to their objectives.

The quick surrender of the first American territory captured in the war held down casualties. For the American military, the preinvasion attacks and invasion day resistance had resulted in the deaths of nine sailors, four Marines, one civilian, and five Insular Force Guards. Civilian deaths are not exactly known, but there were at least 22 and estimates of 30 to 40 are probably closer to the true number. Later Commander Hayashi placed a monument at Trinchera (East Agana), "in memory of 22 Chamorro civilians who died in the fall of Guam."

The Marines were marched to Agana to assemble with the other American prisoners in the plaza. When the Japanese took roll, using the American records, six sailors were missing. The capture of these escaped Americans became an immediate priority. After accounting for all but six men, the POWs were crowded into the Insular Force Guard headquarters, with space for 80 but instead held 450 prisoners of war. Governor McMillin, Navy officers, hospital staff, Mrs. Hellmers and her daughter, five Navy nurses, and American Catholic priests were held at the naval hospital. The prisoner overcrowding eased four days later when the POWs were moved into the cathedral and adjacent St. Vincent de Paul building. Locals who witnessed the move were saddened by this sacrilegious use. Chamorros, including those in the Insular Guard Force, were registered, issued identity tags, and released.

For the captors the limited damage done in the aerial attacks and the invasion proved helpful. The island had been captured largely intact. Two Standard Oil fuel tanks at Sumay had been destroyed by bombs, leaving four undamaged. The five new tanks on Cabras Island, which had just been filled, had not been hit, but two were intentionally destroyed by H. H. Sackers, a civilian Public Works employee. Also, someone destroyed Pomeroy Contractors' large dump trucks. Undamaged were: the piers at the Piti Navy Yard, 41 small boats, shops at Piti and Agana, the Marine Barracks, Pan American facilities, and all government offices and quarters.

1. Japanese monument to the 22 Chamorros killed in the Japanese December 1941 capture of the island.

On January 10, 1942, the American prisoners were marched to the Piti Navy Yard and barged out to the *Argentina Maru*. Boarding this former passenger ship, formerly sailing the Tokyo-Buenos Aires route, and seeing its empty state rooms, lifted prisoner spirits. A comfortable passage to Japan was expected, but it was a false hope. They were herded down to the holds for the six-day trip to Shikoku Island, where they imprisoned in a former military camp at Zentsuji.

For the soldiers of the South Seas Detachment, Guam was quite an experience, the tropical conditions were beautiful. There were coconut trees and trees unknown to the soldiers. Bright colored flowers were in sharp contrast to urban Japan. Agana was described as peaceful and a wonderful place in which to live. Certain native habits were a surprise, one was chewing tobacco instead of smoking it. Not all was perfect, there was a shortage of fresh vegetables.

Civilian life in Guam changed dramatically. A few hundred Americans were replaced by 5,500 Japanese, who took over much of Agana, the schools, and government offices for barracks. The South Seas Detachment commander, General Horii, moved into Government House, while the Navy took over Orote Peninsula military facilities and Sumay Village. Tent and native-type hut camps went up at 13 locations.

Island housing conditions improved with the departure of the American prisoners of war and then the South Seas Detachment, which boarded transports on January 16, 1942, bound for Rabaul. The South Seas Detachment was wiped out in battle on New Guinea. Three hundred men of the Special Naval Landing Force, at Guam, returned to Saipan, leaving behind an occupation force of 200 men. The SNLF was now the 54th Keibitai (Naval Guard Force). Most of the time these Navy men kept to themselves, except liberty days when they explored the island.

Recreation on the island included: visits to local tourist sights, movies, concerts, sports, and "comfort girls" brought to Guam to satisfy the sexual desires of the military men. Over one hundred comfort girls, most of them young Korean girls grabbed out of school lineups, were held in brothels in Agana, Anigua, and Piti. When the South Seas Detachment departed, most of these victims were sent to other bases, eight were held back to service the Navy. Saipan and Tinian also had brothels.

The Japanese civilian occupation included efforts to expand rice cultivation and farming, especially to supply military needs. There was also cultural conversion, turning the island into a Japanese colony. Bowing, the Japanese language, and even renaming places were forced upon the Guamanians. Guam was renamed Omiya Jima, or Great Shrine Island. Agana became Akashi, for the red sun in the national flag. Brutalities were inflicted on the people of Guam, especially in an attempt to learn where the six missing American sailors were hiding.

On invasion day the six Navy men had escaped into the jungle, expecting the Marines to recapture the island in a few weeks. Two of the sailors were off the *Penguin*, Chief Machinist Mate L. L. Krump and Machinist Mate First Class C. B. Johnson. The other four had served at the radio station: Radiomans' First Class George Tweed, Al Tyson, Yeoman First Class A. Yablonsky, and Chief Aerographer L. W. Jones.

Tweed and Tyson escaped in Tweed's 1926 Reo to Yona on the east side of the island. They hid the car and retreated into the jungle. "With the help of Francisco Ogo, a Yona farmer who found them, Tweed and Tyson remained in Yona for several days. There they also met the other Americans who were hiding on the farm of Manuel Aguon, another Yona farmer. Within a few days, several islanders learned of the Americans in the woods and visited them in their hiding places. They brought cigarettes, food, water, reading materials and, of course, news of Japanese activities on the island."[4]

It was not long before the Japanese suspected that the escapees were in the Yona area. Yona residents were arrested and tortured to obtain more precise leads. When the Japanese got close to the hiding place, the group broke up. Tweed went out on his own, staying a short time in the Yona area and then across the island to Upper Tumon. With the help of Guamanians he moved several times.

The first American hideout was discovered on September 12, 1942, when Jones, Yablonsky, and Krump were surrounded in Yona. Asleep they were awakened by Japanese with fixed bayonets. Seeing no opportunity to escape the sailors gave up. They were beheaded.

With three located and killed, the search for the remaining three was intensified. Tweed, learning of the executions, made frequent moves, always depending upon Chamorros for shelter and food. On October 22, 1942, soldiers located Tyson and Johnston. The Japanese surrounded their chicken coop shelter, opened fire, killing both men. Now, there was only Tweed, and his capture assumed a great symbolic importance. For twenty-two months the Japanese tortured those suspected of aiding or hiding Tweed. Despite the beatings the suspects never gave away his location. By July 1944, the Japanese police had a prime suspect and were getting close. They correctly suspected Antonio Artero, but he was warned of the danger, and took his family into hiding on July 12. Even if he had been arrested, the police could not capture Tweed. Two days earlier, on July 10, Tweed signaled the destroyer *McCall* with a mirror and handmade flags, and was picked up on the beach by a small boat.

Father Jesus Baza Duenas was among the people suspected of hiding, or knowing the whereabouts of Tweed. Not only was he suspected of helping the radioman, but he was disliked because of his protesting Japanese mistreatment of Guamanians. About July 8, the Japanese civilian police arrested the priest and his nephew, Eduardo Duenas. Both men were interrogated and horribly tortured over three days; neither supplied information. Early on the morning of July 12, Father Duenas, Eduardo Duenas, and two others were beheaded.

The Minseibu, or civilian government of Guam, behaved in ways which insured hatred of the occupiers, who had called themselves liberators. Lieutenant Commander Homura, the retired officer called back to duty to head the Minseibu, frequently insulted and caused injury to Guamanians. His regular propaganda lectures in the Cathedral Dulce Nombre de Maria were required attendance. By holding them in the cathedral he created hatred, misusing the church. In a further insult, Commander Homura located his office next door in the Saint Vincent de Paul building. What happened to Homura is not known. He was not among the captured, so he may have fought to the end or committed suicide.[5]

THIRTEEN

Preparing a Defense

The Guam defenders had an extra month to ready for enemy landings. It was sufficient time to emplace most of the coastal defense weapons. When the Americans landed only a few guns were in storage. Most of the weapons were installed and operational. However, airfield construction was behind schedule.

To support the decisive sea battle, the first Japanese military construction project was an airfield on Orote Peninsula. Work was started in mid-1943 and on November 10, 1943, the 4th Naval Civil Engineer Department arrived to complete it. They had a 3,600-foot long concrete-coral runway ready in January 1944. Apart from the runway the engineers built only one building, an operations center. There were enough American buildings to meet the airbase needs. When the Navy moved onto Orote Peninsula they the Sumay Village residents, and to this day, they have not been allowed to return. The 4th Naval Civil Engineers moved into the Sumay Village homes. While naval officers moved into the former Pan American Skyways Hotel, in Sumay. The enlisted personnel lived at the Marine Barracks buildings.

Airfield construction was assigned to the 217th and 218th Setsueitai. These naval construction battalions were comprised of 800 Korean laborers and 100 Navy and civilian engineers each. In January 1944 the construction battalions started work on Tiyan field, above Agana. For this project young Chamorro men were employed as laborers, and paid 400 yen ($1.25) for a 12 hour day. Because equipment was limited to one roller and one shovel, the work was done by manual labor. On February 23, 1944, all able-bodied men,

155

sixteen and older, were mobilized for airfield and fortifications construction. During the island campaign Chamorro men were taken to the north to build fortifications. Fifty-one of them were executed just before the island fell.

A third airfield was started at Tanguisson Point (Tomioka) in April 1944. The site was about 50 percent complete at the time of the U.S. invasion. With the landings, the 217th Setsueitai, commanded by Lieutenant Commander Sakamoto, and the 218th led by Lieutenant Commander Masso Arai, were transferred to defense construction. When the battle turned north, they built defenses in the Mount Santa Rosa area.

The September 1943 Imperial Conference addressed the need to reinforce the Marianas. Initially, the combat-tested 13th Division was tapped for the Marianas, and scheduled to depart Central China in November 1943. An advance detachment of 300 was shipped to the Marianas in October. However, the division remained to serve in the South China campaign, in late 1944. The 300-man detachment at Guam stayed.[1] They became part of the replacement division, the 29th Division, commanded by Lieutenant General Takeshi Takashina. In February 1944, the 29th Division was pulled out of the Kwantung Army in Manchuria, and reorganized into regimental combat teams, for duty in the Marianas. Each regiment, the 18th, 38th, and 50th Regiments, was reinforced with attached artillery, and engineers, giving them increased mobility and firepower for independent operations. The division engineer, cavalry, and transport regiments were dropped.

Training of the 29th Division, formed in 1941 with men from the Nagoya District of Honshu Island, had covered large-scale ground maneuvers of an offensive nature. They were well trained and prepared for combat in China. In the offensive-minded Japan military there had been no training in island defense. There would be none in the Marianas, there was neither the time or the inclination. Offense, not static defense, was the precept.

The 29th Division boarded trains at their training camps at Haicheng, Liaoyang, and Tiehling between February 19–21, 1944, and headed for Pusan, Korea. At Pusan, they transferred to transports for passage to Guam. The 18th Regiment, 29th Division, sailed on the *Sakito Maru*; the 38th Regiment and division headquarters on the *Aki Maru*; and the 50th Regiment on the *Togau Maru*.

Additional reinforcements for Guam included elements of the 1st (Tokyo District) and 11th (Shikoku Island) Division of the Kwantung Army. They were formed into the 6th Expeditionary Force, 5,100-strong under the command of Major General Kiyoshi Shigematsu. In March the 6th was transported by train to Pusan, boarding transports bound for the Marianas. This force steamed into Apra Harbor on March 20. In May it was reformed into the 48th Independent Mixed Brigade, comprised of the 319th, 320th, 321st and 322d Independent Infantry Battalions. These battalions were created from the former 11th Division battalions in the 6th Expeditionary. The former 1st Division units of the 6th were made into a two-battalion 10th Independent Mixed Regiment (IMR). One battalion, the 1st of the 10th IMR, was dispatched to Rota with an artillery company and engineer platoon.

Armor for Guam was the 1st and 2d Companies and one-half of the 6th Tank Company, 9th Tank Regiment. There was also the 24th Tank Company with nine Type 95 tanks. The total armor strength was about 38 tanks. Independent antiaircraft artillery included the 52d Field Antiaircraft Battalion and the 45th Independent Antiaircraft Company. Two independent engineer units were assigned, the 2d Company, 7th Independent Engineer Regiment, and 2d Company, 16th Shipping Engineer Regiment.

The 54th Keibitai, Naval Guard Force, was reinforced in early 1944, by an additional company. Other naval units, such as the 217th and 218th Construction Battalions, were on Guam, bringing the total naval ground strength to 4,650. Besides ground personnel there were naval air units. Nearly all of the aircraft sent to New Guinea to reinforce Biak, and those resisting the American invasion, had been destroyed. Therefore the air units, the Southeast Area Air Depot, 263d, 521st and 755th Air Groups, were converted to infantry units.

American submarines discovered the 29th Division convoy. The *Sakito Maru* was sent to the bottom on February 29 with 2,400 soldiers and sailors. All the 18th Regiment weapons and equipment were lost. This mauled regiment was assigned to Guam (except the 1st Battalion on Saipan). The 38th Regiment served on Guam and the 50th Regiment was assigned to Tinian. The total strength at Guam was about 18,500 military.

General Takashina had his troops dispersed around the island until the mid-June U.S. bombardment, which suggested to him west coast landings. On June 16 he realigned his defenses, moving units to the west shore, with reserves to the rear of the western beaches, so they could be moved as needed.

General Takashina's command included Guam and Rota, called the Southern Marianas Group. On June 23 he sent the 1st Battalion, 10th Independent Mixed Regiment, with attached artillery and engineers to Rota. Another convoy carried the 3d Battalion, 18th Infantry Regiment, with engineer and landing detachments, to stage through Rota for counterlandings at Saipan. However, rough seas killed this plan so the regiment returned to Guam. A boat accident on the return sailing cost 100 men drowned and two barges lost.

Guam's island defenses were constructed according to the standard beachline doctrine, with the destruction of the enemy on the beaches. Should seaborne invaders get ashore, powerful counterattacks would drive them back into the sea. At this point the invaders would be destroyed by the Mobile Fleet. This concept ignored the greatest strength of the American invasion forces, their naval and air bombardment capabilities. This type of defense placed the coastal defenses on the beaches where they were most susceptible to bombardment. Despite the evidence from Saipan that this doctrine was terribly flawed, and one extra month to correct it, there was no change at Guam.

There was sufficient time on Guam to install most of the coastal defense guns, only four 140mm coastal defense guns and six 120mm guns were in storage at the time of the invasion. Takashina, also had more time to install mines, beach obstacles, and beach trenchworks, than did the Saipan garrison. Since the Guam defense was nearly complete, it was closer to the textbook beachline defense than Saipan.

The defense starts offshore with stone-filled crib obstacles in the waters between the fringing reef and beach. Mines were also placed on the reef and reef entrances. Nearer the beach were steel poles as anti-landing craft barriers, and on the beach were zigzag trenchworks with machine gun emplacements on their leading points. In the trenches were rifle positions, shelters, command posts, and ammunition storage bunkers, constructed with log roofs covered with sand or soil. To the rear of the first line, the trenchworks, were antitank ditches.

Pillboxes for 37mm guns were sited at the ends of the beaches to fire enfilade on the beach. Along the beaches were pillboxes for 20mm and machine guns. At strategic locations, strongpoints were established. The 200mm antiboat guns were emplaced on promontories for interlocking fire on the inner reef and bays. The remaining coastal defense guns (120mm to 6-inch) were installed on the ridges behind the beaches. When possible they were placed in caves, but there was not a large-scale tunnel construction program. Everywhere the camouflage effort was intense and often very effective.

A second infantry line of defense was located on inclines and ridges behind the beaches. Where valleys or ravines offered a route to the interior, machine guns and mortars were emplaced to defend these passages. On the reverse slopes of hills or hidden in the

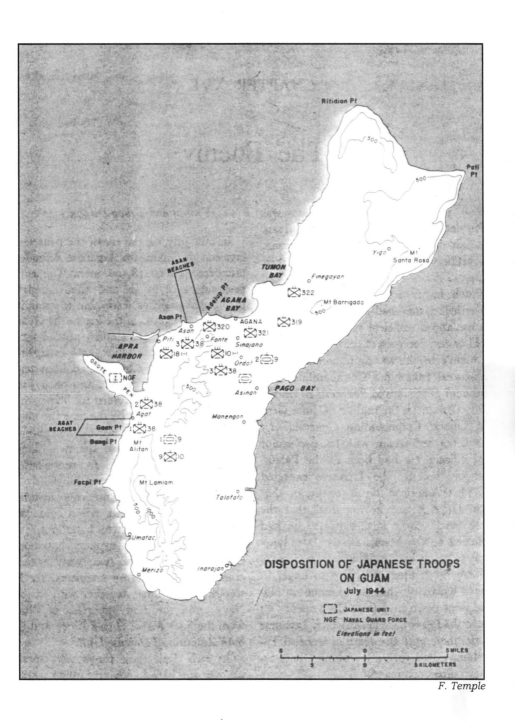

DISPOSITION OF JAPANESE TROOPS
ON GUAM
July 1944

☐ JAPANESE UNIT
NGF NAVAL GUARD FORCE

Elevations in feet

5   0   5 MILES
5   0   5 KILOMETERS

F. Temple

2. General Takashina (right), island commander, and Colonel Suenaga, commander of the 38th Infantry Regiment, inspect the Agat Beach defenses.

National Archives

cliffs were artillery and mortars. There were also command and observation posts on the ridges. Guam's main observation post was on Mount Chachao above Asan. From here the western landing beaches and maneuver areas were visible.[2]

Mount Tenjo (1,022 feet), which still had trenchworks and gun platforms from the Marine defense, was unused. This error is even more glaring considering the greater firepower of World War II. It would be much harder to hit with naval gunfire and the central massif had a commanding view of the western beaches and Apra Harbor. Heavily fortified, the central massif would have been a powerful defense.

Also, the Marianas climate was not considered in the defense plan. Both seasons of the year could be used against an invasion force. The monsoon season turned roads into muddy morasses. With intentional cross-rutting and destruction, the roads could be denied an enemy. Water shortages are the problem during the dry season. A prolonged defense would create water shortages among the landing troops, while the island garrison could store water. When the Americans landed, it was the rainy season, but none of the roads or bridges had been destroyed.

Starting in the north, above the narrow waist from Agana to Pago Bay, there was only one adequate landing beach, Tumon Bay, which was defended. Most of the north shore is sheer cliffs pounded by the ocean, and the few beaches, such as Taraque, are too small and lack maneuver space. Tarague was defended by a few machine guns and infantry positions, to repel small raiding groups.

A land attack against the north was extremely difficult. To reach the north from the southern landing beaches required crossing the exposed waist, from Pago Bay to Agana. At Agana, wide wetlands had to be crossed, below an incline with many places for commanding gun positions. Enemy troops able to get onto the north plateau would find few roads and trails, and they were surrounded by dense jungle, channelizing the invaders into narrow corridors to be ambushed by waiting defenders. Also, maneuver in the north was under the observation of three mountains, Mount Barrigada (674 feet), Mount Santa Rosa (870 feet), and Mount Mataguac (600 feet). They provided excellent observation and guns on them could hit all the routes into the north. General Takashina had the advantage, in the rough terrain of northern Guam, had he developed its potential.

Tumon Bay was the most likely landing area, north of Agana. A Japanese landing force had come ashore here in December 1941, so its value was apparent. Accordingly, General Takashina had extensive fortifications. They included two Type 3 (1943) 200mm antiboat guns at Gongna Cove on the north end of the bay (today,

Gun Beach), sited in escarpment cavities with concrete blast walls for shields. Above Tumon Bay, at Dededo, were four 120mm Type 10 guns for antiaircraft and ground fire. Six more 120mm Type 10 guns at Tanguisson Point protected the under construction airfield. On the north side of Tumon Bay was an antitank barrier. In the cliffs above the beach were more than 70 guns, 13mm to 75mm, and infantry positions. Two 120mm Type 10 guns were at Oka, on the point of land creating the south boundary of Tumon Bay, for interlocking fire with the 200mm guns on the north side.

To the south of Tumon Bay, just above the waist of the island, was Dungcas Beach, or Recreation Beach, a few miles east of Agana. It was here that the Special Naval Landing Force landed in 1941 and rushed to Agana to capture Guam's main city and the island. Dungcas had real advantages as a landing site. The most important was its proximity to the beach road, providing rapid access to Agana. A disadvantage was its narrow maneuver area with sheer cliffs, only fifty to two hundred yards to the rear of the beach. Takashina used this narrow access to create a trap. He had roadblocks and cliff guns to lay crossfire on it. In the cliffs above the beach were two 200mm antiboat guns in caves, and two 120mm Type 10 guns were on the west end of Dungcas Beach. Nearby, at the narrowest point, where the coastal plain narrowed to road width, was a roadblock. Supporting fire for Dungcas Beach and Agana beaches was provided by dual purpose guns at Tiyan Airfield. Ten 120mm Type 10 guns and seventy 13mm to 75mm antiaircraft guns defended the airfield and the beaches below. To draw attention away from these camouflaged guns were dummy AA guns at the field. There were few defenses on the airfield against a landward attack, since any enemy was to be destroyed long before they could advance by land to the airfield.

There was only a narrow reef entrance at Agana Harbor, so a major landing was not expected here. A few pillboxes and two 20mm gun pillboxes were constructed at the Navy Yard, a small repair yard with a small boat dock. Agana was not defended, for the same reason that Tiyan Airfield did not have a land defense; the enemy would be destroyed at the landing beaches, not in the towns or airfields. No provisions were made for a city defense to take advantage of narrow streets, rivers, bridges, and rubble from the American bombardment. Construction in Agana was limited to large shelter tunnels, in the cliffs, behind the Plaza de Espana. These tunnels were large enough to shelter the government workers and headquarters military staff. Defending Agana and Tiyan Field were two 75mm Type 88 antiaircraft guns on the cliff above Government House.

Guam's strongest fortifications were on the west, from Adelup Point to Facpi Point, which included Asan Beach, Piti, Orote Peninsula, and Agat Beach. Along these ten miles of beach (Guam had a total of 15 miles of potential landing beaches) were the best landing areas and they were so protected. The limestone promontory, Adelup Point, was one horn of a "devil's horns". Asan was the second, and between the horns was Asan Beach. Before the Japanese capture, there was U.S. Navy housing on its flat landward side, and on the seaward knoll was the Kroll house, where owners of an import company lived. In 1944 the Navy housing was occupied by Commander Homura and his staff. All the houses on the point were destroyed in the preinvasion bombardment. Around Adelup's broken and jagged coral shore cliffs were natural caves and cavities converted into gun positions for 37mm and 47mm guns, and 70mm howitzers. Machine gun pillboxes were emplaced on the limited beach areas. On the southwest side were two 200mm antiboat guns in open, but well-camouflaged, positions. Supporting fire for Adelup came from machine guns emplaced on the escarpment above the Pigo Cemetery and Chonito Ridge.

One hundred yards to the rear of Adelup Point is Chonito Cliff, running parallel to Asan Beach. Its defensive value was maximized with infantry and artillery positions along its entire length. On the top of the cliff above Adelup Point was a battery of three 6-inch guns in open earthen emplacements, covered with camouflage nets. This deception effort was not sufficient, the guns were spotted and destroyed in the American preinvasion bombardment. Near the gun battery was an observation post with a view of the entire Asan area. On the reverse slope of Chonito was a 200-man shelter cave, of great value during the preassault bombardments.

Chonito Cliff was an eastern foothill of the central mountain massif, from Chonito and Fonte above it, there were encampments to Mount Chachao, where the island's main observation post was located. General Takashina installed fortifications on the approaches to Fonte, where his cave command post was located. On the road from Adelup Point to Fonte were three 120mm guns in pillboxes, 75mm artillery, and numerous machine gun placements.

Antilanding devices at Asan Beach included offshore stone-filled cribs, but no mines, only Dadi Beach, on Orote Peninsula, was mined. Unmolested American Underwater Demolition Teams (UDTs) destroyed 940 obstacles at Agat and Asan beaches. Private First Class Teruo Kurokawa, in the 1st Squad, 2d Platoon, of the 320th Battalion, reported that all units had been instructed not to fire on the UDT's, since this would give away their positions. His 47mm gun position at Asan waited and held its fire, only to be destroyed by preinvasion bombardment. There was a limited supply of barbed wire, so little was used as a barrier at the water's edge. A few coconut palm logs were driven into the sand and cable strung between standing trees as antitank barriers. A long antitank trench was dug in the village of Asan, from the beach to the ridges to block armor headed for Agana or Fonte.

Two 200mm antiboat guns were concealed in the forest on the lower Chonito Cliff, four hundred yards west of Adelup Point. At the midpoint of Asan Beach, a ravine separates Chonito Cliff and Bundschu, and provides the easiest route to the top. Takashina had machine gun nests on both sides. Bundschu Ridge, as named by the American, had artillery, mortar, machine gun and infantry positions, hidden in the thick forest.

Japanese troops assembled in the east slopes of the central mountains stayed alert for landings at Pago Bay, the back door to the Mount Chachao assembly area. Farther east were mobile defenses, including two Type 95 tanks in revetments, not far from Yona in the Maneggon Hills. Both dugouts were open at the back so the tanks could pull out to return to their more mobile role.

The second horn of the Asan Beach devil's horns was Asan Point, the limestone promontory creating the western end of the beach. Like Adelup Point, guns were sited to fire across the 15- to 30-foot-wide sandy beach and the inner reef area. These guns could lay heavy barrages on the obstacles where enemy landing craft might be stalled. On the east side of the point were two 120mm, 37mm, 47mm, and machine guns. The west side had three 200mm antiboat guns, two in cliff line cavities and the third on the tip of the promontory, partially sheltered by concrete walls. Trees and vegetation on the point were left undisturbed to hide the emplacements. This deception worked, the guns survived the preinvasion attacks.

Tepungan and Piti, the next beaches below Asan, were well defended. The 200mm antiboat guns on Asan Point were to fire on landing vessels approaching these beaches. On Laulaug Ridge, above Tepungan, were three 140mm coastal defense guns, with elaborate concealment of palm fronds, canvas, and vegetation. The palm fronds and plant material were changed regularly to keep them fresh and green. Only one, not so well camouflaged, was spotted and damaged by American gunfire. Today this gun battery is a tourist site. One 200mm antiboat gun was installed at the Masso River in Piti.

Two more 200mm antiboat guns were set up in sandbagged revetments next to the Sasa River. These guns guarded the Piti Road and the inner Apra Harbor. There were also six 80mm guns, pillboxes, and local defenses along the road and the beach from

Tepungan to Piti. In open storage, next to the Masso River, were four 140mm coastal defense guns and six 120mm Type 10 guns.

Landings were expected at Agat Bay, between Facpi Point in the south and Orote Peninsula on the north. Agat was similar to Asan with shallow water between the reef and shore, one to four feet deep, a coastal plain allowing for maneuver but mountains with fantastic fields of fire covering the beaches. Dominating the Agat beaches were Mount Alifan (869 feet) and Mount Tenjo plus numerous knobs and small hills with strongpoints.

Defenses at Facpi Point, on the southern edge of Agat Beach, included machine guns and infantry. The heavy firepower started at Bangi Point. Two 200mm antiboat guns and machine gun pillboxes turned this point into a powerful fortification.

Gaan Point, a small rock outcropping at about the midpoint of Agat Beach, was strongly defended. There were two concrete pillboxes built into the rocky knoll. One held a Type 94 75mm gun, and the second a 37mm gun. Around the rocky mount were rifle and machine gun positions, and on the reverse slope were shelter and command caves. All were completely hidden by preserved natural vegetation, shielding them from U.S. aerial snooping. Gaan Point caused serious problems for the Marines, stopping nine LVTs (amphtracs). Gaan Point machine guns and riflemen extracted numerous casualties among the landing forces.

Continuing along Agat Beach, 200 yards in the direction of Agat village, were two 20mm guns in pillboxes on the water's edge. In the coconut grove behind these guns was one 200mm antiboat gun. Agat Beach had trenchworks along its length, dug in the sand and coral, 50 feet inland of the high waterline. A total of 25 pillboxes were built along the beach from Bangi to Apaca Point, at Agat Village.

Apaca Point was the north anchor of the Agat defense. Installed in natural cavities of this rocky point were gun positions improved with concrete embrasure walls, but harmonized into the setting. One surviving pillbox here demonstrates its harmony with the environment. It was built into a small soil mound on the edge of the beach without altering the natural setting. The only evidence of a defense is a small embrasure, and it has a rough concrete face blending it into the terrain.[3]

Small knobs and hills behind Agat Beach were turned into stalwart defenses and supporting artillery locales. Coastal defense guns were installed in open earthen positions on Mount Alifan. Here were two 6-inch Whitworth-Armstrong Model 1900 guns and four 120mm Type 10 guns. Efforts to hide the guns with palm fronds

3. Bangi Point, Agat, stripped clear by bombardment. The 200mm antiboat gun emplacement is visible at the tip of the point.

National Archives

and canvas failed. They were detected and destroyed in preinvasion bombardment.

Orote Peninsula was unique as Takashina's only defense in depth in Guam. This was a carefully designed defense, such that a superior force could be denied the ground by the use of terrain and well-sited defenses. Access to Orote was limited to Dadi Beach on Agat Bay, Gabgab Beach on Apra Harbor, and two mainland roads. All these approaches were strongly defended, beginning with roadblocks on the Agat-Sumay and Piti-Sumay Roads, and artillery on Orote, at Piti, and in the hills to the east, to fire on invaders moving towards Orote. A defensive line, 3,000 feet long, from Dadi Beach to Abo Cove, extended across the neck of the peninsula, commanding the rice fields in front of the line. The Orote Peninsula guns were so effectively camouflaged that few were detected or destroyed prior to the invasion, and many survived until overrun during the battle for Orote.

The most likely landing beach on Orote Peninsula was Dadi Beach, on Agat Bay. Accordingly, it was the best defended beach, with offshore mines and obstacles, barbed wire at the beach, reinforced concrete and palm log pillboxes, and guns in caves at Tipalao Point. On the high ground above Dadi Beach on Tipalao Point were two 200mm antiboat guns and artillery. The second possible landing site was Gabgab Beach on the Apra Harbor side. Since it had little maneuver room, Gabgab Beach had only machine gun pillboxes in the cliffs.

A second Orote Peninsula line was 300 yards beyond its neck. At this point the two roads merge into one road which continues on to Sumay. On one side of the road junction (RJ 15 on U.S. battle maps) was a mangrove swamp and on the other side were wetlands, channelizing the enemy onto the mined road. Mortars, machine guns, and rifle positions, on a ridgeline 100 yards west of the junction, turned the junction into a formidable obstacle. To prevent a flanking move by an advancing enemy, the dry land beyond the wetlands on the south side of the junction was defended by trenches and gun positions in a coconut grove.

A third line, and the most awesome, ran across the peninsula on a bluff, from the south side of the rifle range across the Marine Barracks to Sumay. On the forward edge of the line were trenchworks, and 250 positions. Behind the line were dual purpose guns including four 120mm Type 10 guns, fourteen 75mm Type 88 guns, and sixty 13mm and 25mm guns, some in fuel drum walls with vines growing out of the drums.

At the end of the third defense, where it touched Sumay, the guns had been emplaced in caves to fire on an enemy in Apra

Harbor. Two 25mm guns were installed on the Apra Harbor breakwater and a dummy gun placed in a former U.S. 6-inch gun coastal position on Cabras Island. Finally, antiaircraft guns were placed in the former U.S. 7-inch gun pits on Orote Point.

Takashina had few worries south of Agat, since southern Guam is characterized by tall peaks, with Mount Lamlam at 1,334 feet its highest. Heavy surfs pound the shoreline and the bays while potential landing sites did not have good road networks to link them to the main target areas of Orote Peninsula and Agana. Landing forces would be immobile, so no landings were expected in this area. Only a few pillboxes and infantry positions dotted the southern coast.

Takashina had the following guns installed: eighteen 200mm antiboat guns; six 6-inch coastal defense guns; three 140mm coastal defense (and three 140mm guns in storage); five 120mm coastal defense guns; twenty-eight 120mm dual-purpose guns; and fourteen 75mm antiaircraft guns.

While Guam had more than twice as many coastal defense guns as Saipan, it had a larger front. The Japanese Self-Defense Agency, in its analysis of the battle for Guam, calculated guns per kilometer of battle front. At Guam there were 56 guns on a 32 kilometer front, or 1.6 guns per kilometer. The Saipan defense had 20 guns on 8 kms., or 2.5 per kilometer. Far more impressive was Iwo Jima with 108 guns on a four kilometer front or 27 per km.[4]

The construction program was regularly harassed by American carrier aircraft raids. Leading Private Koko Murano, 2nd Battalion, 10th Independent Mixed Regiment, whose unit arrived on March 21, experienced his first air attack on April 25. At the time, Murano's company, the 11th, was billeted at the Pago Elementary School, and was building obstacles in Pago Bay. This raid missed his work detail, but hit an ammunition dump.[5] Also slowing construction were material shortages, especially cement and steel bar to casemate the guns. Instead, many guns had to be sited in open earthen emplacements, or in caves when available. Given the inability to casemate guns camouflage became more important, with examples of superior endeavors, especially above Piti and on Orote Peninsula.

To get materials to the Marianas, the Matsui Transport, a regular shipping service, was established. Matsui ships brought guns, gasoline, rice, and timber. For example Guam received 20 120mm guns, offloaded from the *Sanshu Maru* on May 25. A few days later the *Sugiyama Maru* arrived with ten more 120mm guns and food. But, many of the Matsui transports became victims of American submarines, losing valuable weapons and supplies. These inbound losses included: April 2, *Tosei Maru* loaded with weapons; May 14,

Whangpoo Maru with cement for casemating; May 17, *Nichiwa Maru* with troops of the 9th Expeditionary Force; and May 17, *Fukko Maru,* carrying food and guns. Convoys on their return trips evacuated civilians, about 300 of the 450 Japanese on Guam got off the island on these voyages. It is not known how many reached Japan. The outbound convoys had a lower priority for the American submarines, but were attacked when there were not more attractive targets.

American naval bombardment, on June 16, appeared to be the prelude to an enemy invasion. Second Lieutenant Imanishi, 38th Regiment, wrote,

> For the first time I saw the enemy fleet and was under its gunfire. I regret very much that we are powerless to do anything but look at the enemy which came in barely 10,000 meters away. They shelled us steadily for two hours. Our positions were hit fourteen times. Fortunately, none was injured... We think that at last the enemy will land tonight, and so we will observe strict alert all night. We were issued hand grenades and are waiting for the enemy to come.[6]

The next day was quiet. The frustrated lieutenant noted in his diary, "If the enemy is coming, let him come. The spirit to fight to the death is high. We are anxiously waiting but nothing unusual has happened so far as dawn breaks."[7]

The diaries of various soldiers had similar entries concerning the preassault bombardment. Lieutenant Imanishi found it "pitiful that we cannot control the air. We can only clench our fists with anger and watch."[8] Leading Private Koko Murano wrote of troops unable to leave their shelters to repair damage or finish important work because of U.S. planes. Corporal Tai Suzuki was bitter that the enemy was so arrogant with their air power. Others spoke of only seeing American planes, asking, "Where are our planes?"[9]

The day before this very heavy bombardment, Guam received word of the invasion of Saipan. That day Major General Kiyoshi Shigematsu, at his headquarters in Sinajana, issued his defense order to destroy the enemy at the water's edge. From the 31st Army came orders that "all units should in perfect unison deliver a decisive and crushing blow at the enemy, positively and resolutely, and annihilate it on the beach at one swoop."[10]

Four days later the Battle of the Marianas, the carrier battle west of the Marianas, directly touched Guam. On June 19, about 40 Japanese planes were destroyed at Guam, and the Orote and

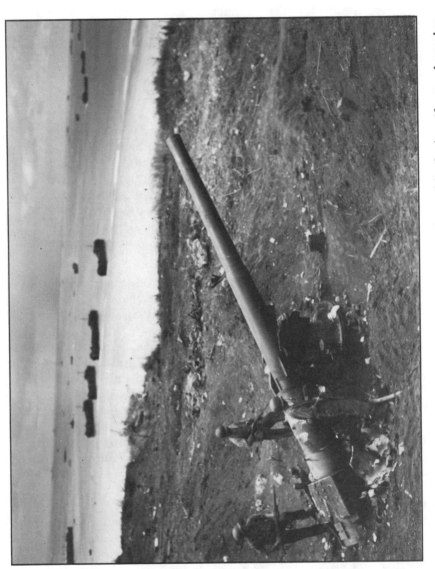

4. A 6-inch gun on Chonito Cliff destroyed by a direct hit during the preinvasion bombardment. Not one large caliber coastal defense gun was firing during the landings.
National Archives

5. Thick camouflage material covers the 140mm coastal defense gun near Piti.
National Archives

6. A log dummy gun sits in former American 6-inch gun position, on Cabras Island, in Apra Harbor.

National Archives

7. Type 10 120mm gun in coconut log-lined emplacement

National Archives

8. Fireblock guarded the Agat Road access to Orote Peninsula.

National Archives

9. Dadi Beach was strongly defended, gun caves can be seen in the rocky point at the end of the beach.

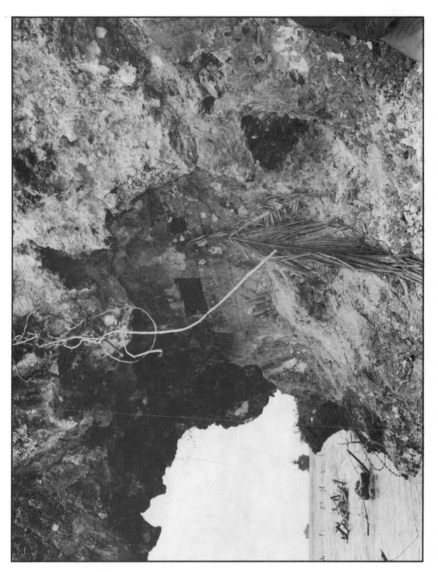

10. Close-up of gun positions in the point at the west end of Dadi Beach, Orote Peninsula. Offshore obstacles are also visible.

National Archives

11. Trenchworks at the Marine Barracks, the ruins of the old Marine Barracks are in the background.

National Archives

12. Fuel drums with live plant material help to camouflage these positions.

National Archives

13. 200mm antiboat gun at South Tipalao, at the west end of Dadi Beach. Offshore obstacles are visible in the bay below.

National Archives

Tiyan fields received extensive damage. Some of the diaries demonstrates that the troops heard misinformation or wild rumors. Second Lieutenant Kanemitsu Kurokawa, 1st Mountain Artillery Company, 38th Infantry, passed on these optimistic accounts to his diary. He wrote that on June 17, morale was high, 30 Japanese planes arrived. Two days later he noted that three U.S. carriers had been sunk. On June 27 he recorded the loss of 316 U.S. planes, shot down from June 11 to June 25. Of course, he had no way of knowing that his sources were terribly wrong, the Japanese were suffering the heavy losses.[11]

In the first months of the build-up, General Takashina had his troops dispersed around the island with most of them at the western landing beaches. The west coast targets of the U.S. naval bombardment of June 16 confirmed the west as the landing zone. Therefore, he reorganized his troop disposition, moving units to the western beaches or placing them in mobile reserve in the center of the island where they could respond to landings anywhere. To hold Guam, General Takashina had a defensive force of about 18,500 men. Days before the American invasion, his troop distribution was:

Tumon Bay:
> 322d Independent Infantry Battalion, 48th Independent Mixed Brigade (IMB)
> 10th Independent Mixed Regiment Artillery (1 $\frac{1}{2}$ battery) assigned to 48th Artillery

Agana Bay:
> 321st Independent Infantry Battalion, 48th IMB
> 319th Independent Infantry Battalion, 48th IMB, in reserve Tiyan Airfield for Tumon-Agana defense
> 48th Independent Mixed Brigade, Artillery Unit
> 10th Independent Mixed Regiment Artillery (1 $\frac{1}{2}$ battery) assigned to 48th Artillery
> 3d Battalion, 38th Regiment, at Mount Chachao, for duty at Agana, including 3d Battery, 38th Artillery

Asan:
> 320th Independent Infantry Battalion, 48th IMB, Adelup to Asan Point
> 10th Independent Mixed Regiment, less 1st Battalion and 9th Company, Fonte-Ordot
> HQ 29th Division, Fonte, General Takashina, C.O.
> HQ 48th IMB, Fonte, General Shigamatsu, C.O.

Piti:
> 18th Regiment, (less 1st Battalion on Saipan), could shift to Asan if landings there)

Orote Peninsula:
   54th Naval Guard Force
   60th Antiaircraft Defense Unit
   755th Genzen Air Unit (converted to ground defense)
   52d Antiaircraft Artillery Battalion (dual-purpose guns)
   2d Battalion, 38th Regiment, at neck of peninsula
Agat:
   1st Battalion, 38th Regiment
   HQ 38th Regiment, Mount Alifan, Colonel Tsunetaro
      Suenago, C.O.
   1st Company, 9th Tank Regiment, reserve Mount Alifan
   9th Company, 10th Independent Mixed Regiment, reserve
      Mount Alifan
Sinajana-Ordot reserve forces:
   29th Tank Unit, Ordot
   2d Company, 9th Tank Regiment, Sinajana
   24th Tank Company
Other Units:
   29th Division Ordnance, Ordot
   29th Division Transport, Ordot
   29th Division Field Hospital, Fonte
   29th Division Quartermaster, Ordot
   29th Signal, Fonte
   265th Independent Motor Transport, Ordot
   521st (Otori) Air Group, Tiyan, converted to ground defense
   217th naval construction
   218th naval construction[12]

Despite the naval bombardment and the invasion of Saipan, Takashina forecast a great success. In the enlisted ranks Corporal Tai Suzuki, expressed concern, saying:

Today, I saw the much hoped for air battle. Our planes shot down some enemy planes in a short time. I heaved a sigh of relief. Since our planes had attacked enemy ships, fuel was running low and ammunition was exhausted after eleven hours of continual flight. Just before they landed, enemy planes attacked them and they made forced landings. I wonder how they felt. I hear that there are a number of pilots who are only 17 or 18!!! . . . I heard that the enemy has 500 ships and 7,500 planes in the Central Pacific Area and that the climax of this battle will come in about a week. I am worried as no word has been received since the landings were made on Saipan.[13]

Naval bombardment was heavy on June 27 as shells pounded Orote Peninsula. Private Murano told his diary of great hardships resulting from the raids. These hardships increased with each of the June raids. As guns were hit, dummy positions were installed to draw fire away from camouflaged guns. On July 11, Murano wrote that his unit had been told that the landings would be in the Piti-Agana area, so his regiment, the 10th Independent Mixed Regiment, was transferred to Agana on July 13, but his company, the 11th, stayed at Pago.

The preinvasion bombardment was a destructive rain of shells and bombs. Private First Class Teruo Kurokawa, 320th Independent Infantry at Asan, recorded that "the bombardment was almost unendurable." Private Murano wrote that "on this island no matter where one goes the shells follow." Other diary entries questioned, "Where is the Combined Fleet?" or spoke of seeing only enemy planes. There were also optimistic entries of reports of large numbers of U.S. planes downed, U.S. carriers sunk, and rumors that the Combined Fleet was on its way. Guam diarists wrote with less confidence and more fear than the Saipan writers. This may been a reaction to the loss of Saipan and the heavier bombardment. Lieutenant Imanishi wrote "our positions have been almost completed but they have not been done as we hoped. ...great effort was put into the construction but we still have been unable to complete the cover...we are in a terrible fix."[14] The long preinvasion bombardment of Guam had a psychological impact. Lieutenant Colonel Hideyuki Takeda remembered the troops in Guam suffering in Seishin, or psychological well-being. As the bombing and naval gunfire continued, there were "scattered outbreaks of serious loss of spirit." Just before the invasion, some men could no longer "perform their duties in a positive manner."[15]

Heavier U.S. bombardment meant that the troops on Guam were more dazed and disorganized than soldiers at Saipan. However, the warrior spirit and belief in a divine blessing was not easily destroyed. The defenders held on to Shiki, or the will to die in combat. They were ready and prepared to die with honor. As one soldier expressed in his diary, "I will not lose my courage, but now is the time to prepare to die! If one desires to live, hope for death. Be prepared to die!...What an honor it is to be born in this day and age."[16]

Only about one hundred men had been killed by the preinvasion bombardment, but weapons losses were high. Most of the coastal defense guns in open emplacements had been destroyed, and overall, one-half of the large caliber weapons were out of commission. Nearly all the antiaircraft guns, most pillboxes, fireblocks, and cave gun positions were intact. However, surviving guns had to be conserved. They could not be fired against UDT activities, shipping, or other targets for fear of giving away their locations. The gun crews had orders to hold their fire until the landing troops were near the beaches. How frustrating this was for the gunners of the 54th Naval Guard Force, responsible for the coastal defenses of Guam. These delays in firing resulted in many guns firing only a few rounds before the Marines had rushed past. Many guns were simply abandoned and made no contribution to the island defense.

General Takashina received word of the fall of Saipan on July 9, 1944. There is no evidence that this event altered his thinking. The beachline defense was retained, but already lost were many guns. His sticking with a beachline defense may have resulted from the strong reluctance to divert from tradition or existing doctrine. This is suggested by the failure to change strategy and the feasible alternative of moving guns to the central massif, where caves and natural features could conceal and cover them. Already, the approaches were defended with machine guns, mortars, and artillery.

Guam's military leaders expressed optimism. General Shigematsu told his soldiers: "The enemy, overconfident because of his successful landing on Saipan, is planning a reckless and insufficiently prepared landing on Guam. We have an excellent opportunity to annihilate him upon the beaches. We are dedicated to the task of destroying this enemy, and are confident that we shall comply with the Imperial wish."[17]

Fourteen

Defense at the Beaches and Counterattacks

Despite the failure of the beachline defense at Saipan, the Guam command stayed with this defense. General Takashina's defense reflected the traditional methods, of linear lines and counterattacks to disrupt the establishment of an enemy beachhead. With the landings Takashina followed with a mass counterattack, and with it, lost many of his best soldiers in one night.

Intense U.S. naval bombardment, starting at 0530 on July 21, 1944, identified this as the U.S. landing day. On the receiving end, Takashina's troops were hunkered down in caves and anywhere else that would offer some shelter from this horrible experience. They were hit by carrier aircraft and naval bombardment, the heaviest to date, in the Pacific. Bombs, rockets, and strafing made the ground tremble, while smoke and dust from the bombardment turned a clear sky hazy. Finally, when the bombardment lifted, the defenders left their shelters to man their weapons. Soldiers in the beach defenses thought that further naval or air bombardment was impossible, since the enemy had expended all their ammunition. They were so wrong.

At 0830 American Marines hit the beaches. The 1st Provisional Brigade came ashore at Agat and the 3d Marine Division at Asan. Regiments of the 3d Marine Division landed on 2,500 yards of beach between the devil's horns of Asan and Adelup Points. Landing alongside Adelup were the 3d Marines (Regiment) facing Chonito Cliff. In the center were the 21st Marines and in the west nearest Asan Point landed the 9th Marines.

184

The defenses on Asan Point had been hurt but not destroyed by the preinvasion bombardment. Machine guns and 37mm guns stalled the 9th Marines alongside the Point. It was not enough to prevent the landing of American armor. Meanwhile, the defenses in front of the 9th Marines fell quickly, allowing the 9th Marines to acquire maneuver room. As the 9th Marines pushed to the west behind Asan Point crossing the bridge over the Matgue River, they came into the sights of machine gunners in natural cavities on the west side of Asan Point. Withering fire drove back the Marines. The 9th Marines had been allowed to get ashore and move inland some, but at a high cost of 231 casualties, including 20 officers killed or wounded.[1]

Climbing through the ravine, dividing Chonito and Bundschu Ridges, was the 2d Battalion, 9th Marines. As the Marines started their climb, soldiers of the 48th Independent Mixed Brigade, opened fire. The defenders could not halt the Marines, but the heat and terrain did. The hot sun was too much for many of the Marines, who had spent long periods of confinement aboard the transports, waiting for the delayed Guam operation. Some of the strongest made it to the top, then Japanese machine guns on the next higher ridge, opened fire on them. Also mortars dropped rounds onto the newly-acquired positions.[2]

In the center area of Asan, the 21st Marines got off the beach and headed up the Asan River Valley. They also were sprayed with machine gun and mortar fire. By opening fire the machine gun strongpoint and mortar positions identified themselves. Naval gunfire rained down on the mortars, putting them out of business. A powerful Marine charge overran the source of their immediate problems, destroying the Japanese strongpoint of fourteen machine guns and six mortars. While the main center of resistance had been defeated, the Marines still had to climb the steep cliff. They were exposed and vulnerable, but a fine defensive opportunity had been missed, there were no guns on the top of the cliff to fire down on the Marine assault. Undisturbed in their climb the 21st Marines stopped and dug in for the night. During the night, mortar fire was dropped into their area. Small, unsuccessful counterattacks were tried to drive the Marines off this ridge.

Defenders on Asan's east side made good use of Chonito Ridge and Adelup Point. Since they had sheltered in caves on Adelup and in the 200-man cave on the reverse slope of Chonito Cliff, soldiers of the 48th Independent Mixed Brigade were in good shape. They were ready to fight the 3rd Marines. As the Marines approached the beaches, artillery and mortar fire destroyed some LVTs. Fortunately for the Marines at Asan, the 6-inch guns on top of Chonito Cliff and all other large caliber guns had been knocked out before the invasion. Still, the defenders laid heavy fire on the beaches. Once the Marines pinpointed their cave firing spots, it was only moments until tank gunfire and flame throwers responded. The Chonito caves were neutralized by noon. Also, on the east at Adelup Point, the 37mm and 47mm guns were still firing. They also were discovered and subjected to heavy attack. In the center, machine guns on Bundschu Ridge forced heavy casualties among the seaborne invaders. Two machine guns on the ridge, sited to fire enfilade, resisted repeated attacks.

To contain the invasion at Asan General Takashina moved reserves from the central massif to Asan. He also transferred his headquarters to a Mount Mangan cave, above Bundschu Ridge, 345 yards west of Fonte. From here he had a much better view of the Asan beach area, and the manganese mine shafts offered good protection from American bombardment. General Shigematsu had already moved his command post to a mine shaft in the nearby Mangan quarry, 540 yards west of Fonte.[3]

Further American advance this first day were hotly contested. Casualties among the 3d Marine Division were heavy, but slowly the Asan defenses fell. As Chonito Cliff was neutralized, one gun at a time, the American situation improved in other ways. U.S. artillery came ashore, greatly enhancing their staying power.

Defending the southern landing beaches, at Agat, was the 1st Battalion, 38th Infantry. These defenders occupied trenches, and strongpoints on small knobs inland of the beach, backed up by mortars and artillery in the foothills. As Marine LVTs moved over the reef, artillery and mortar fire fell on the landing vehicles. When the Marines were close to shore, Gaan Point and other powerful infantry positions opened fire ripping into landing craft and inflicting death and injury among the seaborne invaders. Gaan Point alone knocked out nine landing craft. Still the Marines kept coming, and soon they had their tanks on the beach. A team of tanks and infantry silenced Gaan Point with a charge to its unprotected rear. Soon after Gaan was overrun another knoll fortress, 400 yards inland of the beach, fell to a Marine assault.

As the Agat defenses fell, defenders who could withdraw were used to create a new line of resistance. Some took up positions in the Agat village ruins. These ruins were overrun by an American tank-infantry attack that afternoon. Next, the Marines attacked a machine gun nest northeast of Agat. This nest of "concealed machine guns swept the open area and forced the Marines back to the trenches."[4]

Artillery and an 80mm gun in the foothills behind Gaan Point fired on Marines in this sector, halting the 2d Battalion, 22d Marines. Defenses between Gaan Point and Bangi Point put up powerful resistance, but not enough to stop the Marines. This left a forward stronghold on Hill 40, inland of Bangi Point. On this low hill were machine guns on its forward slopes and mortars on its reverse slopes. Although Hill 40 defenders fought hard, they just did not have the firepower to stop a tank attack. The hill fell.

By the first evening, most of the Agat strongpoints on the beachline had fallen, and the situation worsened as U.S. tanks and artillery came ashore. The time to counterattack was now, or had already passed. Marines at Agat had maneuver room and heavy firepower. Colonel Tsunetaro Suenaga, commander of the 38th Regiment, reviewed the situation and developed plans for night counterattacks. There would be a three-prong attack, designed to push the enemy into the sea.

Colonel Suenaga's first prong hit just after midnight with reserves coming down Harmon Road from the Mount Alifan assembly area. As the troops advanced to the 4th Marine lines, mortar rounds were dropped onto the Marine front. Charging the Marine lines with determination, the attackers expected surprise and speed to bring victory. The Marines held and defeated this charge.

A counterattack striking Hill 40 at 0100 succeeded in driving the Marines off this tiny hill. The Marines regrouped and drove off the Japanese. Again, the Japanese attacked and regained Hill 40. With reinforcements, the Marines took the hill for a third and final time.

The Japanese also tried infiltration. Small groups sought out gaps in the lines with the intent to get behind the Marine lines to destroy artillery, armor, and ammunition dumps. While these groups harassed Marines, they were unable to blow up any artillery or tanks. American illumination shells played a crucial role in exposing infiltration teams before they could do damage.

The most serious counterattack was a second thrust down Harmon Road. At 0230, four Type 95 tanks, gun-mounted trucks, and infantry, struck the Marine roadblock on Harmon Road at Agat. Private First Class Bruno Oribiletti, 4th Marines, hit the two lead tanks before he was killed. His action disrupted the Japanese push, creating time for American tanks to get to the scene, and finish off the rest of the tanks and the trucks. This left the infantry lightly protected, and they were cut down.

At the same time as the Harmon Road charge, Suenaga led a frontal assault against the center of the Marine lines. His goal was to break through the line, rush to the beach, and destroy the artillery here. As the colonel and his troops hit the line, he was struck in the thigh by a mortar shell fragment. Despite his wounds, he kept going. A bullet to the chest killed him. His troops almost reached their target, but were stopped short by Marine artillerymen. In this vicious fight, over 200 Japanese were killed.

Unclear was the motive for another mission, where 12 soldiers with four machine guns marched up to the Marine frontlines with no attempt at stealth. The 12 attackers, in a death march, were easily killed by Marine fire.

General Takashina had artillery moved from Dededo to Fonte to lay barrages on the 3d Marine Division. The 4th Battalion of the 48th Independent Mixed Brigade, moved from Agana to Adelup Point. During the night, the 2d and 3d Battalions of the 48th IMB relocated from Agana and Tumon to Fonte, in readiness for counterattack and reinforcement duties.

In an effort to slow the Marine beach unloading at Asan, mortar and artillery fire targeted the beach resupply missions. The gunners were able to halt unloading this night. There were also small counterattacks along the Asan Marine lines. All these Japanese actions succumbed to artillery, naval gunfire, and Marine readiness. A more powerful counterattack in the Chonito and Bundschu areas hurt the Marines, but could not penetrate their frontline. Takashina's most effective weapons were his artillery and mortars, which inflicted heavy casualties among the 3d Marine Division. During the first two days, the Marines lost 615 men and made only limited progress. On the Japanese side, heavy fighting had not pushed back the invaders even one inch.

General Takashina held a staff meeting at 1500, July 23, to consider what to do next. A summary of the battle to date noted the loss of many senior commanders, the failed counterattacks, the steady progress of the American forces, and his large troop losses. For example, at Agat, the 38th Infantry had lost 80 percent of its soldiers and most of its artillery. General Takashina discussed the human factor, wondering how much longer his troops could psychologically hold on. They were all under frequent artillery and naval gunfire with its destructive and stupefying effect. Based upon this review, General Takashina concluded that two options existed. First, a decisive counterattack to drive the invaders into the sea. Second, was a withdrawal to the very defensible north with the potential for a future counteroffensive. After listening to staff officer comments, Takashina selected the first option. A massive counterattack was set for the night of July 25–26, to begin at 2400.

Work was started on operational plans and preparation of map overlays to coordinate the various units. It was a well-planned assault and also the largest of the Central Pacific. Planners identified specific objectives with destruction of artillery and armor a high priority. On July 24, as planners were putting together the mass counterattack, the 3d Marine Division reached the heights just below the Fonte assembly area. In the south the U.S. Army's 77th Infantry Division landed and expanded the Agat beachhead. Also this day, the 22d Marines challenged the Orote Peninsula defenses. On Orote Peninsula, Commander Asaichi Tamai, Imperial Japanese Navy, 263d Air Unit, now commanded the peninsula forces, with the death of its former commander, Colonel Suenaga. Tamai's troops were dug in, they included remnants of the 2d Battalion, 38th Infantry, two companies of antiaircraft companies, and 600 airmen with no planes, for a total of 2,500 men.

When the 1st Battalion, 22d Marines, reached the Agat-Piti roadblock, they received a nasty welcome. Artillery and mortar fire poured into the Marine road formations. Five Type 95 tanks came up the road to the enemy, where they were blasted by Sherman tank fire. Marine determination and the Sherman's doomed the southern roadblock. Next, naval gunfire moved in to destroy artillery along Agat Bay which had contributed to the deadly fire on the 22d Marines. LCI(G) gunships sailed into Agat Bay, firing at guns at Dadi Beach and the Tipalao area. Gunship *LCI(G) 366*, while attacking Orote positions, was hit by one of the Tipalao guns with the captain and executive officer among the dead. Another gunship, *LCI(G) 439*, was also attacked by guns at South Tipalao. Six men were killed and 28 wounded on the gunships. When the naval shelling lifted, the Sherman tanks and 22d Marines broke the roadblock. Machine gun fire slowed the Marine advance onto the peninsula.

The next day, Commander Tamai attempted to evacuate some of his troops, loading them onto barges at 1700. As the barges crept away from the Sumay dock and into Apra Harbor, American artillery and planes attacked. The escape attempt was destroyed.

Movement beyond the southern roadblock was tough. Artillery at South Tipalao rained down on the Marines, the gunships had yet to knock them out. Heavy casualties experienced by the 1st Battalion, 22d Marines, forced its replacement by the 1st Battalion, 4th Marines. Not only was the south side an effective fortress but the north sector also put up strong resistance against the Marines trying to get onto Orote Peninsula. The series of pillboxes and machine gun nests on the north side were meticulously blended into the forest. It took time to locate and neutralize each position.

At the end of July 25, the Marines took up positions in front of a large mangrove swamp on the north side of Orote Peninsula. The Marines on the south side had yet to reach Dadi Beach. At Agat, the beachhead was expanded, and the Asan invasion troops moved to the slopes just below Fonte.

During the morning of July 25, counterattack orders went to the unit commanders. They identified Asan and Orote as the target areas. At Asan, Colonel Hiko-Shiro Ohashi's 18th Regiment (less the 1st Battalion at Saipan) was to strike at two points. His 2d Battalion, led by Major Chusa Maruyama, was to move from Fonte along the east side of the Asan River to the Asan coastal plan and then turn left to attack Marines at Asan Point. The 3d Battalion, 18th, route was down the hills between the Nidual and Asan River to the high ground directly inland of Asan Point, and then attack the Marines below. Flank protection for the 18th was to be provided by a company from the 10th Independent Mixed Regiment, creating a line on the west, near the Tatgua River.

On the east side of Asan, the 48th Independent Mixed Brigade had the assignment to destroy the battle-weary 3d Marines at Bundschu Ridge. Once they had overcome the 3d Marines, then special explosives team were to blow up ammunition dumps and artillery near the beach. Commander Tamai's role in the counterattack was to wipe out the Marines at the northern and southern approaches to Orote Peninsula.

Tamai's northern force had a celebration before the attack. The consumption of beer and sake loosened up the soldiers, who became loud, broadcasting a warning to the Marines. While the attackers on the south of the peninsula quietly prepared. The northern Orote charge struck on time, at 2400, running into a wall of gunfire and hail of grenades from the alerted Marines. As the assault neared the lines, pack howitzers opened fire at almost point-blank, ripping apart the attackers. A few survivors sought cover by retreating to the mangrove swamp, but the artillery followed them.

The attack on the south was destroyed as it crossed the clearing in front of the Marine lines. Very few of the attackers reached the Marine foxholes. Those who made it were killed in hand-to-hand combat. Now, the Orote Peninsula defenses, which had allowed only minor Marine gains, were seriously weakened by large losses.

Meanwhile at Asan, small reconnaissance teams located gaps and weakly defended routes. Artillery and mortar fire were dropped on the Marines. At 2400 hours the 2d Battalion, 18th Regiment, hit the Marine perimeter, and by 0400 had broken through. As the Marines fell back, they pivoted into two flanks, forcing the attackers through a gauntlet. Major Maruyama's men rushing down the gauntlet suffered heavy casualties but some soldiers made it deep into Marine territory. The lead element made it to the 1st Battalion, 21st Marines, command post and mortar positions, punishing the mortarmen until they regrouped and shot up the attackers. Also, the special demolition squads were stopped and killed, near the beach, at the 3d Marine Division hospital.

Major Setsuo Yukioka's 3d Battalion, 18th Regiment, successfully captured two Marine machine gun positions, but the 3d Battalion, 21st Marines, fought back and recaptured the guns. Another element of Yukioka's attack penetrated the frontline and swung around to smash the lines from the rear, while other attackers raced to the command post at Asan Point. At the command post headquarters' personnel fought back and defeated this element of the 18th Regiment operation. Throughout the 18th Regiment zone of attack, Marines counterattacked and regained their lines. Major Yukioka's 3d Battalion had few survivors, but one enterprising group positioned a machine gun and mortar on the hill above Asan Point to lay deadly fire on the command post and assembly area. That morning it fell to a Marine charge. The 3d Battalion, no longer existed.

On the east side of Asan the 48th IMB fought hard to break through the 2d Battalion, 9th Marines. Seven times the 48th attacked and stopped each time. Losses were heavy on both sides, but the Marines held. That morning, Marines had enough strength to start up the cliff to Fonte, in this movement they ran into and killed Major General Shigematsu, the 48th IMB commander.

Everywhere this well-coordinated and massed counteroffensive had failed. Survivors limped back to Fonte with the depressing news. General Takashina's staff compiled the reports and sorted out the situation to brief the general. They concluded that this assault had not achieved any of its goals. Worse yet, the losses in the officer ranks were near one hundred percent among the participating units. These brave men were often at the head of the columns leading their men, so they were among the first to die. There was so much confusion and break down in control that new leadership could not come forward, men fought in uncoordinated small group and individual efforts.

American firepower was too great, and the Marines displayed quickness, and flexibility. Whenever Japanese success seemed at hand, Marine reinforcements would appear, and this included cooks, engineers, and hospital staff fighting as infantry. General Takashina knew little of Marine traditions or tactics, and this cost him dearly.

Losses in the counterattack were 3,500 soldiers, many of General Takashina's best troops. His offensive capability was seriously depleted. General Takashina radioed the Imperial General Headquarters at 0800, July 26, reporting the failed counterattack. Staff meetings during the afternoon of July 26 dealt with the crisis situation and the need for a new response. Lieutenant Colonel Hideyuki Takeda, chief of staff, 29th Division, summarized the conference conclusions. He concluded that it was no longer possible to expel the American forces from the island. It would only be possible to inflict losses on the American forces, fighting in the interior of Guam. This was the only viable option given the loss of up to 95 percent of the officers of the units in the counterattack. Unit strength was so reduced that some companies were down to several men. There were also huge losses of weapons. Additionally, there was no expectation of reinforcements. The capability for counterattack was gone. The only solution was to employ the natural terrain to fight defensively, killing as many Americans as possible.[5]

On Orote Peninsula, the survivors of the counterattack had only a short rest, before American artillery, naval gunfire and aerial bombardment hit them. At 0700 the 4th Marines came against the center of the Orote defense, now only lightly defended, given the heavy losses, a few hours earlier. Rough terrain and the guns at Tipalao and the airfield retarded the Marine movement. Fired in unison with American artillery, the Japanese guns went undetected, and frustrated the Marines who believed that it was friendly fire. On the north side, once the Marines recovered from the artillery attack, they waded into the mangrove swamp and shot the few snipers present.

By afternoon the 4th and 22d Marines were at Orote Peninsula center road junction (RJ15), halted by a minefield, placed where the road channelized into a narrow corridor with a mangrove swamp on one side and marsh on the other. On the ridgeline and mounds west of the junction were mortars, machine guns, and infantry positions dropping intense fire onto the road junction. American armor returned fire, but could not locate all the defenses, especially mortars on the reverse sides of the mounds. American artillery fire searched out the mounds and silenced the mortars. The minefield remained a barrier.

Despite the unrelenting artillery barrage falling on the Orote defenders, they reacted on July 27, when the Marines started moving again. Once they advanced 100 yards, the machine gunners opened fire, hitting a number of the invaders. There was little the Marines could do. They had only a narrow strip of land, bordered by swamp and thick undergrowth on the other side, and the minefield on the road. A bomb disposal officer, under the cover of a smokescreen, removed the mines. Armor moved forward and within range of the Japanese defenses, working over the ridge defenses.[6] Sherman tanks drove up to the defense line, firing into caves, pillboxes, and bunkers. The absence of adequate antitank defenses doomed the Japanese as much as anything. Machine gunners in the ridgeline were killed. The next defense, in the coconut grove 500 yards beyond the destroyed ridgeline, held out longer as tanks had difficulty working their way into the grove. When the tanks got into the grove, there was a fierce fight. Soon all the defenders here were dead.

As the defensive positions in the center fell, the defenses on the slope below the Marine Barracks laid intense fire on the 4th Marines. Soldiers of the 38th Infantry Regiment manning the barrier below the Barracks had the Marines seeking shelter. However, days of fighting and terrific bombardment had taken a heavy toll. Many defenders were shell shocked, as demonstrated by their behaviors. For example, one dazed officer attacked a Sherman tank with his sword.

On the afternoon of July 27, the center defenses of Orote came under a devastating U.S. air, naval, and artillery bombardment. It was too much for the already dazed men. Many ran, abandoning these well-prepared positions. The 22d Marines rushed in to occupy the line. Only, the defenses at the rifle range of the Marine Barracks and at Sumay held. They fought hard and caused heavy casualties among the 4th Marines. How they were able to stand up to the regular artillery barrages and an extremely intense artillery attack on July 28 is unknown. At one point, the defenders had the 4th Marines alongside where they were able to lay flanking fire into a Marine company. Again, the Marines pulled back, called up armor, and launched a mass tank-infantry attack, destroying this fine defensive complex, with 250 pillboxes and dugouts. Orote Peninsula, Guam's strongest defense, had fallen.

The Marines occupied the ruins of the prewar Marine Barracks. In a significant gesture, one of two Marine Barracks bronze plaques, found in the wreckage of the camp, was displayed at the flag-raising ceremony at 1530 on July 29. This plaque stayed on Guam after the war in a place of honor at a new Marine Barracks.

14. Marines ashore at Asan Beach

15. Marines proudly display the old Marine Barracks plaque, found in the Barracks rubble.

National Archives

16. Irving, or Nakajima Gekko night fighters abandoned on Orote Airfield.
National Archives

17. Marine Air Group 21 takes over Orote Field.

18. Piti Navy Yard in ruins after the battle

National Archives

FIFTEEN

Northern and Final Defense

When the U.S. troops reached the heights of the central massif, the southern portion of Guam was lost. General Takashina recognized the failure of the beachline and central defense, so he ordered a withdrawal to the north to take advantage of its defensible terrain. There would be no final mass charge, but an effort to kill as many Americans as possible, from gun positions in the forests and hills of northern Guam.

On the morning of July 27, General Takashina held a staff meeting to detail his northern defense. He had existing operational plans, which had been developed on July 23, when it was considered as an option. The idea was to have the remaining troops prolong the battle and inflict maximum casualties on the enemy. This defense was a line across the island, from Dededo to Barrigada, with strongpoints behind it at Mount Santa Rosa and Finegayan. To create this line, General Takashina needed time, so rear guard forces stayed back at Fonte, Mount Chachao, and Ordot to retard the U.S. push.

Early on the afternoon of July 27, Takashina issued the northern defense orders. Some units were instructed to withdraw north and others left behind as delaying parties. The field hospital at Fonte was evacuated to the north side of Mount Santa Rosa. General Takashina closed his Mount Mangan command post and started walking to a new Ordot headquarters. Accompanying the general was his chief of staff, Lieutenant Colonel Hideyuki Takeda. At 1400 hours, as they approached a stream on the north foot of Mount Macajna, they came into the sights of a Sherman tank machine

199

gunner. A hail of bullets flew around them, with General Takashina hit and killed. Lieutenant General Hideyoshi Obata, the stranded 31st Army commander, assumed command.

The retreat to the north had troops scattered over the foothills between Fonte and Ordot. There were pathetic scenes of bandaged, wounded men limping to the new battleground. Colonel Takeda saw one man with no legs crawling over two miles to Ordot.[1]

On July 27, delaying forces waited at Fonte in a bowl depression, and on nearby Mount Chachao. Marines were nearby, in an effort to drive them off the slopes, a counterattack of 150 Japanese charged and died in the assault. Meanwhile, in the south, the U.S. Army's 77th Infantry Division was advancing on Mount Tenjo from Agat.

The next day, the defending infantry company in caves and foxholes at the Mount Chachao observation post was wiped out. An undefended Mount Tenjo was occupied by the 305th Regiment, 77th Division. The next day, the Fonte depression came under an intense bazooka, machine gun, and tank gun shelling. Each cave was shelled, and then hit by infantry. Fifty defenders died without inflicting any Marine casualties.

Japanese casualties for the campaign through the fall of the central massif were about 8,400 killed. There were 50 prisoners. This left Obata with about 6,000 combat troops and 2,500 other military.

General Obata received a brief respite on July 29–30, when the Americans paused to rest and regroup. Hurriedly, Obata placed his delaying line across the waist of the island and directed construction of the fortifications. Short of time and troops, Obata left good fighting locales unused, including the ruins of Agana and the commanding slope above the Agana wetlands, and the Pago River in the east.

On July 31 the Americans started their north push, passing through Agana, capturing Ordot with its depots and the cross-island road. The following day, a small number of defenders on Tiyan Airfield attempted to repel the Americans. These defenders were killed and Tiyan Airfield captured the next day. Soon, it was in operation as a U.S. fighter field.

General Obata had a delaying force of 1,000 infantry, 800 naval personnel, and 2,500 men from headquarters and support units, trying to hold back the Americans. Realizing that the delaying force would soon collapse, Obata left Ordot on July 29 to go to his northern command post on the northwest side of Mount Barrigada.

Obata had his troops build strongholds at Dededo, on the west, and Barrigada, on the east side. He had fall back positions at Ipapao,

5,000 yards northeast of Barrigada, and a last stand defense near Mount Santa Rosa.

The island command post was moved, on July 31, to a cave complex at Mount Mataguac. This would be Obata's final CP. Here he prepared defense plans for the "grand sounding" Mount Santa Rosa Garrison Force, remnants of naval, air, and support units. These included the 263d Air Unit, the 521st Naval Air Unit, the 217th and 218th naval construction battalions, the 5th Field Hospital, the 5th Construction Unit, a weather unit, air depot, air ordnance, and the 30th Labor Unit. Obviously, the Santa Rosa force was far from a cohesive fighting unit. Not only was it comprised of diverse units, but it was spread over two large defense sectors. One sector was Mount Mataguac and the second was Mount Santa Rosa consisting of dummy positions and one infantry company. His last defense would be a stand at Mount Mataguac.

Before the northern defenses could be established, the 77th Infantry Division on the east and the 3d Marine Division on the west were on top of the Japanese as they were digging in. On July 31, the 77th Division surprised units in Yona while the 3d Marine Division overran Ordot. The July 31 loss of Agana, Ordot, and Yona meant the destruction of the delaying line, but more importantly for the U.S., it put the cross-island road under their control. This road was needed as a supply route, especially to resupply the 77th Division on the east coast, and it became the main U.S. supply route.[2]

On August 2, the strongpoint at Barrigada was assaulted by the 77th Infantry Division. In an initial assault Sherman tanks knocked out a machine gun nest roadblock. After this the defenses did much better, taking advantage of jungle behind a large, cleared field. The U.S. soldiers were at a disadvantage, they were exposed, but the Japanese were invisible in the forest. More defenders were hidden in the village buildings on the southeast corner of the clearing, at a road junction. There were a few huts, a church, and the largest building was a green colored frame building.[3]

The defenders at Barrigada demonstrated fire discipline by shooting short bursts, often in concert with American fire to avoid discovery. GIs of the U.S. 77th Division on the exposed fields had no protection. For an entire morning these hidden defenses caused heavy American casualties. That afternoon, a hut was set ablaze, and in the hut was a Type 97 tank. With his discovery, the tank commander, making the most of a bad situation, pulled out of the burning hut. He drove into the field, and he sped along, fired at the American soldiers. Near the road junction, a 77th Division machine gun on the second floor of a building opened fire on the tank. The tank drove into the building, smashing through the wall. He came out the other side firing its machine gun. The U.S. infantry returned fire, with everything they had, but failed to stop it. Even when it got briefly hung up on a log, the American gunfire was ineffective. After a few moments the tanker got free and raced through the U.S. lines, firing as he escaped, and leaving behind numerous casualties among the 307th Infantry. Next, the tank drove through a battalion command post, aid station, and command post. No one could stop it. From Barrigada the tank moved west into the 3d Marines sector. Here it was destroyed by two Sherman tanks.[4]

The Barrigada defenders had lost one of their main weapons, the stashed tank, but still had the upper hand. When an American light tank came forward to probe the jungle it was hit and disabled. Next, four Sherman tanks came up to the clearing and fired their 75mm guns to defoliate the forest, while uncovering another tank, a Type 95. Once exposed it was immediately destroyed by the superior American firepower. Finally, enough of the jungle defense had been neutralized, for the U.S. infantry to make a frontal attack. However, it was too late in the day.

That night, the Barrigada village positions were abandoned. They knew the next day would bring artillery and armor assaults. Between the village of Barrigada and Mount Barrigada, the thick jungle was used in conjunction with roadblocks and snipers to slow the 77th Division. Mount Barrigada was not strongly defended, and put up little resistance.

Finegayan was the main defense in the west, a stronghold was built of trenchworks on both sides of the coastal road, just below the village. Occupying the trenches were 200 defenders armed with rifles and machine guns. Even this well-sited blocking position could hold only thirty minutes, falling at a cost of 105 dead Japanese. A second roadblock, north of this defense, nearer the village could do no better.

What slowed the Americans was the jungle, not Obata's defenses. The end was near. On August 3, in the west, the 9th Marines overran the Finegayan defenses, and on August 4, the 77th Infantry Division captured the village of Barrigada, in the east. The collapse of these critical locations left the jungle the main impediment, plus artillery and heavy rains to slow the assault. Japanese artillery firing was effectively used during the rain squalls to hide their guns. It was the heavy rain and the thick jungle, however, which most slowed the Americans on August 5. That dark night, two Type 97 tanks supported by a dozen men struck the 77th Division lines, at about 0200 hours. American gunfire cut down the infantry, but the tanks penetrated, spraying the bivouac with machine gun bullets. Twenty soldiers of the 77th Division were killed, and both tanks escaped undamaged.

These tanks pulled north to cover the trail, which the U.S. infantry took the next day. That morning, the 77th Division walked into the trap. Halted by the deadly fire, a Sherman tank accompanied by infantry came forward, only to be driven back by heavy gunfire. A mortar barrage thrown at the Japanese tanks encouraged their crews to leave them.

Sniping, infiltration, roadblocks, and tank-infantry tactics became the tactics of choice. American casualties were light, but among them was Colonel Douglas McNair, chief of staff, 77th Division, killed by rifle fire in Ipapao on August 6. Less than two weeks earlier, on July 25, his father, Lieutenant General Lesley McNair, had been killed by friendly fire in France.

At Yigo, on Mount Santa Rosa Road, was a strong roadblock comprised of two 47mm antitank guns, two Type 95 tanks, eight machine guns, and infantry. As the 77th Division approached this stronghold, on August 7, the defenders fired a great barrage against the GIs, disabling four American tanks.

Another tank-infantry assault was planned by the defenders for the night of August 7–8. Two tanks hit the 306th Infantry at about 0300, but their noise identified their arrival. A rifle grenade knocked out one tank and machine gun fire stopped the other. U.S. casualties were six dead and 13 wounded, while the raiding party lost at least 18 killed.

Mount Santa Rosa was abandoned, except for a small delaying unit. Nearly all the defenders in this area escaped during a terrific naval and aerial bombardment on August 8. At the time, there were about 3,000 survivors in the northern jungle.

On August 8, the Marines had more difficulty clearing their way through the jungle than with the Japanese. The Marines discovered a truck containing the beheaded bodies of 30 Chamorros. Another 21 executed Chamorros were found the next morning. These young men had been brought from the Yona Concentration Camp to build northern fortifications. When the fortified areas fell, these laborers were executed.

A Radio Tokyo News broadcast, the evening of August 8, warned the Japanese people of defeat, reporting that Americans held nine-tenths of Guam and were patrolling the rest of the island. When Marines reached Ritidian Point the next morning, they were on the northernmost point. Fighting remained. A tank counterattack of five mediums struck at the 2d Battalion, 3d Marines, but the Marines safely escaped into the jungle. The tanks dashed north.

On August 10, two Japanese tanks were destroyed by Marine armor, and seven more Type 97 tanks were found in the woods.

According to captured Captain Hideo Sato, commander of the 24th Tank Company, they had been "scuttled" for lack of fuel. All of the original 38 Japanese tanks on Guam had been destroyed or captured.

General Obata, knowing the end near, sent a final message to Imperial Headquarters on August 10. Obata stated that he was:

> overwhelmed with shame. . .most of the island has been lost and we are without weapons, ammunition, or food. The achievement of the original mission is now hopeless. I do not know how to express my apology. I will, with the remaining officers and men, engage the enemy in the last battle tomorrow, the 11th!![5]

At 1131 on August 10, Guam was declared secure by General Geiger. There remained dying for both sides. As the 77th Infantry Division hurried north, they were told of a concentration of soldiers or a headquarters about three-quarters of a mile northwest of Yigo. It was Obata's headquarters, where a fortified basin depression, 100 yards long and 40 feet deep, guarded the command post. In the thick brush were riflemen and machine gunners. When the 77th probed the bowl its defenses came alive. A violent firefight ensued. The 1st Battalion, 306th Infantry, pulled back at dusk, with losses of 8 killed and 17 wounded.[6]

The 1st Battalion reviewed the situation, and on August 11 resumed the assault with tank support. This combination overwhelmed those in the brush. There were more defenders in the cave command post, and they opened up on the 1st Battalion. Explosive charges, and finally, four 400-pound blocks of TNT, were used to seal the caves. Four days later, the caves were opened and 60 bodies counted, including General Obata, with a bullet wound suggesting suicide.

American losses in the Guam campaign were 2,124 killed in action or died of wounds. Japanese losses were over 17,000 killed. There were also 1,100 military, and 150 civilian prisoners. Guamanians had suffered greatly, there were 700 Guam civilians killed in the war, most dying from Japanese atrocities. Very few had died as a result of the preinvasion bombardment.[7] The bombardment death toll had been limited by the July 12 evacuation of the population to interior concentration camps. This evacuation has never been explained, it may have been to remove the people from areas where they could assist the American invasion troops.

An American declaration that Guam was secure on August 11 had little meaning to the many Japanese hiding in the jungle and caves. The island command launched large search and destroy missions to sweep hiding areas. On August 26, the sweeps were dropped in favor of quiet, focused searches by a jungle-wise Local Security Patrol Force, comprised of Guamanians and Marines. In November 1944 this search duty was assigned to a special police squad.

The holdouts were not a serious military threat, but they did disrupt civilian return to the contested regions. Cattle losses and dangerous encounters with civilians were two reasons to hunt down the stragglers. A Navy corpsman killed at Mataguac on November 10, 1944, in brief diary entries indicates that they were focused on survival, not war:

> 11 August — Had rice to eat but no water.
>
> 12 August — Fled into a palm grove feeling very hungry and thirsty. Drank milk from five coconuts and ate the meat of three.
>
> 14 August — Eat once a day.
>
> 15 August — Tried eating palm tree tips but suffered from severe vomiting in the evening.
>
> 16 August — I am weak from being sick, cooked some rice.
>
> 23 August — Along my way I found some taro plants and ate them. All around me are enemies only. It takes a brave man, indeed, to go in search of food.
>
> 10 September — This morning I went out hunting. Found a dog and killed it. Compared with pork or beef it is not very good.
>
> 19 September — Our taro is running short and we can't afford to eat today.
>
> 2 October — These days I am eating only breadfruit. Wentout in search of some today but it is very dangerous.
>
> 15 October — No food.[8]

In October his situation became acute, after he had gone days without food. His final entry was October 24, when he may have been too hungry to keep up his diary from this day to his death on November 10, 1944. He was one of the many killed by the Guam police patrol, made up of 15 islanders led by Staff Sergeant Juan Aguon of the Guam police. The patrol conducted daily searches from early November to May 1945, killing 117 and capturing five Japanese. Only two of the patrol died, one in a fall and the other hit by a Japanese bullet. Starting in May, they conducted searches when stragglers were reported.

There were two organized groups best able to resist. Major Kiyomachi Sato, communications officer, 29th Division, led one 100-man group, in south Guam. In February 1945 in a major action they killed six submariners exploring the jungle near Camp Dealey. By the spring of 1945, attrition had reduced this force to 35 men, and they came to the realization that further resistance was hopeless, so surrendered on June 11, 1945.

A second organized group, in the north, was commanded by Colonel Takeda, the former chief of staff, 29th Division. After learning of Japan's surrender of Japan the colonel decided to surrender his group. This force of 67 officers and men came out of the jungle, one-and-a-half miles southwest of Tarague on September 4, 1945. One week later, Colonel Takeda ordered another 46 men to surrender.

The Takeda and Sato groups were the last large groups. In the immediate postwar years farmers who lost crops and cattle knew there were small groups of stragglers still hiding out. A few were killed in 1946 and 1947. One straggler surrendered in April 1948, and another was killed the next year. On September 26, 1951, four stragglers were encountered asleep on Anao Beach, on northern Guam's Andersen Air Force Base. Three got away, but one was captured. The captured straggler, Taira Koshin, an Okinawan civilian worker, helped the Guam police talk out his comrades. Three other stragglers in a nearby hideout heard the loudspeaker broadcasts and surrendered.[9]

Still there were more. In 1953, the Japanese government launched a massive leaflet-dropping program to safely bring in stragglers. Despite physical evidence of more men in hiding, none responded to the leaflets. No more stragglers were caught until May 21, 1960, when Bunzo Minagawa was apprehended by two Guamanians at Talofofo. Minagawa then led a U.S. Navy team to his hiding place where his partner, Masashi Itoh, surrendered. One week later, the two men, the last holdouts, were flown to Japan.

What a shock, when on January 24, 1972, Sergeant Shoichi Yokoi was captured by two local fishermen. Sergeant Yokoi had spent 28 years hiding in the jungle, eight of them alone. His last home was a hole in the thick jungle in the Talofofo Falls area.[10]

These last three holdouts all gained national fame in Japan and have made return visits to Guam.

Sixteen

After the Battle

Defeat in the Marianas

Fleet Admiral Osami Nagano, chief of the naval general staff and advisor to the emperor, lamented that with the fall of Saipan "Hell is on us." Defeat in the Marianas and especially Saipan ruptured the home island defense. One blow was the crippling of carrier air capability in the sea Battle of the Marianas, when three carriers, two fleet tankers, and 426 planes were lost. Second, the Marianas became forward American naval facilities, so the U.S. fleet was not at the end of its tether. Resupply, support and logistics from Apra Harbor, Guam, projected the naval arm to the west. Also, American sea power in the Marianas blocked the sea routes and isolated bypassed garrisons such as Chuuk (Truk). These bypassed garrisons became a heavy drain, requiring resupply missions while contributing nothing to the war effort. A third, and the most destructive impact, was regular very heavy bomber attacks on Japan from the Marianas. The first raid from the Marianas hit the home islands on November 24, 1944. By the end of the war there were 1,000 B-29s in the Marianas to carry out raids on Japan.

The defeat in the Marianas rattled the military overconfidence. A belated use of lessons learned was one outcome. In recognition of the overpowering American artillery, air and naval bombardment, Iwo Jima and Okinawa employed a dug-in defense. Soldiers in their caves and heavily shielded bunkers had orders to stay glued to them. There would be no more mass charges.

Japanese holdouts in the Mariana jungles proved tough to locate and capture or kill. Those captured were held in stockades,

207

but left each day for work details, unloading supplies, and cleaning up the battlefields. Korean prisoners, under the direction of their stonemasons, built dry stacked stone walls, some of them surviving to the present. In 1946 the prisoners were returned to their homes.

There had been serious war crimes against American military and civilians in the Marianas. These crimes included: the executions of Father Duenas and other Guamanians, the executions of 51 Chamorro laborers in northern Guam; mass murders of Chamorros in southern Guam; the executions of American sailors who escaped in December 1941; and soldiers who may have killed civilians or other soldiers trying to surrender. Prisoners were interrogated, but the investigations did no go far. There were too few survivors to identify the responsible parties, and usually they had died in battle.

While the prisoner labor was significant in cleaning up the islands, it paled in contrast to the massive U.S. Navy Seabee and Army Engineer construction programs. Rushed to completion were B-29 bases, naval facilities, and support bases for the final stages of the War in the Pacific. The islands of Saipan, Tinian, and Guam became huge military islands with facilities from one end to the other. Expansion happened at many former Japanese bases. Aslito (renamed Isely) Field at Saipan was given two long runways for B-29 operations. An American improved Orote Airfield saw limited service, then abandoned as unsafe because of crosswinds. Ushi Field on the north end of Tinian was the largest B-29 base of World War II. The small field at Oleai, Saipan was not used due to dangerous crosswinds. Marpi Field became North Field.

Bulldozers cleared the bombed-out main cities of Agana and Garapan. In their place went up Quonset hut camps. Agana became the administrative center on Guam. Garapan was the site of a supply depot. Susupe was the Saipan administrative center. In Agana only 24 of the 3,500 buildings had survived the bombardment. The American military government employed these few standing structures. Even fewer structures were intact at Garapan: a hospital, jail, school building, church tower, and the statue of the Sugar King, Matsue. The battle devastation and bulldozing of the towns were so extensive that there are today few reminders of the war. Bullet damage to the Matsue, "Sugar King" statue, and shell damage to the few surviving Garapan buildings are silent testimonies to the Battle of Saipan.

Island-wide destruction left thousands of refugees. Temporary camps were erected to house them. As quickly as possible these people left the camps to return to their lands and rebuild their homes. Many could not return, their lands having been taken over for military base construction. The village of Sumay was not resettled, the ruined village site was within the Naval Operating Base, Orote Peninsula. Sumay's 2,000 residents were relocated to the new village of Santa Rita.

While the rubble of the towns was cleared and bases built, there were areas untouched by military construction. This was due to the topography and how it had figured into the battle. The initial linear defense was thin, concentrated at the beaches, and here were few American construction projects. Two shorelines, at Tanapag and Apra Harbor, were major project sites. Usually, the defended beaches were little affected by the U.S. 1944–1945 military construction program. Recreational activities that involved little demolition or construction occupied many war beaches.

It was a different story for the coastal plains, to the rear of the beaches. These flat properties were ideal for base construction, as village sites, and military cemeteries. The American military cemeteries were placed at Asan, across the beach road from Asan Point, at Agat landward of Gaan Point, in Saipan at Oleai, and near Agingan Point. In 1949 these cemeteries were closed since the Mariana Islands were too difficult for relatives to reach. The burials were returned to stateside cemeteries or the Punchbowl in Hawaii, at the wish of the next of kin. Mass graves and sealed caves became the Japanese resting places. Over the years Japanese bone collecting missions have visited the islands to recover bones of the deceased. Recovered bones are cremated in a religious ceremony and the ashes returned to Japan. Towns and government facilities occupy much of the coastal plain. Surviving features are now subsurface. They are encountered during construction. For example, home building in the Tanapag, Saipan, has exposed burials from the final mass assault.

Battle artifacts are more common in the central mountain ranges since they are less desirable building sites. The less rugged mountains, such as Mount Barrigada and Mount Fina Susa, are now residential districts. Mount Mangan, where General Takashina had his headquarters, became the U.S. Navy's Marianas headquarters, and named Nimitz Hill. Despite extensive Navy construction Nimitz Hill is rich in battle reminders. There is: the untouched Fonte depression; Mount Chachao with its littered battlefield around the extant observation post; Mount Tenjo; and the ruins of the American Radio Direction Finding Station at Libugon. A short walk into the jungle from Navy housing is a Type 94 75mm gun at Fonte.

Those areas now built upon by the Americans in 1944 quickly reforested, with the assistance of air-dropped seeds. Soon the battle-scarred land was greened over by the jungle. Also, as military bases or portions of the bases became surplus to Cold War military missions, they were abandoned and reclaimed by the jungle. This process of jungle reclamation had a positive effect, to hide and save relics. Unfortunately for preservation the tanks, guns, and aircraft left behind became valuable as scrap in the 1950s. Scrap became the main economic pursuit in Saipan, Tinian, and Rota. It was less important in Guam, since the Cold War bases provided employment and income. Surprisingly forty-one Japanese coastal defense and antiaircraft guns survived and can be seen today.

Since war scrap was not a renewable resource, it did not create a long-term economic base. Once the scrap was gone, there was nothing to replace it. Economic development turned to tourism as a new source of income. The 1960s witnessed a local effort to develop tourism, first in Guam and later at Saipan, Tinian, and Rota. Tourism provided the economic foundation to support the long struggle for self-determination. Guam achieved several political victories in their goal of self-determination. In 1950 the island obtained territory status and the residents became U.S. citizens. Twenty years later, in November 1970, the people of this American territory elected a governor for the first time. A separate political struggle was under way on Saipan. After the war and the military occupation, the former mandates became the Trust Territory of the Pacific Islands (TTPI). The TTPI, formed in 1947 to replace the military occupation government, was not aggressive in creating the conditions for economic growth and independence. The people of the Northern Marianas, in their fight for self-government, negotiated for political independence, culminating in a plebiscite on June 17, 1975. In this vote, the residents of the Northern Mariana Islands approved the establishment of a Commonwealth of the Northern Mariana Islands in Political Union with the United States of America. On March 15, 1976, President Gerald Ford signed the covenant making the Commonwealth a reality. This covenant made Northern Mariana residents U.S. citizens with self-governing privileges under U.S. laws.

Meanwhile tourism flourished bringing safe and regular air service to all the islands. This air service opened the islands to those interested in visiting war relics. Today, the Marianas are a textbook of the War in the Pacific. Each island has some well-reserved wartime features, so by visiting the four main islands you can observe the full range of military installations. Saipan and Guam have intact beach defenses. Saipan and Tinian have the best preserved Japanese airfields in the Central Pacific. Guam has a well-preserved central massif, and Rota has its unique defensive complex. And, the four together contain, *in situ*, most of the coastal defense weapon types of the Japanese arsenal.[1]

Saipan Artifacts

Today, the landing beaches on western Saipan are popular tourist spots or islander fishing locales. They are clean with little war material. In the shallow water offshore of Oleai are two Sherman tanks and three LVTs. On invasion day these Marine tanks were flooded out when discharged in too deep water. Now, at low tide, the turrets are exposed. Both are within wading distance of the beach. Near the tanks are LVTs, stopped by artillery.

On Managaha Island at the entrance to Tanapag Harbor are three 140mm coastal defense guns in their unfinished casemates. These are the guns that fired on the *Maryland*, and were then silenced by American warships. The weakness of these positions is readily apparent. They are exposed and the casemating in progress was too weak. Near the 140mm's is a Type 96 25mm gun. In the waters of the harbor between this small island and Saipan are underwater relics: three Japanese planes, one of them a Kawanishi Flying Boat; and five Japanese vessels, a transport, a subchaser, a landing craft, and three barges.

Back on the Saipan shore of Tanapag Harbor are defenses at Puntan Muchot. There are two pillboxes, of reinforced concrete with stone facing, to harmonize them into the terrain, and a casemate which held a 120mm coastal defense gun. This casemate shows the scars of receiving many U.S. projectile hits. Today, it is a wind surfboard rental shop. Standing alone, with no terrain or added shielding, it was doomed.

Only a few pillboxes survive along the western landing beaches, from Muchot Point south to Agingan Point. On the south edge of Garapan is a 20mm gun pillbox, easily recognized by its long rectangular shape. Two stone machine gun pillboxes are nearby. A single mount Type 96 25mm gun is located at the Nissan dealership at the intersection of Beach Road and Guerrero Road. Also at this intersection is a simple monument to fallen U.S. troops and two Type 1, 47mm antitank guns. Until recently this was the only monument to the Americans, but a flurry of U.S. monument building has taken place in the 1990s. American visitors had for years wondered why there were numerous Japanese monuments and so few honoring those who liberated the islands. However, the disparity was not so surprising. The Marianas are closer to Japan than the mainland United States, with many more Japanese visitors. Additionally, the culture and religious values of Japan emphasize erecting monuments to the dead. The fiftieth anniversary of the battles brought many American veterans to the islands and the erection of impressive monuments.

At Oleai starts a straight stretch of beach road to Susupe, the site of a Japanese runway. This stretch of modern road is built on top of the World War II runway. There are no trace of airfield gun positions. Also, gone is evidence of the second line of infantry defense behind the beach. Housing and government offices occupy this site. Aeftna Point has lost its network of defenses to a first class hotel.

In Susupe the inter-island radio station, target of the June 16-17 tank-infantry counterattack, survives. The wetlands where the tank-infantry assault was stopped cold by Marines holds small relics of the battle. The destroyed tanks have long since been removed. In the town of Susupe are relics of the post-battle camps for the Japanese, Koreans, Chamorros and Carolinians. In residential yards are objects from these camps including sinks, cooking stoves, and building foundations.

The southwestern beaches have few surviving fortifications. A pillbox, which held a 37mm gun, is on the Chalan Kanoa beach. All that remains of the sugar mill is the granary, now within the Mount Carmel School. Former sugar company duplexes are current day homes and businesses.

Agingan Point has its two 6-inch gun casemates. They are heavily damaged, and devoid of guns. The least damaged casemate, farthest from the sea, is unique in containing a fire control center within the structure. On Agingan Beach, to the southeast of the point, is one of the circular blockhouses designed to hold four 20mm guns. Like the other two blockhouses, it was sited on the beaches for fire seaward, and enfilade up and down the beach. All three examples on Saipan are in fair condition, none seriously damaged. The Agingan Beach blockhouse is within a beach park at Coral Ocean Point Resort. It can be reached by a trail from the golf course. Signage in the park details the history of this defense. What is absent is the elaborate camouflage given to these units. They were completely covered by vines growing on a dried vine lattice, and on top was soil with native plants. All the uncovered parts were camouflaged painted. A second blockhouse is on the next beach to the east, Obyan.

Also in the south region of the island is Nafutan Point, one of the toughest defenses in the Marianas. Along its shore and on Mount Nafutan are caves which were very effectively used to hold off the U.S. Army's 27th Division. There are also the empty concrete emplacements for 127mm dual-mount, dual-purpose guns, which were never emplaced. On the peninsula are two extant guns from the 140mm and 6-inch Whitworth-Armstrong batteries. Today, housing has moved onto the peninsula easing access, but also destroying its integrity. On the north side of Nafutan, at Puntan Dandan, were two 200mm antiboat guns, sited in the rocky cliffs at the tip. The guns are gone, but the positions are intact.

At the midpoint of Unai Laulau is the third circular blockhouse. This blockhouse, unarmed at the time of the landings, was untouched until American troops fired on it from the rear. It is in the best condition of the blockhouses, with its steel observation turret, steel shutters, and pulley system to raise and lower the shutters, in place. To the rear of the blockhouse are the shallow outlines of an extensive trenchworks. Observers will note that they are of a zigzag design so an enemy could not fire enfilade across the entire trench.

Northwest of the Laulau blockhouse, on a small point, is a 120mm gun in a casemate. The gun was hit by naval bombardment and knocked off its base. To the rear of the casemate is a demolished ammunition bunker, and nearby is an open position for a second 120mm gun. The revetment walls and foundation of the battery commander's station and fire control building are 150 yards to the northwest. Adjacent to the fire control station are the concrete posts of barracks and garrison buildings. In the cliffs above Laulau Beach are machine gun positions, a destroyed searchlight, and the rock walls of a dummy position.

Pillboxes of the Laulau Bay defense have survived and are excellent examples of skillful camouflage. For example, one pillbox is constructed between two emerged sea stacks, with a rock face blending it into the limestone cliffs. Additional pillboxes are cut into the rocky cliffs at the edge of the beach. On the northwest tip of the Laulau Bay are two caves, which had been ammunition bunkers for two 200mm antiboat guns in front of the caves. Construction of an American fuel tank farm removed the gun positions. On the peninsula above had been Kagman Field, an American fighter base. This base covered and removed evidence of the battle for this point of land. One significant exception is a U.S. M5A1 Stuart light tank, resting where it was halted by mines and antitank fire. The blown tracks sit alongside the tank, and the bullet holes in the tank recall the antitank fire it took.

To the north of Kagman are Tank and Marine Beaches (Brown Beaches). Many dummy positions were constructed in these areas, but evidence of the flimsy counterfeits has rotted away. A few real pillboxes, blended into the rocky shore, survive. North of here no fortifications were needed since the shore is so rugged.

Coastal and antiaircraft guns were installed on the north tip of the island, but they have been removed. Some of them made it to the Last Command Post Park (a cave here is incorrectly identified as the final command post, the real CP was to the south in the Valley of Hell). On park display are: a 140mm coastal defense gun,

200mm antiboat gun, three Type 10 120mm guns, and a 37mm gun. A battle damaged Type 95 tank pulled out of the jungle is another exhibit. Adjacent to the park are impressive Japanese, Okinawan, and Korean peace monuments. To the north of the park is the site of the Banaderu Airfield, which Seabees finished as North Field.

During their visits to this north tip Japanese tour buses stop at Marpi cliff, or "suicide cliffs", where hundreds jumped to their deaths in 1944. At the cliffs you can get close to the 800-foot high bluffs to see the boiling sea and jagged coral rock below.

The only surviving large caliber artillery piece is a Type 4 150mm howitzer on Hill 500. This is one of the guns which caused such suffering for the Marines. It is now displayed at a monument near its original emplacement.

Of the three Japanese airfields, Aslito was until recent years the most intact and best preserved Japanese field in the Pacific. However, expansion of the Saipan International Airport has intruded into the abandoned airfield site. A number of Aslito buildings survive, including an oxygen plant; air raid shelters; semi-underground ammunition bunker; a number of foundations; the concrete streets of the facility; four large fuel drum storage bunkers; a bombproof power plant; a water catchment system to collect run-off water from the runway; and a pharmacy building. At the Saipan International Airport terminal is the former operations building which has been made into offices. Some of the other buildings are also reused. The power plant is the local Red Cross office, and two fuel drum bunkers are offices, one housing the Marianas Visitors Bureau (where maps showing the Saipan World War II features are available), and the second is a Historic Preservation facility. In front of the Marianas Visitors Bureau offices is a monument to Captain Sasaki, who commanded the June 27 counterattack against American held Aslito field.

Some very valuable artifacts from Aslito survive in the mainland United States. When the field was overrun intact a dozen repairable aircraft were recovered and shipped to the United States for evaluation. Of this group, three Zeros remain in existence. One hangs from the ceiling of the National Air and Space Museum, Washington, D.C., with the tail number 61-131. Another is in a private collection in Florida (this one from the 261st Kokutai), and the third with the tail marking 61-120 is in the Planes of Fame collection in Chino, California.[2]

At Flores Point are: air raid shelters; the two seaplane ramps; and a reinforced concrete ammunition bunker. This was all that remained standing when the island was captured. The U.S. built

Camp Calhoun, a Quonset hut camp on the site. After this camp was closed in 1949 the area was abandoned. In 1970 the area became the Lower Base Industrial Park. The war features are mixed in with the contemporary industrial buildings.

On the north edge of Garapan, in the American Memorial Park, are the remains of Admiral Nagumo's estate. A fish pond and garden in the jungle recall this once elegant residence. They can be reached by a marked trail at the entrance to the park.

In the central mountains can be found hundreds of caves. Many of them littered with flotsam of war. Caves can be explored in Death Valley, Mount Tapotchau, and the Valley of Hell. There are so many caves, and none very different, that it is difficult to determine which were General Saito's five cave command posts. On top of Mount Tapotchau is the Japanese observation post and debris from a 1944 American radar station. Its observation value is obvious as you look below to the beaches and routes into the central area.

Garapan was destroyed in the war and bulldozed to make room for a U.S. Navy supply depot with many 40x100-foot Quonset huts. Present day Garapan has replaced the Quonset hut camp. Among the few prewar buildings are: the jail (where some have claimed that Amelia Earhart was imprisoned); the hospital; a school building at Central Park (also called Sugar King Park); and the statue of the "Sugar King", Huruji Matsue. Displayed in the park is a sugarcane train locomotive. Nearer the ocean, in the shopping district near Muchot Point, is a small Shinto shrine, which somehow missed destruction. On its white walls are inscriptions left by American servicemen in 1944–1945. One sailor, Robert Rickett, off the *Nebraska*, wrote, "look me up and I will take you for a couple throws".

Much of the gyokusai battlefield, above the village of Tanapag, is a lush green forest. On its south edge is housing and on the north a resort hotel. Within the undeveloped area are distinguishing features noted in the final days of the battle—the dry creek, the railroad and road bed survive. A limited excavation of the battlefield has recovered Japanese human remains and study of artifacts has answered questions regarding the mass attack.[3]

1. 120mm coastal defense gun in casemate on Laulau Bay
Photo by author

2. Muchot Point 120mm casemate, now a windsurfing rental shop
Photo by author

3. Circular blockhouse on Agingan Beach

Photo by author

4. Type 97 medium tank on exhibit at the American Memorial Park in Garapan

Photo by author

5. Japanese Air Operations building at Aslito Field, today the Saipan International Airport

Photo by author

6. Japanese bunker for fuel drums in use in 1945 by the 874th Bomb Squadron

National Archives

7. In 1981 the fuel drum storage bunker stood empty.

Photo by author

8. The Marianas Visitors Bureau repaired the bunker and opened their offices here.

Photo by author

9. Bombproof power plant at Aslito

Photo by author

Tinian War Objects

The unexpected American landings at Unai Babui (White One) and Unai Chulu (White Two) set the stage for a great victory. A visit to these pocket beaches makes clear the winning American gamble. The well-organized landings came across beaches normally too small for an invasion force. At White Two were defenses capable of resisting a small raiding party, not a full invasion. Two pillboxes stand on this beach, recalling its defense. The northern pillbox has extensive damage, especially on the rear side where the Marines attacked it.

Most of the Japanese weapons of Tinian have disappeared. A 140mm gun is in a cave position at Peipeinigul, below West Field. One of the six-inch guns from south of Tinian Town is now displayed at the airport. Also at the airport display is a Type 96 25mm gun, and aircraft parts.

With respect to existing fortifications, there are gun caves at Fabius San Hilo, to the southwest of the White Beaches. The remainder of the rugged coast to San Jose (Tinian Town) did not require defenses. On the northwest edge of San Jose is a pillbox for a 75mm gun. The pillbox was discovered empty when the Marines captured the town. In all likelihood the gun was pulled out to be used in the southern defense. In addition to this pillbox are only about ten Japanese buildings in San Jose (Tinian Town), which was virtually destroyed by American bombardment. The fire station, jail, a couple commercial buildings, school, company houses, and a sugar mill building survive.

Development to the south of San Jose has removed the six-inch gun caves. On the northeast side there are numerous defensive positions on Asiga Bay. Colonel Ogata had considered this beach the second most likely landing site, after Tinian Town. There are more fine examples of pillboxes harmonized into the terrain. Some 25 pillboxes and gun positions can be seen in the low cliffs at the edge of the sandy beach.

On the north end of the island fortifications can be seen at Puntan Tahgong. They guarded the north approach to the island, for both the Japanese and then the B-29 base. The Ushi/North Field region is rich in cultural resources from both eras. Japanese features include: the Asahi shrine; 1st Air Fleet Headquarters Building; Operations Building, with World War II graffiti such as "G. Koly, Campbell, Ohio, 11-4-44"; power plant; air raid shelters; a large underground storage bunker; and hangar and barracks foundations. Inland of White Beach Two was a Japanese village at Lake Hagoi. There is a considerable amount of surface debris at the village site.

North Field American features include the two loading pits for the atomic bombs. The bombs were too large to roll under the planes, so they were lowered into the pits and hoisted into the bomb bays. Some other features of North Field include: the four U.S. runways, the campsite of the 509th Composite Group which had dropped the atomic bombs, and an LVT 2 (amtrac) disabled by Japanese gunfire. Today, North Field is a National Historic Landmark and a military training area, with annual exercises and landings at White Beach Two.

Tinian with its large flat areas was ideal for base construction. Much of the island was turned into camps and depots to support the B-29 operations. Many of the battlefields were cleared for new construction. The flat summit of Mount Lasso was used as an Army hospital site. Where evidence of the battle can be found are the slopes of the Mount Lasso, the central area, and in the south redoubt area. The caves along the south tip shoreline are littered with Japanese canteens, cooking utensils, scraps of clothing, and bones. These southern caves recall the men who refused to surrender, staying and dying in these caves.

Those who surrendered were held in camps in the Chulo (Churo) area in north central Tinian. Within this jungle are relics of the

1. White Beach Two pillbox neutralized by an attack from the rear.

Photo by author

2. Pillbox blended into the Asiga Beach cliffs.

Photo by author

3. Inter-island Radio Station building being used as a slaughterhouse for a Tinian cattle ranch.

Photo by author

camp, including a standing police station on 96th Street, east of 8th Avenue (In 1944 the U.S. engineers laying out the roads on Tinian copied the road network of Manhattan Island; the two islands are similar in size and shape). The inter-island radio station, now a slaughterhouse, is located on Broadway at 96th Street.

Rota Defenses

This island has the most unique defensive works in the Marianas. Located at Ginalangan, this complex is one mile long with caves and a firing and blast wall along a steep cliffs. Positions in the cliff held machine guns, 25mm, 37mm, 75mm and 120mm guns. This complex reflected better consideration of American strengths. An especially useful element was the provision for water collection and storage. Troops in this defense could hold out for long periods of time. The caves, pillboxes, and artifacts of the defensive complex, undamaged by warfare, exist on the cliff. Relics at the encampment site, at the base of the escarpment, include cooking stoves and a light tractor, RO-KE model, an unarmed artillery prime mover. It is the only known surviving example of this type of tractor.

The RO-KE was certainly missed at Saipan and Guam to relocate artillery in danger of capture.

A modern airport has been constructed over the Japanese airfield. Some barracks foundations and an observation tower are extant near the present day airport. Artifacts were turned up by airport construction. They included Japanese aircraft engines and a Type 96 25mm gun, which are displayed at the airport terminal.

A 120mm Type 10 gun is in a cave at Sabana Fanlagon. This weapon was placed at the cave entrance so it had some protection and still could fire antiaircraft missions. Above the harbor, 2.5 miles east of Songsong, is a 140mm coastal defense gun in a cliff cavity. In Songsong Town are some Japanese objects and the ruins of the sugar mill. Sunk in 60 feet of water in the harbor is the *Shoun Maru*, hit by U.S. aerial bombardment.

Pagan Island, 280 miles north of Guam, had an airfield with a 2,500-foot long runway, to support patrolling the north. The airfield and other relics exist, but portions of the island are covered by

1. Type 10 120mm dual purpose gun at entrance of cave to protect it yet retain land and antiaircraft uses

Photo by author

2. A 140mm gun defended the harbor.

Photo by author

3. Japanese Air Operations and control tower

Photo by author

ash from recent volcanic eruptions. These relics include: a Type 88 75mm gun, a Nell, Judy, and Zero aircraft, and aircraft debris.

Guam War Features

Guam has intact beach defenses to help us visualize the Japanese battle plan. Starting at Facpi Point, at the southern end of the west coast defenses, are positions which provided flanking fire on Agat Beach. The premier Agat defenses were sited at Bangi Point. This point has its unfinished 200mm antiboat gun position, devoid of its gun. Intact at the point is a reinforced concrete pillbox which held a 7.7mm machine gun.

The next significant feature was one of the most effective beach defenses in the Marianas. This is the Gaan Point strongpoint with pillboxes for 37mm and 75mm guns, built into this small rock mound. Both pillboxes are intact, and show the damage from U.S. attacks. On its reverse slope are shelter and command caves. Standing at this strongpoint one realizes that camouflage was critical. Without camouflage it would have presented an easy target. Two guns displayed here may be moved to the Newman Center, a 200mm antiboat gun and Type 96 25mm. The National Park Service has signs telling the story of this strongpoint.

Hill 40 inland of Agat Beach, a small hill where there was bloody fighting, cannot be recognized as a battlefield. Farming on the hill has erased all traces of its wartime appearance. This is not the case for Mount Alifan which has gun positions, the 38th Infantry Regiment cave command post, gun caves, and the open 120mm gun revetments. These emplacements are so exposed that it is clear why they were destroyed in the preinvasion bombardment.

Agat Beach above Gaan Point has been altered by post-war rebuilding. Pillboxes and gun positions are gone. However, on the north end of Agat at Apaca Point are remarkable defenses. This point has fine examples of pillboxes harmonized into their settings. One pillbox at the edge of the beach is built into rocky point, the only visible constructed feature is its tiny firing embrasure. Seaward of this position are gun positions in the rock crevices. One of the gun positions is a concrete embrasure filling in the space between two rocks.

Next is Orote Peninsula, reached by the old Agat to Sumay Road. This peninsula was the only Marianas example of a defense in depth. There were fireblocks at its initial access, the two roads coming onto this point of land. Beyond the fireblocks was a line across the entire neck. Additional defensive lines and guns were located on this well-defended point of land. On the potential landing beaches were strong defenses. Construction of the Naval Operating Base in 1944–1945 removed most of the Japanese objects. Where Japanese features have survived, is in the cliffs and on the beaches. In the Dadi-Tipalao area above Agat Bay are 13 gun caves, including the cave strongpoint on the west end of Dadi Beach. Along Dadi Beach are a stone pillbox and reinforced concrete pillbox, both hidden in the jungle at the edge of the beach. Also in the jungle are Korean-built stone steps and walls done by prisoners in 1946. These stoneworks graced the American Palm Beach recreation area.

On the north shore of Orote Peninsula, gun caves and a hospital cave are only a few feet from the road at Sumay. All that remains of the village is its cemetery, with gravestones shattered by shelling and the church site marked by a cross. In the jungle above the west end of Sumay is a Type 96 25mm gun from the Apra Harbor defense. Along the shore beyond Sumay is Gabgab Beach, a possible landing place. Three pillboxes exist in the escarpment above the beach; three more were removed during the construction of recreational facilities in 1945. Farther west is Orote Point, the only Japanese defense was an antiaircraft gun in a prewar, and intact U.S. seven-inch gun pit.

Displayed at the naval station (formerly the Naval Operating Base) is a Japanese Type A midget submarine, *Ha-51,* which got stuck on the east coast reef off Togcha Beach. Seabees helped the submariners at the Camp Dealy rest center at Togcha pull the *Ha 51* ashore. The captured submarine was exhibited at Camp Dealy until the camp was closed in 1950. Then the submarine was moved to the Naval Station on Orote Peninsula, where it is today.

When the Marines recaptured Orote their former Marine Barracks was in ruins, but found in the rubble were both station bronze plaques? One plaque was exhibited during the July 1944 flag raising. When a new Marine Barracks was built on Orote Peninsula in about 1950, the plaque was placed on a concrete pedestal, at the headquarters building. With the recent closing of the Guam Marines Barracks the museum branch of the Marine Corps acquired the plaque. It was returned to Guam in July 1994.

There are more than sixty known and identified underwater relics in Apra Harbor and the Agat Bay shoreline of Orote Peninsula. A few of the more significant underwater features are:

Tokai Maru. On August 23, 1943, she was hit by two torpedoes fired from the *Snapper.* The *Tokai Maru* settled to 140-foot depth in Apra Harbor next to the *Cormoran,* now at Buoy 1.

SMS Cormoran. This World War I German warship was scuttled during World War I to prevent its capture.

Kisogawa Maru. This transport was under repair when attacked by torpedo bombers from the *White ·Plains* on June 24, 1944. She was hit and sank in 150 feet of water. This ship is intact, her bow gun still in place.

Nichiyu Maru. It is not clear if this transport was sunk by torpedoes or aerial attack during the preinvasion bombardment. She rests in 50 feet of water at the GORCO pier.

Aichi D3A2 Dive Bomber. Shot down in a dogfight, this aircraft sits in the harbor along the breakwater.

Penguin. Scuttled during the Japanese air raid on December 8, 1941, this ship is in deep water, one and a half miles off Orote Point.

Aratama Maru. Across the island from Apra Harbor, on the east shore, is this ammunition ship. She was hit by a U.S. submarine-launched torpedo, on April 8, 1944. The *Aratama Maru* limped into Talofofo Bay, and sank here.

In the inner harbor area was the Piti Navy Yard. The Japanese had used this facility as its Guam Naval Base, but it was destroyed in the 1944 battle. Only pieces of the dock exist.

On the ridge above the village of Piti are three 140mm coastal defense guns. The guns were in especially open positions, but photographs taken after the capture of the island show elaborate camouflage. The guns were covered with palm fronds, canvas and local plant material. One gun was hit, fired on by advancing Marines. These were probably not fired because the after-the-battle photographs show the guns completely covered with camouflage. A trail from the Catholic Social Hall in Piti leads to the guns.

Within view of the 140mm guns is Asan Point. On the Piti side of the point were two 200mm antiboat guns, one was dug into the cliff face shielding a concrete wall. While the position is intact, the gun is gone. The second position in the west cliffs is no longer identifiable. A third 200mm position at the seaward tip, to fire seaward and against ships approaching Piti and Asan, is present. The rock hollow gun dugout and blown-up concrete blast walls suggest that it was destroyed in the preinvasion attack. Naval bombardment missed the two 200mm guns to fire on the Piti beaches. They were no danger to the invasion since there were no landings within their sights. While not all the coastal defense guns were destroyed before the invasion, not one large caliber gun was firing when the landings took place.

The village of Asan has been rebuilt removing most of the surface war relics. One Asan battlefield feature is the bridge over the Matgue River, at Asan Point, where Marines came under terrific machine gun fire. Bullet holes in the railings of this abandoned bridge recall the battle. In Asan Village is the Stell Newman Visitors Center with museum and archives.

A region of Guam rich in material of the War in the Pacific is the central massif, the foothills of Asan and the mountain tops.

This includes Chonito and Bundschu Ridges, Fonte, Mount Mangan, and Mount Chachao to Mount Tenjo. Hidden in the dense foliage of the ridges are caves, battlefields, and discarded soldiers' gear. In the Fonte depression are the gun caves destroyed by tank gunfire. On the approach to Fonte is the early 29th Division headquarters cave, which was expanded after the war into a civil defense shelter cave. A 75mm gun rests in the Fonte woods where it guarded the route to the headquarters camp. More reminders can be seen at Mount Chachao where the observation post is intact on the summit, and directly below it are gun caves. A trail from Mount Chachao leads to Mount Tenjo. Visitors to Mount Tenjo will find prewar Marine trenchworks, a battery commanders station building, platforms for coastal defense guns, and a dam which collected water for the Marine camp and gun battery.

At the east end of Asan is Adelup Point. On its west or Asan side were 47mm guns and machine guns. Caves and rock cavities' positions are present. On its east side is a reinforced concrete machine gun pillbox.

While landings over the rough seas on the east coast were not likely, they were possible. Therefore protection was required. Pillboxes, infantry positions, and dummy works guarded the back door, or eastern approaches to the central area were infantry positions and two Type 95 tanks in revetments on Maneggon Hill. These tanks were in their revetments until 1985 when one disappeared. In 1992 the second tank was moved to a recreated revetment a few hundred yards away, to make way for a resort complex. Not far away is the "tank farm", a collection of two Sherman tanks and three LVTs, all heavily shell damaged. A local account had a major World War II tank battle at this feature. In fact, the landing craft and tanks were brought here in 1946 as targets for U.S. Marine training.

The western beaches from Adelup Point to the east side of Agana were not likely landing sites, so they had few defenses. A 20mm gun pillbox is at the site of the Agana Navy Yard, adjacent to the small boat harbor. In the city of Agana are shelter caves and one large cave complex near Government House. The American 1944 bombardment destroyed Government House, leaving only a porch and foundation. In front of the foundation is the base of the Government House flagpole, where the Japanese raised their flag in December 1941. Two 47mm antitank guns are displayed at the Guam jail on the plaza.

In 1962 telephone linemen working in the Agana swamp, on the east side of the city, discovered a crashed Zero. The A6M5 was in good condition and restorable. Still visible on its tail was 43-188, or a plane of the 343d Kokutai, and 188 identifying it as a carrier plane. Further research indicated that its pilot was Lieutenant Commander Nobuya Ozaki, who on June 19, 1944 was wounded in a dogfight over Guam. Trying to save the aircraft he made a soft crash landing in the wetlands. Found alive, Ozaki was taken to an aid station where he died. The Zero (serial number 4,685) was donated by the governor of Guam to the people of Japan. It was restored and is exhibited at Hamamatsu Air Base, Japan.

The Tiyan field was built into a U.S. Naval Air Station and the Guam International Airport. Only a few stone culverts are left from the Japanese period. The Orote Peninsula Airfield was expanded into a naval air station with no trace of the Japanese period. In the jungle along the runway is a crashed Corsair of Marine Air Group 21 (MAG-21), but its history is unknown. A third Japanese field under construction near Dededo became a U.S. military base, and there are no known Japanese features here.

The present day Marine Drive is approximately the same route as the prewar beach road. Along this road from Dungcas Beach came the 1941 Special Naval Landing Force. A park on the road, just outside East Agana, was used by the Japan for the erection of a wood monument in memory of "22 Chamorros who died in the 1941 liberation of Guam". Surviving the 1944 battle, the monument was removed but saved, finally it was lost in Typhoon Pamela on May 21, 1976.

Dungcas Beach (East Agana) has become a business and hotel district. When clearing land for the Onward Agana Hotel a cave with a 200mm antiboat gun was discovered. The gun was relocated to a display at the hotel swimming pool.

The next potential landing beach was Tumon Bay. Tourism development has completely altered this region. Three 120mm Type 10 guns found in the jungle during hotel construction have been saved. Their final exhibit place is not known, while they wait in storage at the Black Construction Company. Another 120mm Type 10 is displayed at the Hilton Hotel on Tumon Bay. At Gun Beach on Tumon Bay is an *in-situ* 200mm gun in the rocky bluff.

Unfortunately the battlefield sites in the north have been lost to massive U.S. military construction, residential communities, and golf courses. The battle site at Barrigada is occupied by the P. C. Lujan Elementary School. Mount Barrigada and Mount Santa Rosa's lower portion are covered with residential housing. On the top of Mount Santa Rosa is an Air Force installation. The Finegayan battlefield is now a Naval Communications Station. Located on this station is Radioman George R. Tweed's shelter at Haputo Point. The simple shelter was a natural crevice covered with a piece of corrugated iron shielding Tweed from the rain and hot sun. General Obata's final command post complex is near Yigo, next to the Japanese Peace Monument.

The shelter of the 28 year holdout, Sergeant Yokoi, is also preserved. It is a hole in the ground in the Talofofo region. Some of his personal artifacts, handmade fishing tools, trapping devices, cooking utensils, and handmade clothes are exhibited at the Guam Museum. They recall his long tenure in the jungle, and the eight years of solitary life before his capture. A crashed Val dive bomber, near the Fena Reservoir, is on the tour route of safari vehicles to Yokoi's shelter.

Guamanians have not forgotten their own who suffered so much in the war. Memorials to the victims of Japanese brutalities are located at appropriate places. The body of Father Duenas was recovered from his execution site and buried in Saint Joseph's Church in Inarajan. Tai, where he was murdered, is the location of the Father Duenas Memorial High School. The mass murders in the south at Merizo are remembered by a memorial there.

1. One of three 140mm guns at Piti

Photo by author

2. A damaged 140mm at the Piti battery

Photo by author

3. A 200mm antiboat gun on Tumon Bay, it gave this beach its name, Gun Beach.

Photo by author

4. Pillbox on Dadi Beach, Orote Peninsula

Photo by author

5. Midget submarine captured at Togcha Beach, now displayed on the Guam Naval Station, Orote Peninsula.

Photo by author

6. A cross identifies the site of the prewar Sumay church.

Photo by author

7. Battle damaged gravestone in the Sumay cemetery

Photo by author

INTRODUCTION

1. The discussion of Japanese military values and their negative impact on the defense of the Marianas draws heavily on Inega, *The Pacific War.*
2. The five available inventories of Japanese weapons on Guam are: III Amphibious Corps Report Guam, Incl D, G-2; Takeda letter, 4 October 1946; RG 127, Box 65, Reel 1, USMC, Captured Weapons, pp. 1183–1277; USMC Reel 5, pp. 1832–1835; Disposition of Japanese Forces and Gun Installations. These documents are available at the U.S. Marine Corps Historical Center, except the last listed inventory, which is at the War in the Pacific National Historic Park, Guam.
3. General Saito's burial with full military honors was unusual. No other Japanese officers received this special recognition.

CHAPTER ONE

1. Tourism has brought development and the need to clear lands. The historic preservation laws require archaeological investigations, and these studies have provided considerable data on the prehistory of the Chamorro people.
2. Sanchez, *Guahan*, 40–48.
3. Peattie, *Nanyo*, 24.
4. Peattie, *Nanyo*, 25.
5. Peattie, *Nanyo*, 43–44.
6. Russell, *Rising Sun*, 2.
7. Peattie, *Nanyo*, 124.
8. Russell, *Rising Sun*, 27.
9. Denfeld and Russell, *Home of the Superfort*, 7.
10. Crowl, *Campaign in the Marinas*, 54; and Crowl and Love, *Seizure of Gilberts and Marshalls*, 207.
11. Peattie, *Nanyo*, 252.
12. Lighthouses have survived at Chuuk and Saipan. The lighthouse on Moen Island, Chuuk, retains its historical integrity. It was a 200mm coastal defense battery fire control station. A restaurant has taken over and modified the Saipan lighthouse.

CHAPTER TWO

1. Crowl, *Campaign in the Marianas*, 54.
2. The description of the Japanese capture of Guam is from Sanchez, *Guahan*; McMillin, *Surrender of Guam*; and U.S. Army, *Japanese Studies in World War II*, Vol. 48.
3. Prange, *God's Samurai*, 107.
4. This account of convoy interception is from Blair, *Silent Victory*, and Parillo, *The Japanese Merchant Marine in World War II*. Parillo demonstrates that logistics was shortchanged, monies went to ships for the big battle.
5. The reinforcement of Saipan and the battle for the island is fully recorded in Hoffman, *Saipan*, and Crowl, *Campaign in the Marianas*.
6. Jones, *Oba*, 18.
7. Chief of Staff, 31st Army to COS, Central Pacific Area Fleet, Translation 116, USMC.
8. Cook and Cook, *Japan at War*, 282. Yamauchi emphasizes that he was different, one of the few not wanting to die in battle. He may not be representative of the soldiers in the Marianas.
9. Chihaya, *Fading Victory*, 425.
10. U.S. Army, *Japanese Studies in World War II*, Vol. 55, 19–20.
11. U.S. Army Engineers, Report on Japanese Defense Plan for the Island of Saipan, 1944.
12. Contrary to many reports, British 6-inch and 8-inch guns in the Pacific were not captured Singapore guns. The Japanese had purchased these naval guns from the British in the early 1900s, and during the war in the Pacific removed them from obsolete ships for land emplacement.
13. Crowl, *Campaign in the Marianas*, 41.
14. Denfeld, "The Battle of Attu", 374–376.
15. Smith, *Approach to the Philippines*, 301.

CHAPTER THREE

1. Cook and Cook, *Japan at War*, 283.
2. Translation No. 10,238, CINCPAC-CINCPOA. The translated Japanese diaries are on file at the Naval Operational Archives, Navy Yard, Washington, D.C. The Marine Corps Historical Center at the Navy Yard and the War in the Pacific, National Historic Park, have additional translated diaries and captured materials. Hoffman, *Saipan*, used many of these translations.
3. Translation No. 11,405.
4. Translation No. 10,051.
5. Crowl, *Campaign in the Marianas*, 76–77.
6. Translation No. 15,282.
7. 31st Army Msg. File, No. 1,027.
8. Translation No. 10,238.
9. Translation No. 10,410.
10. Hoffman, *Saipan*, 50.
11. Cook and Cook, *Japan at War*, 285.
12. Hoffman, *Saipan*, 51.
13. 31st Army Msg. File, No. 1,038.
14. Hoffman, *Saipan*, 87.
15. Hoffman, *Saipan*, 89–90.
16. Translation No. 9,983–85.
17. Hoffman, *Saipan*, 91.
18. 31st Army Msg. File, No. 115 and 1,046.
19. Cook and Cook, *Japan at War*, 287.

20. Translation No. 9,983–85.
21. Translation No. 18,238.

CHAPTER FOUR

1. Chihaya, *Fading Victory*, 418.
2. Morison, *New Guinea and Marianas*, 216. Morison was the main source for this chapter.
3. Chihaya, *Fading Victory*, 428.

CHAPTER FIVE

1. Translation No. 10,238.
2. Ito, *End of the Imperial Japanese Navy*, 224.
3. Hoffman, *Saipan*, 130.
4. Translation No. 9,983–85.
5. Translation No. 9,983–85.
6. Translation No. 9,983–85.
7. Hoffman, *Saipan*, 140.
8. Translation No. 9,983–85.
9. Translation No. 11,405.
10. Translation No. 9,983–85.
11. Crowl, *Campaign in the Marinas*, 172–73.
12. Translation No. 9,983–85.
13. Hoffman, *Saipan*, 143.
14. 31st Army Msg. File, No. 1,102.
15. 31st Army Msg. File, No. 1,101.
16. Hoffman, *Saipan*, 162.
17. Hoffman, *Saipan*, 168.

CHAPTER SIX

1. Translation No. 9,983–85.
2. Jones, *Oba*, 54.
3. Jones, *Oba*, 54.
4. Crowl, *Campaign in the Marianas*, 257.
5. Photographs of the burial of General Saito are held in the National Archives Still Photography Collection.
6. Jones, *Oba*, 57.
7. McCandless, letter to author, September 7, 1987.
8. U.S. Navy, Commander Fifth Fleet, "Rpt. Japanese Counterattack at Saipan", July 19, 1944.
9. Sheeks, "Civilians on Saipan", 111.

CHAPTER SEVEN

1. Ienaga, *The Pacific War*, 49.
2. Kitaoka, "The Army as Bureaucracy", 84.
3. Chihaya, *Fading Victory*, 419.
4. Hoffman, *Saipan*, has a summary of Japanese failures. Isely and Crowl, *Marines and Amphibious War*, also discuss tactics of both sides.
5. Kitaoka, "The Army as Bureaucracy", 85.

CHAPTER EIGHT

1. Sanchez, *Guahan*, 39.
2. Price, *Japan's Islands of Mystery*, 47.
3. Farrell, *Tinian*, 11.
4. Hoffman, *Tinian*, has a complete order of battle.
5. Memorial Service Association for Deceased Compatriots Overseas, Seoul, Korea.
6. Translation No. 11,405.
7. Translation No. 11,962.
8. Takayoshi Yamagaki Diary, War in the Pacific National Historic Park.

CHAPTER NINE

1. Morison, *New Guinea and Marianas*, 361–362.
2. Some accounts list six tanks in this counterattack. One tank may have escaped, five tanks were discovered on the battlefield.
3. Hoffman, *Tinian*, 65.
4. Chihaya, *Fading Victory*, 438.
5. Hoffman, *Tinian*, 105.

CHAPTER TEN

1. Crowl, *Campaign in the Marianas*, 329.
2. Moore and Hunter-Anderson, "Report on Ginalangan", 128.
3. Moore and Hunter-Anderson, "Report on Ginalangan", 26.
4. *Guam News*, July 2, 1951.

CHAPTER ELEVEN

1. Sanchez, *Guahan*, 30. Sanchez is the most complete history of Guahan.
2. Peattie, *Nanyo*, 235.
3. Morison, *Rising Sun in the Pacific*, 32–34.

CHAPTER TWELVE

1. U.S. Army, *Japanese Studies in World War II*, Vol. 55.
2. McMillin, "Surrender", and Morison, *The Rising Sun in the Pacific*, provided the details of the Japanese capture of Guam, 186.
3. Sanchez, *Guahan*, 180.
4. Sanchez, *Guahan*, 208.
5. Sanchez, Guahan, 194.

CHAPTER THIRTEEN

1. Lodge, *Recapture of Guam*, 9–11; and Crowl, *Campaign in the Marianas*, 331.
2. Lodge, *Recapture*, 86.
3. The War in the Pacific, National Historic Park, Guam, has opened access to the Apaca Point defenses as well as other surviving relics of the war.
4. Japan Self-Defense Agency, *Guam*, 128.
5. Translation No. 10,996.
6. Translation No. 10,802.
7. Translation No. 10,802.
8. Translation No. 10,802.
9. Translation No. 10,802.
10. Translation No. 10,377.

11. Kurokawa diary, War in the Pacific, National Historic Park, Guam.
12. Unit notebooks, Guam, War in the Pacific, National Historic Park, Guam.
13. Translation No. 10,802.
14. Translation No. 10,802.
15. Crowl, *Campaign in the Marianas*, 337.
16. Translation No. 10,802.
17. Crowl, *Campaign in the Marianas*, 339.

CHAPTER FOURTEEN

1. Lodge, *Recapture Guam*, 39.
2. Lodge, *Recapture Guam*, 41.
3. Japan Self-Defense Agency, *Guam*, 160.
4. Lodge, *Recapture Guam*, 50.
5. Takeda file, War in the Pacific, National Historic Park, Guam.
6. Lodge, *Recapture Guam*, 89.

CHAPTER FIFTEEN

1. Japan Self-Defense Agency, *Guam*, 194.
2. U.S. Army, *Guam*, 74.
3. U.S. Army, *Guam*, 79.
4. Crowl, *Campaign in the Marianas*, 392.
5. Japan Self-Defense Agency, *Guam*, 207.
6. U.S. Army, *Guam*, 131.
7. Guam War Repatriations Commission, Agana, Guam.
8. Diary Navy Corpsman, War in the Pacific, National Historic Park, Guam.
9. Kahn, *The Stragglers*, 12–13.

CHAPTER SIXTEEN

1. The Guam and Saipan Historic Preservation Offices and the Visitor Bureaus of the islands have identified a large portion of the World War II features in the Marianas.
2. Mikesh, *Broken Wings of the Samurai*, 177.
3. Russell and Fleming, *A Bulwark in the Pacific*, 26–27.

BIBLIOGRAPHY

Blair, Clay Jr. *Silent Victory: The U.S. Submarine War Against Japan.* Philadelphia: Lippincott, 1975.

Chihaya, Masataka, Donald Goldstein and Katherine Dillon, eds. *Fading Victory: The Diary of Admiral Matome Ugaki,*1941–45. Pittsburgh: University of Pittsburgh Press, 1991.

Cook, Haruko and Theodore Cook. *Japan at War: An Oral History.* New York: New Press, 1992.

Crowl, Philip. *The War in the Pacific: Campaign in the Marianas.* Washington, D.C.: Office of the Chief, Military History, 1960.

Crowl, Philip and Edmund Love. *The War in the Pacific: Seizure of the Gilberts and Marshalls.* Washington, D.C.: Office of the Chief, Military History, 1955.

Croziat, Victor. *Across the Reef.* London: Arms and Artillery Press, 1989.

Denfeld, Colt. *Japanese Fortifications and Other Structures in the Central Pacific.* Saipan: Micronesian Archaeological Survey Reports, Number 9, 1992.

———. "The Battle of Attu". *Builders and Fighters: U.S. Army Engineers in World War II.* Fort Belvoir, Virginia: Office of History, 1992.

———. "Korean Laborers in Micronesia During World War II". Seoul, Korea: *Korea Observer,* Volume XV, Fall, 1984.

Denfeld, Colt and Scott Russell. *Home of the Superfort.* Micronesian Archaeological Survey Reports, No. 21, 1984.

Farrell, Don A. *Tinian.* Guam: Micronesian Publications, 1989.

Harries, Meiron and Susie Harries. *Soldiers of the Sun: The Rise and Fall of the Imperial Japanese Army.* New York: Random House, 1992.

Hoffman, Major Carl. *The Seizure of Tinian.* Washington, D.C.: Historical Division, USMC, 1951.

———. *Saipan: The Beginning of the End.* Washington, D.C.: Historical Division, USMC, 1950.

Ienaga, Saburo. *The Pacific War: World War II and the Japanese, 1931–1945.* New York: Pantheon Books, 1968.

Isely, J. A and P. Crowl. *The Marines and Amphibious War.* Princeton: Princeton Press, 1951.

Ito, Masanori with Roger Pineau. *The End of the Imperial Japanese Navy.* New York: W. W. Norton, 1950.

Japan Self-Defense Agency. *How the Guam Operation was Conducted.* Tokyo, 1962.

Jones, Don. *Oba, The Last Samurai.* Novato, California: Presidio Press, 1986.

Kahn, E. J. *The Stragglers.* New York: Random House, 1962.

Kitaoka, Shinichi. "The Army as Bureaucracy: Japanese Militarism Revisited". *The Journal of Military History,* October, pp. 67–86.

Lodge, Major O. R. *The Recapture of Guam.* Washington, D.C.: Historical Branch: USMC, 1954.

McMillin, Captain George, USN. "Surrender of Guam". On file, War in the Pacific, National Historic Park, Guam.

Mikesh, Robert. *Broken Wings of the Samurai: The Destruction of the Japanese Airforce.* Annapolis: Naval Institute Press, 1993.

Moore, Darlene and Rosalind Hunter-Anderson. "Report on the Ginalangan Defense Complex, Rota". Saipan: Historic Preservation Office, Commonwealth of the Northern Mariana Islands, 1988.

Morison, S. E. *History of U.S. Naval Operations in World War II, Vol. 8: New Guinea and Marianas.* Boston: Little, Brown and Company, 1953.

———. *History of U.S. Naval Operations in World War II, Vol. 3: The Rising Sun in the Pacific.* Boston: Little, Brown and Company, 1950.

Owings, Kathleen, ed. *The War Years on Guam: Narratives of the Chamorro Experience.* Guam: Micronesian Area Research Center (MARC), University of Guam, 1981.

Parillo, Mark. *The Japanese Merchant Marine in World War II.* Annapolis: Naval Institute Press, 1993.

Peattie, Mark. *Nanyo: The Rise and Fall of the Japanese in Micronesia, 1885–1945.* Honolulu: University of Hawaii Press, 1988.

Prange, G. with Donald Goldstein and Katherine Dillon. *God's Samurai: Lead Pilot at Pearl Harbor.* Washington,D.C.: Brassey's, 1990.

Price, Willard. *Japan's Islands of Mystery.* New York: John Day, 1944.

Richard, Lieutenant Commander Dorothy. *U.S. Naval Administration of the Trust Territory of the Pacific Islands.* Washington, D.C.: Office of the Chief of Naval Operations, 1957.

Russell, Scott. *From Arabwal to Ashes: A Brief History of Garapan Village, 1818–1945.* Saipan: Micronesian Archaeological Survey Reports, Number 19, 1984.

———. *Rising Sun Over the Northern Marianas: Life and Culture Under the Japanese Administration, 1914–1944.* Saipan: Division of Historic Preservation, 1983.

Russell, Scott and Michael Fleming. *A Bulwark in the Pacific: An Example of World War II Archaeology on Saipan.* Columbia, Missouri: Museum of Anthropology, Monograph 10, Archaeological Studies of World War II, 1991.

Sanchez, Pedro. *Guahan: Guam, The History of Our Island.* Agana, Guam: Sanchez Publishing, n.d.

Sheeks, Lieutenant Robert. "Civilians on Saipan". *Far Eastern Survey,* pp.109–113, May 9, 1945.

Smith, General Holland M. and Percy Finch. *Coral and Brass.* New York: Bantam, 1987.

Takeda, Lieutenant Colonel Hideyuki, IJA. Letters to Director, Marine Corps History, 1946 and 1952.

U.S. Army *Guam: Operations of the 77th Division.* Washington, D.C.: Center for Military History, 1990.

———. *Japanese Monographs, Operations in the Central Pacific.* Volumes 48 and 55. Washington, D.C.

U.S. Navy. Japanese Translations, CINCPAC-CINCPOA.

———. *ONI-99: Strategic Study of Guam.* Office of Naval Intelligence, 1944.

U.S. Strategic Bombing Survey. *Interrogation of Japanese Officials,* Volumes One and Two. Washington, D.C.: Government Printing Office, 1946.

243

940.5426 Denfeld, D. Colt.
D
          Hold the Marianas.

DATE			